DELIVER *from* SEXUAL DEMONS

Freedom from Sexual Addictions

BY Peter Hobson

DELIVERANCE FROM SEXUAL DEMONS
FREEDOM FROM SEXUAL ADDICTIONS

Part of the Christian Deliverance Series

by Peter and Verlie Hobson

Copyright ©1996, 2014

SECOND EDITION

Formerly entitled:
SEX, DEMONS & MORALITY

FULL SALVATION FELLOWSHIP
ISBN: 0947252088

National Library of Australia

I.S.B.N. 0947252088

DEDICATION

To:

The ***Rev. Fred Nile M.L.C.***, a Christian Minister of the Congregational Church, and a courageous Christian voice in the midst of our N.S.W. State Parliament, many Members of which have eyed him as a missionary is eyed by heathen cannibals.

An extraordinary Christian soldier, he is a modern-day John the Baptist who, together with his wife ***Elaine Nile M.L.C.***, continues to battle in the political arena with spirits of mockery, ridicule and unbelief as well as with the gods of socialism and humanism, which have seized and held sway over the minds and hearts of many of our past and present legislators, to the detriment of Christ's Kingdom and people.

God help him, and us.

CONTENTS

CHAPTER 3 - DEMONS AND UNCLEAN SEXUAL MANIFESTATIONS

CHAPTER 4 - THE WRATH OF GOD—FACT OR FICTION?

CHAPTER 5 - YOUR WAY OF ESCAPE-WHAT YOU DO NEXT

CHAPTER 6 - THE WAY AHEAD—GOD'S MORALITY

APPENDICES

PREFACE

I write this preface some twelve years after this book began to take shape. All the trends that it records have continued so, although some statistics might be outdated, the message remains as up-to-date as tomorrow's newspaper.

It is especially tomorrow's message because lust and demonic activity continue in ever-increasing measure in the world. The purpose of this book is to expose the spiritual forces at work, and show you how to get out of their clutches! It is the result of more than twenty years in full-time Deliverance Ministry and I trust the sharing of these revelations will be invaluable to you and the Body of Christ.

My special thanks to the Rev. Allan Alcock, Th.L., Dip.R.E. (New Covenant Ministries) and Dr John Rockey, D.Phil., Ph.D., (Jesus Healing Ministries) for their reading of the text and making helpful suggestions, some of which have been incorporated. However responsibility for the final text is mine and mine alone, before God and man.

To God be the Glory!

Peter Hobson
Crows Nest, Sydney
1st July 1995

"MISGUIDED GROPE WAS ACT OF GOD"

A RANDY priest who fondled a woman's breasts told a court it wasn't him, but "the hand of God".

Frisky Father Jean Ricateau, 47, groped a 17-year-old churchgoer after choir practice, then tried to make her fondle his own tackle through his cassock.

When Fr Ricateau appeared in court, his defence was: "I couldn't help it; my hand was guided by the Lord. It was Him, not me, who did this."

So ran the item in a Sunday Telegraph report by Bruce Loudon, their London editor (Sydney, 9 Feb. '97). Thank God we don't go to Ricateau's church!

1
INTRODUCING THE VISIBLE PROBLEMS

1.1 THE DECLINE OF COMMUNITY STANDARDS IN WESTERN (CHRISTIAN) CIVILIZATION SINCE 1940 A.D.

This century's sexual revolution in democratic societies (usually thought of as *western cultures* which are influenced by Christian principles of morality) has created such an enormous change in "acceptable" standards of sexual behaviour that long-standing Christian principles are no longer considered "acceptable" or desirable for such communities as a whole. This current trend, of course, is not new. History tells us that the Roman Empire disintegrated some sixteen centuries ago because of its descent into sexual licence on a broad scale.[1] In 1787 the atheist *Gibbon* completed his book "*The Decline and Fall of the Roman Empire*", in which he listed five reasons for that fall:

1. The rapid increase of divorce; the undermining of the dignity and the sanctity of the home, which is the basis of human society.

2. Higher and higher taxes and the spending of public money for free bread and circuses for the populace.

3. The mad craze for pleasure; sports becoming every year more exciting and more brutal.

4. The building of gigantic armaments when the real enemy was within, the decadence of the people.

---

1 "The Failure of the Roman Republic" by R. E. Smith, Chapters 13 & 14.

5. The decay of religion—faith fading into mere form—losing touch with life and becoming impotent to guide the people.

It is said that history is constantly repeating itself—not in detail but in general. Can we learn anything from Gibbon's conclusions?

A GENERATION OF CHANGE

Today's decline in standards can be illustrated by a comparison of disciplinary problems experienced by school teachers in the United States. *Gabler's Educational Research Newsletter*[2] lists the relative problems that existed in 1940, with those of ONE generation later in 1982:

In 1940 the main problems teachers faced in disciplining their classes were talking and chewing gum.

By 1982, the main problems were rape and robbery.

These are among the statistics of a Gallup Poll on education, taken in America. They show a drastic change in children's behaviour, and the top discipline problems, during 42 years, in the twentieth century.

1940

1. Talking	5. Getting out of turn in line
2. Chewing gum	6. Wearing improper clothing
3. Making noise	7. Not putting paper in waste-paper baskets
4. Running in halls	

2 Reprinted in "Challenge Weekly," New Zealand.

<u>1982</u>

1 . Rape	10. Vandalism
2. Robbery	11. Extortion
3. Assault	12. Drug abuse and drug pushing
4. Burglary	13. Alcohol abuse
5. Arson	14. Gang warfare
6. Bombings	15. Pregnancies
7. Murder	16. Abortions
8. Suicide	17. Venereal disease
9. Absenteeism	

Many attitudes have changed greatly since World War II. Some twenty years ago I listened with great interest as an Anglican Clergyman recalled how he had visited an open air music festival on the outskirts of Sydney where drugs and bare bodies were everywhere. As he talked to many hippies about the Lord Jesus, some listened with interest. One said "Man, you've got beautiful thoughts," but when faced with the challenge of marrying their lovers or alternatively refraining from "free" sexual intercourse, they found this to be too great a stumbling block and their interest was dashed. "Man, that's hard!" they said.

For those who have continuously exercised sexual licence it IS hard to exercise self-control and restraint. There is no question that were it not for the need to regulate their sexual activity in accordance with the teachings of the New Testament, many of those hippies would have become Christians.

But they did as Jesus advised, they counted the cost of becoming His disciples **before** they made a commitment (Luke 14:27–33) and the desire of their flesh for continual sexual gratification with all and sundry overruled the desires of their spirits for forgiveness of sins and eternal life.

The apostle John describes these desires as:

1. the lust of the flesh

2. the lust of the eyes

3. the pride of life.   (1 John 2:16).

Some have interpreted these lusts to read *sex, money* and *power*, or *gals*, *gold* and *glory*, and as we can observe today, sexual desires through flesh and eyes exert an enormous influence in the lives of men and women everywhere. So much so that even the forgiveness of their sins by Almighty God is something they pass up so they can continue their sexual lusts, relationships and activities. The human spirit is sometimes willing but the flesh is indeed weak (Matt. 26:41, Mark 14:38), and we will say more in chapter 3.1.

This seems to run parallel with the rise in illegitimate births, which rose over ten years by 88% to almost 48,000 throughout Australia during 1987, according to the *Australian Bureau of Statistics*. *"The Plain Truth"* magazine,[3] no doubt commenting on the American scene, tells us *"there are more illegitimate children being conceived than at any other time in history."*

1.2 THE FINANCIAL COST OF IGNORING THE LAW OF CHRIST

Even Governments, endeavouring to keep the electorate happy, spend millions of dollars on programmes designed to allow people to pursue their sexual preferences without restraint and without having to pay the terrible spiritual and physical price for the abuse of their sexual nature.

But the Government is WASTING its (your) money. Not only do Abortion and other clinics (through Medicare or otherwise) cost the taxpayer a fortune, but there is also a terrible inner burden put upon the human soul when a woman interferes with God's creative processes and destroys the living embryo within her, simply because it is inconvenient or IS a product of lust and/or fornication and not a product of committed love within the family context.

---

3   March 1988

The Right to Life Association in Australia has a telling new car sticker which reads: ***ABORTION—ONE DEAD, ONE WOUNDED!***

Similarly un-married (and here we mean those who have never been married) mothers' pensions cost millions. Right here I would like to make it very clear that I have nothing but admiration for the many single mothers who have lost their husbands through one cause or another, and who are striving to bring up their children to be good citizens in a hostile world of sex, drugs, musical hypnosis, humanistic brain polluting (mistakenly labelled **brain washing**), rebellion, sickness and poverty. Many of them would say it is impossible without the Lord, and His people.

The Word of God tells us that *"**the heart of a child is bound up in foolishness, but the rod of correction will drive it far from him**"* (Prov. 22:15).

This is specifically applied to boys, of course, but nevertheless in humanistic societies where even a responsible and fair use of corporal punishment can actually get you into trouble with the law, parents have little hope. If you obey the law you disobey the Word of God and vice versa.

We also quickly end up with a nation of stupid and lawless people. Children whose hearts are bound up in stupidity then become adults whose hearts are bound up in stupidity, in the eyes of God.

It is hard enough, today, for two parents to succeed with their children's upbringing. It is well-nigh impossible for a single parent, unless they have a strong family support system in place. Fathers, brothers, sisters, mothers can all play a valuable and very practical part.

I am specifically concerned with NEVER MARRIED mothers, and the enormous problems they bring to ANY society or nation, as well as themselves. According to the Daily Mirror (21st January 1985), an unreleased Social Securities Department report reveals N.S.W. then had 57,581 people receiving the supporting parent's benefit— some 5,000 more than the previous year. A department spokesman said **the benefit was the fastest growing pension in Australia**. That made the then pay-out figure more than $7 million a week and rising. Many girls think they can have their baby (toy) to play with and at the same time get paid for it by the Government, by conveniently removing themselves from the work force. Meanwhile, the sweet little baby, without the secure environment of a well balanced family life, may grow into a maladjusted "monster" loosed into an already violent world, and the mother's life soon becomes a living hell. She ends up paying a terrible price emotionally, especially when the "monster" spends most of "his" life in jail, at the taxpayers' expense.

What has happened? In many cases the whole sorry process begins with an act of harlotry by a single girl. She gives birth to an illegitimate child, but because the Government encourages single parenthood by financing single unwed mothers, she refuses to have the baby adopted out into a good home. She enjoys the experience of motherhood and the dependence, love and company of the baby when it is small, and gets paid for it, *as well as going to the front of the government queue for welfare housing*. However, as baby grows up, it often becomes too much for the single mother to discipline adequately and embarks on a life of rebellion, deceit, drugs and stealing. The lass gets a broken heart, and the community foots an enormous bill through law-enforcement services as long as the "monster" lives.

Why "monster"?

The seeds of future disasters were sown in early childhood, when Mum felt lonely at night. Most full parent teams of man and wife pack their little ones off to bed fairly soon after the evening meal.

The little ones don't want to go to bed, of course, for fear of missing out on something, especially the television. But with TWO parents, the adults are glad to get a little time to themselves, without the children being in the centre of everything, and there are so many things that cannot be discussed with children present.

So, with two parents, it's "Off to bed!" which is as it should be. **With one lonely parent the kid(s) get to stay up as long as the adult and watch all the television** shows programmed at a late-evening time slot because of their sex and violence, etc.

Well-known Marriage Counsellor and Sex Therapist *Bettina Arndt* contributed the following in her Sunday Telegraph column:[4]

---

4   15 Jan. 1989

It was humiliating. The assault took place at our front door, where I stood waiting to show them out. The woman cowered in the face of his relentless tirade, ignoring his insults, feebly attempting to persuade him to see reason...

Miss Arndt explains that the mother's seven year old son had behaved normally until his mother arrived. Then the shouts and kicks!

... I didn't realise it at the time, but I have now discovered that social scientists are quite familiar with the abuse that takes place in this particular family structure.

Single mothers and sons have turned out to be a dangerous combination, notorious for all sorts of destructive patterns and behaviour .. .-

Psychologist Mavis Hetherington is the driving force behind the Virginia Longitudinal Study of Divorce and Remarriage, a project which has investigated children's adjustment from six months to six years after the divorce.

In all the permutations and combinations of family members that can result from a divorce it is boys who end up living with their single mothers who are most likely to create havoc and suffer the consequences to their psyche ...

Miss Arndt refers to "declared war" and "a struggle for survival," even six years after the divorce.

Troubled mother-son relationships persist, with many boys showing signs of disturbed behaviour...

The Hetherington research found ample evidence of the difficulty many divorced mothers have in controlling their sons: "Divorced mothers were ineffectual in their control attempts and gave many instructions with little follow-through. They tended to nag, natter and complain and were often involved in angry, escalating coercive cycles with their sons" ...

One of Ms. Hetherington's remarried mothers described her relief at being rescued by her new husband from the conflict-ridden relationship with her son. It was like being dragged from "the vortex of a whirlpool" she said.

Miss Arndt's comments are, of course, equally appropriate to unmarried mothers and their sons as they are to divorced mothers and their sons. Sadly, all this enormous and tragic WASTE of human lives (and workers' taxes) is greatly increased by sex before marriage producing FATHERLESS CHILDREN, followed by irresponsible, humanistic[5] government responses which accelerate rather than solve the problem.

Even when marriage is entered into by those who do not live according to the law of Christ (Gal. 6:2) but according to their own passions and desires, there often results a heavy economic cost to the community, quite apart from emotional hurts and traumas. We learn from ex N.S.W. Liberal politician **Alastair Webster** that the **annual cost of divorce** in Australia had reached **$1.8 BILLION** ($1,800,000,000) according to figures released in Federal Parliament.[6] One could house and/or feed quite a few poor with that kind of money.

1.3 A.I.D.S. BRINGS POVERTY TO ALL

"... keep the Commandments of the Lord, and His Statutes which I am commanding you today ...

                                             ... FOR YOUR GOOD!" (Deut. 10:13)

You may well say the consideration of the financial cost of A.I.D.S. to a nation is inhumane and un-Christian, when so many are dying or suffering in the most dreadful circumstances. Surely **the burden of human suffering** and how best we can alleviate that suffering should be the only consideration?

Yes, certainly that is the PRIORITY and we will be examining that critical matter, but for now we must consider the **financial** cost because if a nation becomes bankrupt of

5   Humanism is the religion in which man is God

6   Daily Mirror 20 April 1988

its resources NO ONE will get the help they need, as far as medical care and services are concerned.

Dr. Julian Gold, the Director of the Sydney AIDS Clinic, on his return from the first International Conference on AIDS in the U.S. made it clear that not only is the disease a deadly killer but it is one of the COSTLIEST diseases ever to combat in terms of MONEY.

He stated that the first 10,000 cases of AIDS in the U.S. had cost close to $5 billion (i.e. $5,000,000,000). The Australian Federal Government Report tabled in Parliament during November 1988 estimates the financial cost to the community during 1988 "was up to $400 million, with the cost growing as the deadly disease spreads."[7] **Professor David Penington**, chairman of the AIDS Task Force was quoted as saying:

> *"By the time AIDS regresses, as no doubt it will, society will be different... we will have learnt a great deal about the problems of human behaviour, how difficult it is for people to change ... there will have been a great many deaths, a great deal of suffering and A HUGE COST TO THE PUBLIC PURSE."* [8]

What are the Workers, the Unions and the Taxpayers going to do about that? What are Governments going to do about that? One thing the N.S.W. Government is reported to be doing is building new jail sections for the **Department of Corrective Services** (previously the Prisons Department) so that suspected AIDS carriers can be isolated from other prisoners. Hundreds of thousands of dollars are again involved in just this ONE comparatively small facet of the epidemic.

Multiply that one area by all the other areas which may include AIDS sufferers and we will quickly discover **the huge financial resources required to implement hygienic measures on every side simply do not exist**. What it all means is that the promiscuity of those who introduced the disease to our society may soon be responsible for the acceleration of poverty, sickness and death amongst us to a degree unprecedented in our history, and possibly the eventual total collapse of civilization as we know it in

7   Sun-Herald 7/11/88

8   Sydney Morning Herald 10/6/85

Australia and beyond.

Newsweek Magazine[9] carried the statement of Dr. Ward Cates of the U.S. Center for Disease Control: "*Anyone ... can see the potential for this disease being much worse than anything mankind has seen before.*"

Dr. Mervyn Silverman, one-time San Francisco Health Director who had been nationally praised for his efforts to treat AIDS patients and contain the disease is reported to have called AIDS "*the most devastating epidemic of the century.*"

As long ago as 1959, when I was converted to Christ, I can remember the world-famous evangelist *Dr. Billy Graham*, warning our prospering Australian nation, that SIN DESTROYS and that moral decay in any nation would destroy it just as Rome's Empire was destroyed by moral decay from WITHIN. Many didn't believe him then, preferring to believe the "It couldn't happen here" philosophy, but it seems our immoral chickens have now come home to roost.

Governments that have legislated or proposed legislation AGAINST the family unit (e.g. pensions and other favoured treatment for fornicators such as unmarried mothers, the de-christianising of our laws relating to homosexual activity, the removal of distinctions made on the basis of sex, i.e. in favour of unisex or homosexuality, and the legitimising of de facto relationships) will need to think again and PROTECT the FAMILY concept against all destructive intrusions and PROMOTE MONOGAMY.

That is, if they don't want to become BANKRUPT! Avoiding economic bankruptcy should NOT, of course, be the main motive for legislating PRO-FAMILY laws and moves against immorality but it is the motive that screams the loudest and hits the hardest where secular governments are concerned.

A few years ago a magazine gave some interesting statistics about two families who once lived in the United States.

> *Max Jukes did not believe in Christianity, and he married a girl of like beliefs. From the studies of 1,026 descendants of this union, 300 died prematurely; 190 sold themselves to vice; 100 were drunkards, and the*

9   12/8/85

family cost the State of New York one million, one hundred thousand dollars (currency values of the 1920s). Jonathan Edwards was a Christian and believed in Christian training. He married a girl who was a Christian. From this union they have studied 729 descendants: 300 were preachers; 65 were college professors; 13 were University Presidents; 6 were authors of good books; 3 United States Congressmen; 1 Vice-President of the United States. The family did not cost the State of New York a single dollar.[10]

The bottom line of all this, is that IMMORALITY BRINGS POVERTY. When we keep the law of Christ, prosperity, health and life abound, but **when we rebel against the law of Christ, poverty, sickness and death abound**. Which will it be? Blessings or curses? (cf. Deut. 28–29, John 10:10).

1.4 GOVERNMENT BY THE LOWEST COMMON DENOMINATOR

It is not good Government to allow Society's laws to sink to the level of the lowest common denominator, i.e. to the level where the LOWEST standards of its citizens are accommodated. This has the effect of bringing everyone down to the miserably low standards of the promiscuous minority, who then infest and infect the majority. Society's laws are not supposed to be accommodating to all standards of conduct but should afford protection of **high** standards of human behaviour for both Christians and non-Christians alike (Rom. 13:1–5). Our laws should PROTECT our CIVILIZATION, not allow it to degenerate to the level of the animals of the jungle.

Humanistic philosophy, which accommodates ALL standards of behaviour because there are no absolute rights or wrongs, leads inevitably into non-standards and the legalising of a wide range of social ills and evils, which inevitably brings the destruction of civilization as we know it. This is what the Bible means by lawlessness, i.e. the absence of law, which is anarchy (2 Thess. 2:1–12) and which Christ predicts will overtake most of the nations of the world before Judgement Day (cf. Matt. 24:9–14).

10 Author unknown

The message that must be put across to all governments is that NO SOCIETY CAN FINANCIALLY AFFORD IMMORALITY. **Australia** and the **United States** cannot afford immorality. **We the people** cannot afford the support pensions, the sickness benefits, the medical resources and the crime generated by immorality, not to mention the EMOTIONAL heartbreak and grief where family units have disintegrated on a wide scale. Therefore NO NATION can afford the luxury of humanistic and hedonistic governments,[11] unless their primary aim is to self-destruct.

For example, the Welfare payout by the Australian Government in the 1984–85 financial year was around $14.2 BILLION (i.e. $14,200,000,000), of which only $5.6 BILLION was for aged pensions. Most of the rest of the money went towards helping people in various kinds of situations which should not normally burden a society living under God's moral laws and blessings, but are more akin to a nation being under a curse, i.e.:

> Unemployed and Sickness benefits $3.5 BILLION (3,500,000,000)
> Invalid benefits $1.5 BILLION (1,500,000,000)
> Family allowances $1.5 BILLION (1,500,000,000)
> Supporting parents $1.0 BILLION (1,000,000,000)

Six years later the blow-out continues, with **$30 BILLION** allocated for Social Security and welfare.[12]

There are enough pressures on the people in our "democratic" society, through television and other media, schools and peer groups, teenage and party-going, and people living in sin and adultery all around us, without governments actively legislating against the family and MONOGAMY.

1.5 THE WORLD IS WRONG—AS USUAL

Thirty years ago just about EVERY young adult in a western "Christian" country

---

11 See Appendix C "Aids, Homosexuality and the N.S.W. Parliament."

12 Daily Mirror 22 Aug. 1990

knew sex before marriage was considered a sin in their society because their social customs then were at least based on the teachings of the historic Christian Church. Today in this age of "independence" against the Church (really rebellion against God), together with the discarding of the social customs of a past age (including Christian teaching) and the embracing of the new witchcraft trends of the occultism and eastern mysticism of the "New Age" movement, etc., we now live in an age when many young people have no sense of shame in going off on a weekend together and living as man and wife.

Some are genuinely startled when told that it is a sin to participate in sexual intercourse before marriage because they have never received that kind of Christian teaching. Such teaching seems contrary to the standards and behaviour of their friends and just about everybody else in their age group and circle of activity. Indeed, living together as man and wife before marriage is viewed as a status or maturity symbol, rather like smoking and drinking to advertise one's adulthood and sophistication—a kind of showing to the world (and oneself) how worldly-wise and grown up we are!

However, the world and its ways are no help in our pursuit of true happiness and fulfilment because we can never find or have a loving relationship with our Father God through worldliness. Rather, the Word of God says that ***friendship with the World is enmity (hostility) to God*** (James 4:4) and there is no safety in numbers.

It may come as a surprise to learn that in SPIRITUAL matters the majority is usually WRONG.[13] ***Archbishop William Temple*** once keenly observed that *"**In the Bible, the majority is always wrong**."*

This point is rather humorously portrayed in an anonymous piece of prose, reportedly circulated around Melbourne by some Roman Catholic priests. It takes the form of a memo directed to Jesus, son of Joseph, by Jordan Management Consultants:

> *"**Thank you for submitting the resumes of the 12 men you have picked for management positions in your new organization. All of them have now taken our battery of tests; we have not only run the results through our computer but have also arranged personal interviews for each of***

13 Refer to Appendix C

them with our psychologist.

"It is the staff opinion that most of your nominees are lacking in background, education and vocational aptitude for the type of enterprise you are undertaking.

"Simon Peter is emotionally unstable and given to fits of temper. Andrew has absolutely no qualities of leadership. The two brothers, James and John, the sons of Zebedee, place personal interest above company loyalty. Thomas demonstrates a questioning attitude that would tend to undermine morale.

"We feel that it is our duty to tell you that Matthew has been blacklisted by the Greater Jerusalem Better Business Bureau. James and Thaddaeus definitely have radical leanings and they both registered a high score on the maniac-depressive (sic) scale.

"One of the candidates, however, shows great potential. He is a man of ability and resourcefulness, meets people well, has a keen business mind and has contacts in high places. We recommend Judas Iscariot as your controller and right-hand man."

The gravity of this kind of "majority error" was illustrated by the **N.S.W. Department of Education's** philosophy on sex education in schools:

In attempting to be "value-free", sex education in Australian schools has become squeamish about marriage, fidelity and traditional values, according to the right-wing Institute of Public Affairs.

Releasing an institute study on sex education, the head of its Education Policy Unit, Dame Leonie Kramer, said Australian sex education guides failed to deal with the notions of sexual restraint and responsibility.

The study, by Dr. Susan Moore, a lecturer at the Sydney College of Advanced Education, examined the NSW and Victorian Governments

AIDS education kits and found them to be far inferior to a recently published United States kit.

The NSW kit, Dr. Moore said, was silent about the place of moral, emotional or spiritual considerations in sex education.

Instead it offered "platitudes" about the importance of values, the desirability of loving and caring and self-esteem.

The Victorian guide approved safe sex by devoting considerable space to it, while ignoring the benefits pupils might derive from sexual abstinence or restraint.

By contrast, the US booklet asserted that sex education should be provided within a strong moral context, "based on fidelity, commitment and maturity and placing sexuality within the context of marriage".

Dr. Moore said traditional values and a declared belief in the desirability of heterosexual over homosexual activity were "out" as far as Australian educators were concerned.

The Australian guides failed to explore the idea that sexuality was an expression of more than physical needs and desires. [14]

This "majority error" principle is consistent with the teaching of Jesus Christ, who said:

"Enter through the narrow gate because wide is the gate and easy is the way leading to destruction and there are many who enter it, but narrow is the gate and hard is the way that leads to life and those who find it are FEW." (Matthew 7:13–14)

Not only is the majority usually wrong and the people of God or the Church in the minority, but overall, down through the centuries, those who become children of God

14 Sydney Morning Herald 28/3/88

and enter the narrow gate (which is Jesus Christ) that leads to life will always be the FEW rather than the MANY, at least until the close of the New Testament Age—Jesus said so!

This scripture means a lot to me, because when I first heard it, May 10, 1959, over the radio, I was convicted by the Holy Spirit that I didn't want to be among the many who were on the broad road that led to destruction. My spirit cried out deep within me that I wanted to be one of the FEW, and as I experienced the fear of God I was also filled with the Holy Spirit. Praise the Name of Jesus!

The prophet *Isaiah* also brings to us a Word from the Lord which explains why "ordinary" people, that is, people who do not study the Word of God, nearly always get spiritual things wrong. We think we have a knowledge of God and that He thinks like we human beings think, but that is not true.

All over the world there are religions founded by men in an attempt to reach out to God. Invariably the teachings of such religions point to a salvation by good works. Man reasons that if his good deeds outweigh his bad deeds he will get a pass mark of 51% and be able to enter Heaven (or the Kingdom of God).

But God doesn't say that. God expects good works, but not as a means of buying our way into Heaven. He has provided a much more certain and achievable gate and way for us. His Name is Jesus, and His sacrifice on our behalf on the Cross of Calvary has purchased us a PARDON and a pass mark of 100%. We'll say more on this later. For the moment it is enough to see that what God said through Isaiah is true:

> *"For my thoughts are not your thoughts, neither are your ways my ways,"*
> *declares the Lord.*
>
> *As the heavens are higher than the earth, so are my ways higher than*
> *your ways and my thoughts than your thoughts."*
>
> (Isaiah 55:8–9)

We can't even get the way of Salvation right without help from the Word of God! Is it any wonder the majority (of the world) is always wrong about matters of life and death?

1.6 GOOD AND BAD SEX

The word of God also says to us:

> *"Do you not know that the unrighteous shall not inherit the Kingdom of God? Do not be deceived: neither fornicators nor idolaters, nor adulterers, nor effeminate nor sodomite... shall inherit the Kingdom of God"* (1 Cor. 6:9–10).

And,

> *"Let marriage be had in honour among all, and let the bed be undefiled, for fornicators and adulterers God will judge."* (Heb. 13:4).

So we can see that when we come to the sexual area, what the world tells us is trendy or acceptable is in direct conflict with God's Word. Who is right—God or man?

I remember a Swedish lady telling me why she had separated from her husband. "Bad sex" she said, clearly indicating that her standards of sexual behaviour were different from his. This is a very common problem between spouses. What is good sex and what is bad sex? What are the standards or criteria by which we should judge? The Christian Church has often been accused of being against sex, any form of sex, especially in the Victorian era when conversation on sexual subjects appears to have been practically non-existent. However sexual activity itself was not dead, as an over-populated United Kingdom amply testifies today.

But, as our texts illustrate, marriage is to be held in honour among all and the Christian standard has always been that sexual intercourse must be experienced within the context of lawful marriage. Fornication (basically, sex between unmarrieds) and adultery are condemned as coming under the judgement (wrath) of God. ***So, at the very beginning we have some guide-lines drawn as to what is good sex and bad sex in the eyes of the Lord.*** His standards should be ours also for we are His creatures and He is our Maker. He knows what is good for us and His laws are for OUR good, not His (Deut. 10:13); He doesn't need protection from hidden dangers but we do. To emphasise this, the apostle *Paul* describes a distinguishing feature of sexual sin. He says that we should:

"Flee (from) fornication. Every other sin which a man does is outside the body, but the fornicator sins against his own body." (1 Cor. 6:18)

and the same principle applies to the ladies, of course.

So, we can say that *"good" sex must be conducted within the context of marriage and all sexual activity outside of marriage by a man or his wife is "bad."* However, the Swedish lady was complaining about "bad" sex WITHIN her marriage, apparently due to sexual practices which she, rightly or wrongly, found unacceptable, so we can see that sexual problems can go far deeper than a simplistic view of fornication and adultery. For example, it is plain that *adultery* is sexual infidelity by or with people who are married (Lev. 20:10) but *fornication* has a much wider meaning, covering many forms of sexual sin, especially sex by non-married (cf. Rev. 21:8, 1 Cor. 6:13–20). Included under the broad meaning of "fornication" in the New Testament (sometimes translated "immorality"— 1 Cor. 5:1), would be *bestiality* (Lev. 21:15–16), *incest* (Lev. 20:11,17), *homosexuality* (Lev. 20:13, Rom. 1:26–27), *sex with occultists* (Lev. 20:6–7) and *sex during* a woman's monthly menstruation (Lev. 20:18), indeed ALL sexual uncleanness, because the word "fornication" means sexual impurity and uncleanness!

1.7 SPIRITUAL (DEMONIC) INFLUENCE

Why are these activities an abomination? Simply because they are unclean and contaminatory physical actions and by definition are inspired by unclean spirits. A simplistic but accurate principle to note well and which will be amply attested to in this publication is that *"What God considers unclean under the New Covenant is inspired by unclean spirits."*

This is a logical extension of a self-evident truth, the eternal "cause and effect" principle, but in this case the cause is spiritual, i.e. invisible, and the manifested effect takes place in the physical realm of creation as we see it, i.e. the visible world. If this causes you any uneasiness, please do not stop reading. One of the reasons this book is written is that both Christians and non-Christians might be encouraged to examine the evidence for themselves and perhaps continue their research beyond the boundaries of this book. However, I can say with enormous confidence that the deliverance ministry confirms these principles one hundred per cent. That is to say, **when people break the moral law of Christ they are invariably infected by unclean spirits**, and that **for every habitual sin in our lives there is a causal spirit** that only Christ can remove, usually through His anointed servants (chosen disciples).

Yes, it's true! Behind every sin (whether habitual or not) there is a spirit which stirs up our flesh—our old nature, our worldly thoughts and emotions, so that we often do what we don't want to do (Eph. 2:1–3, Rom 7:21–8:8).

To conclude on a positive note, THERE ARE REAL AND EFFECTIVE ANSWERS for the tide of moral and social ills plaguing the U.S.A., Australia and indeed, the whole world.

I want you to know that regardless of your spiritual or physical condition at this very moment in time, there are REAL and EFFECTIVE ANSWERS for you. The Almighty God, who may have given you up in the past to the gods of your choosing, is but waiting for you to RETURN to Him. His promise that "whoever shall call upon the Name of the Lord (Jesus) shall be saved (healed, delivered)" (Acts 2:21) is for you. YOU CAN BE CHANGED!

That is why this book has been written. In it we may criticise or condemn various ideas, philosophies and life-styles, **but we do NOT mean to criticise or condemn any human being**, for Christ did not come to destroy but to save. However the time of the Lord's saving grace is almost completed, the wrath of God has begun and the Judgement of God is at hand. NOW is the time to get ourselves right with Almighty God. Now, today, if you wish (see Chapter 5), or at the very latest by the time you have completed reading this book.

So far we have given you a brief introduction to the degeneration of western societies since 1940. Today's newspaper will tell you the same. So let us begin to present what we know about the INVISIBLE problems, that is, **the elemental or creation spirits of the universe**, with which the world we live in is infested.

2
THE INVISIBLE PROBLEM
ELEMENTAL (CREATION) SPIRITS

2.1 ANIMAL (CREATION) SPIRITS

This book has been an easy-read so far, hasn't it?

I believe it will be very worthwhile if you can now apply yourself to study. However, should you find this chapter difficult to get into, I suggest you slip over to chapter 3 and come back to this later. They form a *"cause and effect"* pattern, but some people find looking at effects first helps them understand causes. It's up to you.

The discussion of this whole area of spiritual activity may be a shock to your (belief) system. However, at the end of this section you should find your Christian belief system better informed, enlarged and strengthened, especially if you can also bring yourself to study *Appendix B* carefully.

Let us begin with another church-shaking controversy. Perhaps by the Grace of God we can turn two areas of current theological darkness into a blaze of light! The current so-called *"Toronto-blessing"* is a movement of such magnitude that many sections of Christendom have been forced to respond to it, some positively, most negatively. Such strange behaviour has been manifested in so many churches throughout the world (more than 5000 in the U.K.), that the weight of criticism now being raised against the movement has become enormous.

Recently one of our Deacons brought her husband to a Deliverance and Restoration meeting. When invited to come again he said to her, "I've been to one of your meetings—it was like a night at the Zoo!"

According to witnesses at a Benny Hinn meeting (available on video) people are laughing, screaming, exhibiting hysteria, roaring like lions, barking like dogs and hooting like owls, amongst other things.

Not the normal behaviour, I think you'll agree, for church goers!

The problem lies in the fact that even scholarly Christian leaders don't have the faintest idea of the extent of the existence of **ANIMAL (Creation) SPIRITS** in undeveloped nations, let alone western societies.

Few have any idea of the distinction, indeed conflict, between the human *soul* and the human *spirit*.

Few have any idea of the **demonic nature** of the spiritual disease of SIN with which we are all born.

Few have any idea what is Christ's solution to these problems (they didn't know there WAS a problem to begin with!). So how could they be expected to know what is going on in a 'Toronto-style'[15] meeting? These are the areas on which we believe we can shed some light.

An interesting incident is recorded in the book of Acts where a clairvoyant, occult woman had a **spirit of divination** cast out of her. Literally this should be translated **"the spirit of a python"** (Acts 16:16). We have known many cases where the spirit of a snake (including python) and various other animals and birds have been manifested and cast out of people. There are people who remind us of cats, pigs, frogs, various kinds of dogs, sparrows, owls, various birds of prey (hawk, vulture), snakes and reptiles, etc. and apparently there is no limit to the parallels that are possible from the realm of the flesh to the realm of the spiritual world. Hard to believe? Then ponder again 'the spirit of a python' and ask yourself what the Word of God is saying to us with this revealing phrase.

In fact the whole area of the INVISIBLE creation is one where we have only scanty information from the Word of God but nevertheless it probably has a lot more to

---

15 See "Toronto and the Truths You Haven't Heard Before" by this author, available at
www.impactchristianbooks.com/peter

tell us than we first realised. As well as the revelation of the existence of the spirit of a python which inspired a fortune-teller (above) the following scriptures are worth considering:

The LORD said to Israel: ***"I will restore to you the years that the locust has eaten, the cankerworm and the caterpillar and the palmerworm, my great army which I sent among you"*** (Joel 2:25).

The question is—are these insects a literal and physical army or is the LORD talking about a SPIRITUAL, UNSEEN army? There appears to be no similar prior reference to such insects in the Bible but earlier in the same chapter it seems they make their appearance at the Day of the LORD, that is, about judgement time. Also the New Testament has an interesting revelation on locusts (Rev. 9:7–11) which supports the view that the army is spiritual. We are not denying the physical, but simply emphasising the spiritual. Obviously both physical AND spiritual interpretations are necessary for many passages in the Bible.

The Bible also talks of a spiritual hornet which won victory for Israel in the Promised Land:

"And I sent the HORNET before you, which drove them out from before you, the two kings of the Amorites; not with your swords or your bow" (Josh. 24:12).

In the battles that Israel fought for the Promised Land there is no reference to an army or swarm of physical hornets descending upon the Amorites in order to give Israel victory, but here the LORD plainly says that they did not win the battle by their own physical weapons but by His intervention, probably supernatural and invisible. The earthly battle was fought with sword and bow, but it was won in the heavenlies, in the ***spiritual realm***, by ***God's hornet***.

Similarly the tramping of the Israelites out of Egypt and through the wilderness to Mount Sinai with all its dangers and drama may have been made on foot, physically, but they survived because in the spiritual, invisible realm they were borne on ***eagles' wings*** (Exod. 19:4).

According to one of king David's prophetic psalms, when Jesus hung on the Cross and looked down on the crowd mocking, reviling and abusing Him, ***He did not see*** *people, but animal spirits manifesting THROUGH people*—their teeth bared, nostrils flaring and their lips curled back as they hurled abuse at the Lamb of God. "If you be the Son of God come down from the Cross!" and "He saved others—let Him save Himself." Prophetic Psalm 22 tells us that Jesus saw *bulls* and *dogs* surrounding Him:

> "Many bulls have compassed me
> Strong bulls of Bashan have beset me round
> They gape upon me with their mouth
> As a ravening and roaring lion" (Ps. 22:12–13).

> "For dogs have compassed me
> The assembly of evil-doers have enclosed me
> They pierced my hands and my feet" (v. 16).

Plainly the Lord Jesus was not seeing flesh and blood but was looking into the SPIRITUAL natures of those surrounding Him, perceiving the attack of the unclean SPIRIT world THROUGH *bulls* (Jews?) and *dogs* (Gentiles?).

We hardly need to add that the self-righteous, traditional, religious Pharisees are seen in the spiritual realm of things as *VIPERS* (Matt. 3:7, 23:27–33) and that the harlot church (as distinct from the true Church—the Bride of Christ) is the home of every unclean spirit and every unclean hateful *BIRD* (spirit) (Rev. 18:2).

There is yet another hint of the spiritual nature of things operating invisibly behind the physical elements we normally see in the incident of Jesus stiliing the storm on the Sea of Galilee. He commanded the wind and sea, literally, "Be silent, BE MUZZLED!" He spoke to the elements as if they were some huge invisible animal or beast that was snarling and gnashing its teeth at the disciples in the boat and needed MUZZLING! (Mark 4:39). Have you ever thought of a severe storm in that way?

An Assyrian king, *Tiglath-Pileser*[16] (c.750 B.C.) wrote that he piled up the corpses of his enemies like a storm demon.[17] In another place this king calls himself a storm trooper. This immediately brings to mind the feared Nazi S.S. (Storm-troopers) of

---

16 Bible refs: 2 Kings 15:29, 16:7–10, 1 Chron. 5:6,26, 2 Chron. 28:20.

17 Albert Kirk Grayson "Assyrian Royal Inscriptions" part 2 (pp.6–7).

World War II.

Animals are terrified of storms. The weaker sex (lit. "vessel", perhaps referring primarily to physical strength — 1 Peter 3:7) normally fear storms, and if there is anything that would make a brave man afraid and feel like an insignificant and powerless ant it would be a life-threatening storm.

Storm demons are very nasty and man (without God) feels so very impotent and helpless against them. Another king, **Esarhaddon** (2 Kings 19:37 — c698 B.C.) called himself a **raging wolf** who had a storm demon going before him.[18] **Adolf**, the first name of Adolf Hitler, means **noble wolf**.

Consider the case where a Christian missionary in India told a visiting evangelist that he could tell which god various people worshipped by the way they walked, and illustrated his point by indicating people who worshipped an **elephant** god as those people lumbered by. Like any other unclean spirits, creation spirits stamp their character upon the person they inhabit and this is often observable, even to those without much discernment. It is a **spiritual** truth that we humans often take on the appearance of our **control spirit** (god, the old man—Col. 3:9 etc.) before we become Christians (Psalm 135:15–18). When Jesus comes into our lives, then the Holy Spirit becomes our control Spirit. The more we allow His control the more people see Jesus in us—praise the Lord! The more people impress us in this way, the more cautious we need to be regarding the imagery which they have taken on from Satan (Rom. 1:23–25) instead of the imagery of Jesus, the Son of God (Rom. 8:29), who is also Man made in the image of God (2 Cor. 4:4).

Taking this a step further, and it is a big step, perhaps we have erred in interpreting the **beasts in the book of Revelation** as being metaphorical or pictorial beasts but not real beings. They could well be spiritual beings, like satan[19] himself. It is only our tiny minds and lack of information about the spiritual world—demonic and Godly—which encourages us to settle for lesser but more acceptable explanations of prophecy (see Rev. 13:1–4, 11–15, cf.12:9, 12–17).

18 Daniel David Luckenbill "Ancient Records of Assyria and Babylonia Vol.11 (p.225).

19 We recognise satan as a personality, but do not wish to honour him with a capital S.

Also in the book of **Revelation** we have a clear indication that spiritual creatures are in fact unclean spirits. The **apostle John** writes:

> And I saw three unclean spirits coming out of the mouth of the dragon, out of the mouth of the beast and out of the mouth of the false prophet. For they are spirits of demons, performing signs… (Rev. 16: 13–14a).

What a comfort and a joy it is to know that the good Lord has given His disciples ***"authority to tread on serpents and scorpions and over all the power of the enemy".*** (Luke 10:19). Are these **serpents** and **scorpions** spiritual or physical? Probably BOTH!

Some time ago a Godly lady lay in bed racked with pain. She had been a heavy smoker but when she became a Christian she came under conviction that the nicotine bondage was unclean and so she received successful deliverance ministry for it, coughing up black chunks into the toilet for six weeks.

After this victory she began to experience enormous pain in her ribs, and X-rays showed that they were all twisted out of shape. Apparently the nicotine dosage had nullified the pain but now she had stopped taking the drug her body was sending and receiving warning signals that all was not well, and which hurt!

The pain grew so intense she began to see little scorpions crawling out from the corners of her ceiling towards her. She would rebuke them in Jesus' Name and they would go scurrying back to the corners of the ceiling again, to disappear for a season.

After using Christ's authority for several days, as given in Luke 10:19, she was healed. Praise the Lord!.

Let us re-think yet another passage of scripture. Mr. **Peter Horrobin**, Director of **Ellel Ministries** near Lancaster, England, believes the wild beasts referred to in Ezekiel's condemnation of false and slack shepherds have very real meaning for today, because they are in fact demonic, invisible, spiritual beasts that we fight against, now, in the New Testament Age, and not simply a parable applicable only to Ezekiel's time (Ezek. 34:5,8,25,28). In view of the evidence we have just considered how can any serious Bible student disagree with him?

Our Lord Jesus Christ once said of **King Herod**, the puppet governor for the Romans who had John the Baptist beheaded, "**Go and tell that FOX** Behold, I cast out demons and perform cures today and tomorrow, and on the third (day) I am finished." (Luke 13:32 lit.)

What a strange message to send Herod, who was reported to be seeking Jesus' life at that time. Was it simply a message to tell Herod He was getting out of his territory? Perhaps, but why the reference to healing and deliverance? Was it an oblique prophecy of His coming death and resurrection in which Herod would play a part? Or was it a veiled threat to the unclean spirit in Herod that Jesus was "on to it" and would cast it out if Herod (that is, the **Fox** spirit ruling Herod) gave Him any trouble?

Whatever you decide, one thing is inescapable, and that is that Jesus addressed Herod as a FOX! Was this simply a metaphorical description of a man who exhibited fox-like cunning during his reign or was Jesus referring literally to the SPIRITUAL nature of the man? Once I would have said the reference was metaphorical, but after twenty-one years in deliverance work I now believe it to be a literal, spiritual description.

2.2 THE SPIRIT OF DISOBEDIENCE (REBELLION)

The Bible has some very strong things to say about **human** nature, within which our **sexual** nature is so dominant. Our root psychological problems are exposed and referred to in many places but I doubt if there are a more revelational three verses than Ephesians 2:1–3:

> (V. 1) "And you He made alive when you were dead in your trespasses and in your sins (V.2) in which you then walked according to the age of this world, according to the ruler of the authority of the air, of the spirit now operating in the sons of disobedience (V.3) among whom we all also then conducted ourselves in the lusts of our flesh, doing the will of the flesh and of the mind, and were by nature children of wrath as also the rest (of mankind)." (Eph. 2:1-3)

What a powerful statement this is. It really spells out the world, the flesh and what appears to be Satan's spirit—all linked inextricably together and producing the result of sins and putting the sinner under the wrath of God — and the **spirit of rebellion**, probably referring to the **"old man"** or **"strong man"** within us all.

It is, of course, addressed to Christians who have therefore come out of the darkness of this Age and into the light of Christ, but nevertheless it explains the CAUSE(S) of the darkness. I believe the following points are found in the passage:

1. The **human spirit is in a kind of "dead" state** before it is made alive by the Holy Spirit (i.e. born again).

2. Those not born into a New Covenant-keeping family ALL behave according to:

   (i) the lusts of their flesh

   (ii) the will of their flesh

   (iii) the will of their mind

3. We were therefore **by nature** (soulish instinct) **ALL children of wrath** like ALL mankind, before receiving the saving grace of Christ.

4. This polluted and disastrous spiritual condition of original sin in our lives causes us to behave **according to the ways of the world**—

5. which puts us (our minds and flesh) under the control of the (spiritual) **ruler of the authority of the air** (airwaves—media? sound—music?)

6. — as well as being under the control of the **spirit of rebellion** (against God) which operates IN the sons of disobedience.

7. **Therefore original sin is caused by a spirit of rebellion within us, inherited from Adam** (Romans 5:12).

Clearly the apostle Paul tells us that everyone who has NOT received the HOLY Spirit and therefore been born again in their HUMAN spirit is under the control of an unclean spirit of rebellion or disobedience.

This makes them very vulnerable to the ways of the world with its satanic music and media influences. Our sexual natures are particularly vulnerable to such corruption by spiritual forces, even before we were born (the first time).

Praise the Lord that Paul goes on to tell us of the wonderful grace of God which enables Christians to break free from the foul spiritual chains which have bound them from within in the past, as they apply themselves to becoming like the Lord Jesus Christ! You will need to study the remaining chapters of his letter to the Ephesians to get the full picture.

Please forgive me if I do not spend much time in establishing the sinful and/or demonic nature of the human heart. This has been covered before in several other publications[20] and I would ask you to accept the truth of that statement as it stands, i.e. the human heart is, by nature, sinful and *its spiritual disease of sin is caused by a ruling unclean spirit presiding over an empire of various kingdoms of unclean spirits*, revealed in the Bible under the blanket names of Sin and Death. If you do not accept or like this initial premise and you do not have a copy of one of the other books to refer to, perhaps you could quickly look at Romans 5: 12, 17, 21 and 7:13-25 and tie in these references to the REIGN (as kings and princes) of Sin and Death with other verses which clearly teach that the inescapable warfare of life is SPIRITUAL. The apostle Paul tells us:

> "We are not contending against blood and flesh but against the Rulers, against the Authorities, against the world rulers of this darkness, against the SPIRITUALS (HOSTS) of evil in the heavenlies." (Ephesians 6:12 lit.)

> "For though we walk in the flesh we do not wage war in the flesh (realm or world), for the weapons of our warfare are not fleshly but powerful in God (spiritual) to overthrow strongholds ..." (2 Corinthians 10:3–4)

---

20 "The Re-incarnation Deception," "End-Time Deliverance and the Holy Spirit Revival," Christian Deliverance Book 4 "We All Have Our Demons" — available at **www.impactchristianbooks.com/peter**

2.3 THE TRUTH ABOUT THIS WORLD'S PROBLEMS

When we stop to think about this and begin to take Paul's words seriously, we find they strongly emphasize that the whole struggle of life is a struggle against unclean, invisible, spiritual enemies, i.e. unclean spirits or demons.[21]

Since it is obvious that every day carries its own challenges, indeed Jesus taught us that every day presents us with more than enough evil (Matthew 6:34), we begin to realise we are literally surrounded by the hosts of darkness seeking to trap us wherever possible. Is this being negative? No, we are only saying what the Bible says and the Bible is not a negative book — it is the revelation of God's victory over the spiritual rulers and authorities of this world through Jesus Christ, and how WE can experience it.

Thus Christians who are "in Christ" have nothing to fear—there is no need to hide one's head in the sand rather than look the enemy in the eye. The enormity and complexity of Satan's hosts (armies) are being revealed by the Holy Spirit today in a way no generation before us has ever experienced. We have never understood or even scratched the surface of another well-known Bible phrase *"the whole world lies in (the power of) the evil one"* (1 John 5:19). Would you please read that phrase slowly—three times—and really let it sink in? If you have done that you will more readily and easily understand something of the variety of unclean spirits or demons encountered during deliverance ministry, and how a very large proportion of their attacks against humans are aimed at our vulnerable sexual natures.

2.4 DANGERS FOR OUR CHILDREN

A factor that disturbs me greatly (although it is not at all surprising when we understand who rules the world) is the *increase of films depicting animals or monsters (usually quite hideous) in abnormally close fellowship with human beings.* This theme really seemed to get under way with the film "Planet of the Apes" and since then hideous things with appearances designed to horrify have been presented as poor, gentle, good, misunderstood friends of mankind. I sense that viewers are being

---

21 The term "unclean spirits", "demons" and "the powers of darkness" are considered interchangeable throughout.

programmed and softened up for an invasion of animal spirits, if they are not already affected; or at the very least, our children are being prepared by the evil genius of the destroyer, satan, to accept, communicate and be friendly with every hideous, foul and corrupting thing in his ugly kingdom (compare the film "E.T.", television's *Alf*, and any other friendly alien stories).

We have seen all kinds of children's toys made into cult figures such as:

a) Cabbage Patch dolls, with their witch-like imagery.

b) He-man dolls, a kind of deformed violent mutant from different worlds with telepathic, occult natures.

c) Ninja turtles, arguably the most violent cartoon on television and alleged to average 83 acts of violence during each segment.

d) Barbie dolls with their very materialistic influence and abnormal shapes.

e) Care bears which teach that actions depend on feelings rather than commitment and righteousness.

f) Smurfs, presented as lovable good guys who fight the bad guys for us. The problem is they are full of occult-images of magic and witchcraft.

g) Muppets, now even being presented in full length movies.

All these things seem to have replaced the *fairies* and *goblins* of yesteryear, sowing seeds of fantasy and superstition about the invisible World. No wonder the good Lord said, *"You shall not make to yourself any (graven) image, nor the likeness of ANYTHING that is in Heaven above or in the earth beneath or in the waters under the earth..."* (Exodus 20:4).

This central commandment has to be one of the most ignored and broken commandments in the Bible. This interest in animals and all living things in creation by children is probably a development from their love of a pet in their backyard, graduating to monsters on the television screen. To underline this soulish interest in the very young, we should note that it is customary even in Christian societies to give *dolls* to little girls and *teddy bears* to little boys. One might attempt to justify giving dolls to little girls on grounds of satisfying their basic motherhood instincts, so they can copy their mother and lavish love, care and affection (and perhaps practice a little domination) on a "baby" which, when you think about it, is really the image or idol of a baby. But how do we attempt to justify teddy bears for little boys?

When we stop to think about it we realise such a practice is really quite illogical or irrational. It is difficult to see any training for the future in this at all. One might argue that some little boys would be just as happy with a model puppy dog, but if that is the case WHY do we give BEARS? The answer is partly that BEARS SATISFY the SOULISH and mysterious LONGING of the little one for a relationship of love and protection, which may take years to disappear.

I remember well enough to know I lavished love (and sometimes a little "cruelty") on my own teddy and also at times found great security and comfort in having him in bed with me. What strange creatures we are when even as little children, we can IDENTIFY with, and believe we are protected by, speechless, inanimate objects which can never repay the trust we place in them (cf. Jeremiah 10:3-5). Would it not be healthier, and more obedient, for little children to be taught to trust in the Lord Jesus?

2.5 MANIFESTATIONS TODAY

When we grow up, of course, our relationship with animal or creation spirits can be quite sinister, e.g. a prostitute who received deliverance from unclean spirits drew me pictures of weird, furry animal shapes of the spirits that were tormenting her. *Gary Gilmore*, the American mass murderer who insisted on being executed at the end of 1976 and succeeded in January, 1977 drew pictures of the various animal spirits that were tormenting him in prison and they were published in the American press.

Gilmore wrote to his girlfriend from prison in September, 1976 as follows:

> "I've told you that I haven't slept. The ghosts have descended and set upon me with a force I didn't believe they possessed."

> 'They're slippery, sneaky and get tangled in your hair like bats—demons with dirty, furry bodies whispering vile things, chortling and laughing with a hideous glee to see me toss sleepless."

> "They plan to pounce upon me in a shrieking, mad fury when I leave (this life), with their hideous long toe and finger claws and teeth dripping

with rank saliva… dirty inhuman beasts, creeping, crawling red-eyed soulless beasts."

"They bite and claw, scratch and screech. They beckon with crooked finger. They call: 'You have to come one day. Come now, Gary, you murderous fiend.' Their aim is to recruit me. And their method is to destroy hope, then reason. They won't let me have a night's sleep. I smack them down, but they sneak back and climb in my ears and tell me foul jokes. They want to sap my strength, drain my hope . . . leave me derelict, lost, alone. I just endure and counter-punch when I can. I need a silver sword against them."

"They beset me, but I will shake them yet. I will slay and scatter them with the silver sword of love. You are my Nicole. Love me—give me the silver sword. They will never recruit me. They might attack me, but they will never prevail … never in all their shrieking, screeching insanity."

In the same letter, Gilmore refers to another time the ghosts attacked him years ago. He was chained to a bed in solitary confinement while serving time for robbery in an Oregon prison.

"They jumped on me like fiends when I was chained to that bed. They laughed with glee and made a circle with joined paws and long three-fingered hands. They thought they had me. I endured a constant onslaught of demon fury."

"It left me drained and fifty pounds lighter. They like it when I hurl. And I have been burning lately. I hate to say it, but in the last week they almost got me. They came the closest that they ever have." (National Enquirer, 18 Jan. 1977).

Doreen Irvine in her life story[22] wrote:

"I experienced the most horrific dreams . . . Ugly hairy animals chased me to a dark bottomless pit, hands clawed at my body, my throat. Marks

22 "From Witchcraft to Christ", p.135.

were evident on my body when I awoke."

The truth of the matter is that **creation spirits**—what the scriptures call the **beggarly and elemental spirits**[23] **of the universe** (Col. 2:8,20 R.S.V.) are rife throughout all forms of societies and cultures, INCLUDING CHRISTIAN. It surprises us today that they are there because they have never been exposed before, but they are coming out into the open more and more in these last days, and we are going to be absolutely amazed at the extent of their activities. In other words, the incident of Paul casting out the spirit of a python is not recorded in Holy Scripture so that we Christians might view it as an isolated or rare conflict which we can pass over quickly (by translating "python" as "divination"), but it is recorded for our benefit TODAY as a KEY deliverance, because it opens up our understanding to a widespread area of satanic activity and human need, together with the Lord's powerful solution.

In our ministry experience we have found various snake and serpent spirits are very, very common, and recently my wife, Verlie, received a Word of knowledge to concentrate on "wolf" spirits during a deliverance meeting. There were several obvious manifestations and the results very pleasing.

The Lord Jesus implies that **wolves** will be present in every church or Christian group. Their outward appearance is that of God's sheep (men and women) but INWARDLY (soulishly) they are ravenous **wolves** (Matt. 7:15).

The apostle Paul adds that this attack by spiritual wolves from within an assembly will certainly happen to the Ephesian church. Why? Because it is normal in spiritual warfare for EVERY Christian group (Acts 20:29–30).

Tiger spirits are common where the human problem concerns murder and blood-lust, and where violent sports are engaged in, such as boxing, and even common in the ladies. "Beware the fury of a woman ..."

Manifestations of animal spirits in people are also observable from their attitude to animals, and the clothes they wear. Nobody seems to know why women who are dressed in leopard-skin swimsuits, pants suits and play suits are considered as a sexual "turn-on" for males as well as a female "come-on"; likewise (shiny) leather jackets,

23 See Appendix B for a wider discussion.

slacks and boots, and also animal fur clothes. Apparently there is an area of unclean "kinky" sexual behaviour where animals' furs, skins and other paraphernalia are used. However, we will discuss this further under the heading "Bestiality."

At this point there will be some who are able to nod their heads to most of the general principles we have so far put forward, but there will be others who would like additional biblIcal information for the things we are saying. We have made this available at the end of this book under Appendix B so that theological and Bible students can get their spiritual teeth into it.

Let us now look in some detail at the SPIRITUAL CONFLICT that is now taking place in the sexual natures of millions of people around the world.

3
DEMONS AND UNCLEAN SEXUAL MANIFESTATIONS

3.1 LUST

The thing the world needs to note about the impact of the deliverance ministry upon the sexual area of our lives is the importance of facing up to the fact that our sexuality is probably the most vulnerable part of our personality, involving as it does the lust of the flesh and the lust of the eyes in particular. It is so easy for satan to distort our sexuality, particularly when we are unaware of what is going on. Various lusts are widespread—as is frigidity, and very often we find both problems in the one person.

MORE than a million Australian women are sexually assaulted every year but 90 per cent do not report the offences to police, according to the Institute of Criminology.[24]

The assaults, ranging from bottom-pinching to rape, were revealed as part of an international Victims of Crime survey. Institute researchers surveyed Australian women selected at random from telephone lists.

Senior institute criminologist, John Walker, said Australia had the highest rate of sexual assault of any of the 14 countries which took part in the survey. But it had a significantly lower rate of reporting attacks to police.

There is an enormous amount of sexual interference with young children and there can be no question such interference carries lasting effects and distorts the sufferers' emotions and attitudes throughout their lives—unless Christ's ministry is received.

---

24 Reported in the Sunday Telegraph by B. Bonham 3 Nov. 1991

The spirits that enter and trouble people who have been so abused are called *incubi* (in women) and *succubi* (in men) and basically produce various destructive personality problems flowing from sexual distortion. Such problems as nightmares, frustration, confusion, rages, depression, envy, frigidity and criticism when supported by fears, especially (in women) fear of men, invariably reveal molestation up to primary age, possibly by fathers, step-fathers, "uncles", brothers or sisters. This foul spirit can sometimes be smelt during ministry and sufferer improvement is usually quite dramatic. Some of these folk have suffered nervous breakdowns which increase their depression and would normally be classified as paranoid or schizophrenic. Lust would be one of the most common of all spirits, especially in men.

If satan is to lead men (and women) into rebellion against God and to destruction, it is desirable for him to tighten his grip on the object of his attention, and possibly no area of the personality is more vulnerable and open to distortion than the sexual. Whereas the world views lust as either masculine virility or feminine warmth and passion and therefore a ground for boasting and highly desirable amongst either sex, *God sees it as a gross distortion of a precious creative gift entrusted to mankind for both the procreation of children and the demonstration of human love.* It expresses an intimate commitment which makes man and woman 'one flesh'.

Boundaries have been set by God's Word as to the right use of this gracious gift. What a trust! What a privilege, and how we have abused it! It is true there are people who have enormous problems through spirits causing fear of sex, fear of men and various other forms of frigidity, and there are other blocks to normal sexual activity within marriages based on the Christian ethic. It is also true there are MANY MORE people affected by lust and not only heterosexual lust but homosexual, and bestial etc., expressed by a variety of perversions. The world says "Do what you like—no one should legislate for bedroom behaviour," but the Bible says *"there is a way that seems right to man but the way there of ends in death"* (Prov. 14:12).

The view of the world majority might be acceptable to some if the pervert would stay locked in his bedroom forever, but unfortunately he comes out to mix and influence and infect all and sundry, for his perversion is not simply of the flesh but of the soul also, and his bedroom perversions are but a small manifestation of the corruption of his heart—the tip of the iceberg. He carries the animal monsters of the powers of darkness with him to his factory, his office, his barracks—to his children and indeed down to the third and fourth generation of his seed, and then has the unmitigated gall and hypocrisy to blame God when a child is born less than perfect (see Transvestism).

Lust is not only an enormous kingdom within the heart of mankind, it is also one of the most common. Jesus said:

> Nothing going into the mouth defiles the man, but that which comes out of the mouth, this defiles the man... What comes out of the mouth comes forth out of the HEART and those defile the man... For out of the Heart come forth evil thoughts (dialogue), murders, ADULTERIES, FORNICATIONS... **(Matthew 15:11, 15–19 lit).**

Again the apostle John tells us of the THREE MAIN unclean motivations we have in life. They are recorded in 1 John 2:16:

(i) *The LUST of the FLESH*, which is simply the lust of the eyes and all the other sense organs such as smell TRANSMITTED INTO SOME FORM OF PHYSICAL ACTION, as in the David and Bathsheba story, or in regard to gluttony it is rather like your dog who finally gets your steak bone AFTER staring at you and it throughout your dinner.

(ii) *The LUST of the EYES* (e.g. lusting after a woman in our HEARTS and COVETING material wealth or goods etc.), through SEEING—compare Matt. 5:28 and David's sin with Bathsheba, (2 Sam. 11:2).

Here lusting also includes gluttony BEFORE you hand over the steak bone! I experienced an interesting example of the lust of the eyes recently. I was rushing up the street to keep an appointment with a dear brain-damaged lady who wanted some occult curses broken that had been placed on her. We had agreed to meet and talk in a grassy park plaza just off a busy street, and as I rushed up that street to be on time I looked across to the plaza to see if she had arrived before me.

As I looked, my line of vision was obscured by a very leggy girl in high heels and tight mini-skirt crossing the road. I looked intently, trying to see around her and into the park area where the seats were. "Tut tut, you shouldn't be doing that!" gently admonished a voice in my ear. I looked around to see a man smiling rather red-facedly at me. (I think he was a brother in Christ from the local Baptists). He had noticed the leggy girl also, as had most of the males in the immediate vicinity and thought I had been staring at her in an unseemly way. What was I to do or say? If I had told him the truth—that I was not looking particularly at her and she had walked across my line of vision he would have thought I was a hypocrite trying to justify or lie my way out of a bit of ogling, having been caught red-handed in the act, so to speak.

Further, the true explanation would also have made me out to be some kind of freakish eunuch who was so "holier than thou" (Isaiah 65:5) that I was not affected by a measure of the lusts of the flesh and eyes like other normal or ordinary mortal men—indeed, I was beyond 'temptation, which would have made me greater than the Lord Jesus Christ (Heb. 2:18).

I have been married thirty-five years and have two grown-up sons, so I do not write this book from the viewpoint of one who had taken a vow of celibacy in honour of the Lord, neither from a "holier than thou" philosophy, but from the position of an ordinary man of flesh, with all its burdens and desires, who has sought, and often failed, to walk in the footsteps of the Lord Jesus.

So what was I to respond to my brother-in-Christ? I said very simply, "I'm trying not to." I admitted my humanity and my Christian moral conviction combined in five words—by the grace of God. He very graciously replied, "I know what you mean!"

(iii) *The PRIDE of LIFE* which is all to do with life's power game. Recognition, status, influence and the craving for adulation—to be SOMEONE. One might even call this an unclean LUST or DESIRE also the lust for IMPORTANCE. Suffice to say that the Bible labels two out of three of our unclean motivations as LUST, witnessing to the enormity of this human weakness. Lust is spiritual, as confirmed by the prophet Hosea who says of Israel:

"Whoredom and wine and new wine take away the understanding ... for the spirit of whoredom has caused them to err... **(Hosea 4:11–12).**

"... for the spirit of whoredom is within them and they do not know the Lord." **(Hosea 5:4b).**

Compare this with **Babylon the Great**, which with all her **fornication** with the Kings of the earth, has become a haunt of **every foul spirit** (Rev. 18:1–3). I believe the picture is clear enough, and nearly every subject discussed in this chapter will add to our awareness of the magnitude of the Kingdom of lust in the world.

3.2 MASTURBATION

It may surprise many non-Christians to learn that masturbation is a sin, let alone the work of an unclean spirit, but while the scriptures do not seem to list masturbation specifically in the "sin lists" there are many sins common today that are also not categorised. What the scriptures do describe however, is THE IMMORAL PRINCIPLES WHICH MANIFEST AS SINS. For example, Jesus taught that if a man lusts for a woman (not his wife) in his heart he commits adultery with her (spiritually) (Matt. 5:27–28, cf. Jer. 17:9).

But is this not at the heart of masturbation? **Does it not flow from the lusts of the imagination?** Is it not a form of spiritual fornication or adultery which finds its physical expression in self abuse? Does it not flow from the lust of the flesh and the lust of the eyes? Therein lies the work of the unclean spirit and therein lies the cause of the GUILT that some secular psychiatrists, both professional and amateur, wrongly try to persuade their patients is unwarranted and unnecessary. Notwithstanding the need to overcome spirits of guilt and condemnation, they often err because they neither believe nor understand the Holy Scriptures and therefore they cannot have a fundamental understanding of the human spirit, the human soul and human accountability to a Holy God.

However I should add it is my view that adultery or fornication by masturbation (self-abuse) is a lesser sin than adultery or fornication involving another person. The latter are deadly sins (1 John 5:16–17). The former may also have deadly consequences, such as prostate cancer, but because masturbation is not mentioned in the deadly sin lists of the New Testament (e.g. Rom. 1:18–32, 1 Cor. 6:9–10, Gal. 5:19–21, Col. 3:5–8, Eph. 5:3–6), it **may** not lead to back-sliding and eternal death.

It would appear masturbation is ONE activity that eventually adversely affects the *male prostate gland* which "houses" many of man's spiritual and sexual problems. The unclean spirits activate the sexual imagination (mind) by producing lust in the heart, either during the day through the lust of the eyes (1 John 2:16) or dreams by night.

There is a verse that has always stood out for me from the time I sang it as a little choir boy:

"He has scattered the proud in the imagination of their hearts... " (Luke 1:51).

Clearly the imagination of our hearts is a very powerful influence in our lives. Today, the disciples of "get rich quick" philosophies tell us to tap into it all the time. *Napoleon Hill* set the tone more than thirty years ago when he wrote *"Think and Grow Rich"*. The message of this best-seller was simply to become an "ideas" person and put them to work, make them happen. Another title to it could well have been "Make Money Your God," although it did inspire creativity.

I share this with you in order to show *just how powerful the imagination of our hearts can be,* either to seek wealth, power, prestige and gratification of our unclean sexual desires or to seek the Kingdom (Rule) of God and His righteousness (Matt. 6:33).

No wonder we are told to pray without ceasing! (1 Thess 5:17)—it helps to keep our imagination clean and Christ-centred.

And it is also no wonder masturbation is so widespread and difficult for single people, especially men, to control!

WET DREAMS

As masturbation is resisted, however, the good Lord has arranged things so that the body can obtain its own natural, sexual release during night dreaming. The imagination is still involved but in a sub-conscious way, and wilful sin is avoided. The Word of God specifically recognises this form of sexual release, commonly called wet dreams, and although the actual discharge renders a man spiritually unclean for a short season, this position is quickly addressed and remedied under Old Testament law (Deut. 23:10–15).

Today, as the matter is not mentioned in the New Testament sin lists, no guilt should be entertained in the heart over wet dreams provided:

(i) physical cleansing (washing) is effected soon after.

(ii) the dreams were not centred on a particular object of lust (e.g. a neighbour's sexy wife or a voluptuous film star) about whom the imagination runs riot during the day.

Obviously pornographic voyeurism falls into category (ii) above.

We should also mention that while a Christian may not feel accountable for what happens when he is non-conscious, *the night-dreaming experience nevertheless warns him of the hidden lusts within his soul*, and which need to be crucified with Christ (Gal. 2:20, 5:24, 6:14).

It behoves EVERY Christian to strive to get victory over masturbation during their Christian walk. In the meantime man cannot escape the truth that he is a sinner and falls far short of the glory of God (Rom. 3:23) and needs the continuing forgiveness, deliverance and healing of Christ the Lord (1 John 1 :9).

It is no surprise that prostate cancer is such a killer today. Don't give up!

3.3 PORNOGRAPHY

Back in 1972 the fifty or so members of the Longford Committee Investigating Pornography published its report in England. The *Earl of Longford* was overall chairman, and rarely has a serious, scholarly report had so much ridicule and mockery heaped upon it. Why? Well, basically the rubbishing came from the print media which, of course, has a vested interest in girlie magazines, soft and hard porn. It is amazing how vitriolic the media magnates and their hard-bitten journalists can get when one hits their hip-pocket nerve (where they keep their money). Lord Longford soon became known as *Lord Porn*, and the butt of music-hall jokes throughout the land. Even the porn merchants in Australia joined in, like vultures around a carcass.

Yet the truth, the bottom line is that Lord Longford and the distinguished members of his hard-working Committee did a fine job in trying to warn the nation of a subtle, insidious moral disease that was defiling the nation—Pornography.

What follows in this chapter is a more modern, independent sketch on the same topic but **underlining its demonic inspiration**. A young lad of seventeen who had led a sheltered and civilised life was suddenly exposed to photographs of nude women in a girlie magazine. As he recounts it he was suddenly choking as if an invisible hand had grasped him around his throat in a vice-like grip. His friends were laughing and giggling at the pictures unaware of the trauma taking place in the lad next to them, who was fighting for his breath. When eventually the young man recovered his voice he was too embarrassed about his ignorance of sex to do anything but put on a bold front. Many years later and looking back he testifies to the invasion of himself by spirits of lust on that occasion, and lust was to trouble him for many years—until he received regular deliverance from Christ Jesus.

Mass murderer **Ted Bundy** blamed pornography for starting him on a career of about 100 sex murders.

The following newspaper report sums up his story:

MIAMI: Theodore Bundy, America's most notorious death row inmate, died in the electric chair last night after confessing to the murders of almost two dozen young women.

Last weekend Bundy moved to delay his execution by confessing to about 100 sex murders throughout the 1970s.

After almost 10 years of imprisonment, Bundy, 42, was put to death at the Florida State Prison for the 1978 murder of a 12-year-old girl.

California religious broadcaster James Dobson, who interviewed Bundy on the eve of his execution, said the condemned man told him his murder spree had been inspired by an addiction to hard-core pornography as an adolescent.

"He did say that was the fuel for the fantasies that led him to do these horrible things, and his concern is that other people out there are falling victim to the same things and that innocent women and children are going to be affected by it," Dobson told reporters.

He warned Americans that "there are loose in their towns, in their communities, people like me today whose dangerous impulses are being fuelled day in and day out by violence in the media in its various forms, particularly sexual violence." [25]

Many rapists, including Bundy, and the Moors murderer **Ian Brady** have admitted they used pornography as a spur to commit their crimes. Brady killed five children with **Myra Hindley. John Wayne Gacy** who raped and killed 33 boys in Illinois is another to openly confess that he often used pornography before a crime.

The point to make from Bundy's horrific experience is that anything that is addictive and dangerous either to self or to others, is plainly **demonic**. Addictions control people. Worse, **addictions ENSLAVE people and that is what demons do**. In the Bible people were blighted and enslaved by forces that took them over so those affected were described as demonised, or, as some translations put it, they were demon-possessed. The thought is one where people can no longer control their bodies or their desires or even their thoughts and decisions. Stronger forces have taken over and the Bible describes these as demons or unclean spirits.

It may surprise many people to know that pornography is addictive, as the testimony of Dan clearly indicates:

"At the age of nine, I spent my summer afternoons swimming at the local YMCA. That was where I met a young man in his early 20s. He befriended me and quickly won my confidence. About a week after we met, he talked me into going to a movie one day instead of swimming. After the movie, we walked down by the railroad track and climbed into an empty boxcar. He took some little cartoon books out of his pocket and showed them to me. I had never seen anything like them. They showed several cartoon

25 Daily Telegraph 25/1/89

characters in various stages of fornication and oral sex.

It was during my military tour of duty in Europe that I had the opportunity to purchase actual photographs, books and magazines depicting explicit sex acts. I then resumed my former habit of stimulation and masturbation through pornography. This continued for two years until I met and married my wife. After my marriage, I once again stopped buying explicit material and again disposed of all material I had collected.

However, the demon which had invaded my mind in that railroad car so many years ago would not let me alone. Without any consciousness on my part, I had been thoroughly conditioned to relate pornography with my own sexual experiences ...

During the sixties and seventies, I purchased thousands of explicit sex materials, including books, magazines and 8mm movies. I saw hundreds of films at adult movie theatres. I tried many times to stop my habit and would often dispose of everything I had collected. I would burn the material, hundreds, even thousands of dollars going up in smoke. Only it never stopped. Eventually the urge would come over me, and it would start all over again, each time my appetite becoming more bizarre.

It was at this point I realised I needed professional counselling, which I received. Through professional help, I came to realise that sexually explicit material is very much like substance abuse. The user becomes dependent upon material to satisfy a mental and physical demand. It exercises tremendous control over the mind. Fortunately for me, I was able to recognise my problem and had the desire to overcome it.

In no way is this to suggest that I am cured. What it does mean is I am in control of my habit. I have not purchased sexually explicit material for over four years. But the demon is still there, just waiting for the opportunity to regain control.

I cannot allow myself to be in a situation where I might weaken and once again fall prey to pornography. I cannot and will not patronise a store that displays and sells any type of sexually-oriented material. I must carefully select the television programmes I watch and the movies I see. Sometimes I am caught off guard when someone leaves a copy of Playboy or Penthouse lying around.

I must leave as quickly as possible, because I know if I took so much as one little peek, it would start all over again. I cannot afford to let that happen.

There are thousands, perhaps millions, of men and women just like me who have been enslaved by sexually explicit material and their number continues to grow with increasing availability of X-rated video cassettes and the accessibility of pornography. I personally know many users myself..."

(Light Magazine–Feb. 89)

A porn actor named George testifies to the influence of a father involved in pornography, and the heartless cruelty of those making money out of the industry:

"My daddy always had magazines like Playboy around the house. He also had quite a few X-rated publications. Even as a small child, I would find them and read them. Then as I got a little older, like junior high, my daddy would finish his magazines and throw them on my bed for me to look through. At that time, he would also take me to see R-rated movies at the drive-in.

I gradually got into the porno films industry. At nineteen when I was in college, I started out with dancing and nude modelling. That was in New York. After a while I was approached by a couple of different magazines. I was almost 21 when I finally got involved with X-rated movies—my goal. You know, you get paid to have sex with all these really pretty women. Life in the fast lane. Easy work. Easy money.

And anyway, it was my chance to become an actor. But the reality of what "acting" really meant hit me pretty fast. In the industry, you're not paid by the number of lines you have; you are paid per sex scene; you are paid more for anal; girls are paid more when they are working with two guys.

One thing to keep in mind is that the producer and director just have to get a product out. They really don't care about developing a "skill". They are nothing more than pimps. All they are out to do is make money. They don't give a hoot about the girls or guys. There are no health plans in the porn industry. The whole disease thing is one reason I decided to get out of the business. I personally have been pretty lucky only to have got gonorrhoea a couple of times. The diseases are really rampant out there. And there's the AIDS scare. If you have one person with AIDS, the whole industry can be infected.

Another reason I got out had to do with the way it dehumanises you and the young ladies you work with. I have been friends with a number of porno "actresses" over the years, and I hate seeing what it does to them. It really bothered me the way they were treated. Directors and producers would often, amid a lot of shouting and sometimes throwing of objects, tell them they'll never work again if they don't do a certain scene ...

I have seen real nice, sweet 18 year old girls go through total changes in personality and lifestyle. The industry affects them in really bad ways. And once they get into it they find it real hard to get out, because many of them have a drug or alcohol habit to support. I would say about 80 to 90 percent of the models delve into cocaine, and definitely use pot and alcohol ...

My home life definitely had an impact on me. If I hadn't been exposed to so much pornography, I really wouldn't have had that much interest in becoming a pornographic actor. If I hadn't had that influence growing up, I definitely wouldn't have got into this.

(Light Magazine–Feb. 89)

Pornography is such a harmful beginning to many serious crimes. The head of the Child Exploitation Unit in the Victorian Police has told director of the Australian Federation for Decency, Mr. Jack Sonneman, that **pornography was used in every case of child molestation and rape that has been investigated**.

A study by American psychologist William Marshall at Kingston Penitentiary and Queens University bears this out. In his most recent study Marshall found **almost half of the rapists** he interviewed admitted using so-called "soft core" consenting-sex pornography to arouse themselves in preparation for seeking out a victim.

He found 19 per cent of rapists used forced-sex, sadistic-bondage pornography to incite them to rape, while 38 per cent used consenting-sex pornography immediately prior to committing an offence. Even more strikingly, he found that **55 percent of homosexual child molesters he studied used child pornography to instigate their crimes.**

Dr. Paul Wilson, assistant director of the Australian Institute of Criminology says **the rise in lust killings is due to porno videos**. The Anita Cobby killing bears this out and an English judge has said porno videos turn a common thief into a depraved rapist. (Australia for Christ—Sept. 87)

Even primary schoolchildren can be affected by demonic influence through pornography. The Daily Mirror reported (June 10, 1988) that **three American primary schoolboys** watched pornographic gay movies on late night television before raping a number of their classmates in a school bathroom.

> The boys, aged 10, 11 and 12, "indicated they saw risque movies late at night on cable television", said Miami Beach police sergeant James Mazer.
>
> "Then they decided to try it out on their classmates."
>
> The boys and their alleged victims—some six to nine boys—are all in the same fifth grade class.
>
> "They're older-looking and stronger than their classmates," Sergeant Mazer said.

David and Roslyn Phillips writing in Light Magazine (Feb. '89) perhaps sum it all up for us:

> "In USA, the harm caused by porn is now being recognized. That was not true when the 1970 Presidential Commission on Obscenity and Pornography found no evidence to date that exposure to explicit sexual materials plays a significant role in the causation of delinquent or criminal behaviour. However, the recent Meese Commission on Pornography called the earlier conclusion 'starkly obscene.' Appointed in 1985 by U. S. Attorney General Edwin Meese, the Commission on Pornography published its final report in 1986 and became the first government study to claim that research is 'virtually unanimous' that 'there is a causal relationship between exposure to sexually violent materials and an increase in aggressive behaviour directed toward women.'

> 'In Australia too, the harm caused by pornographic and violent material is now being recognized. The 1988 Report of the Joint Select Committee on Video Material found 'clear evidence' that 'excessive exposure to violent material can have deleterious effects upon some people, particularly children and those predisposed to aggression.' It also found that pornography 'promotes a dangerous sexual mythology' by reducing 'persons to objects or occasions of sexual pleasure.'

> "That pornography should arouse such strong debate should not take us by surprise. Some 3000 years ago, God said to the people of Israel: 'You must not do as they do in Egypt, where you used to live, and you must not do as they do in the land of Canaan, where I am bringing you. There follows a list of all the sexual perversions promoted by modern pornography: incest, adultery, sodomy, bestiality, and the like. 'Do not defile yourselves in any of these ways,' says the Lord, 'because this is how the nations that I am going to drive out before you became defiled'". (Lev. 18:24)

Christians today are called, not to drive the defiled out of the land, but to drive defiling practices and the unclean spirits which inspire them out of both the land and the people who suffer from them.

One of the more encouraging things that happens in the deliverance ministry is the young men who come with their load of pornography to burn. There is usually a sigh of relief as the flames (in a backyard fireplace) begin to take hold, followed by an expression of annoyance as they remember how much they paid for the dirty pictures. "That is $... going up in smoke—oh well—good riddance!"

Have you got dirty pictures? Have they ever done you any good? If you have a lust problem (spirit) why feed it? Why build it up into a bigger monster than it already is? Get rid of it—come to Jesus and be cleansed—let your sexual appetites be controlled by your maker for ennobling, honourable and elevating fulfilment of your God-given sexuality, to be used according to God's laws. If you keep your dirty pictures you will inevitably be caught up with lust of the imagination and commit adultery and fornication in your heart, which is the same snare that satan sets for the masturbator. If you persist in this "voyeurism" you will be setting a course for your life that will destroy others, and eventually yourself.

Dean Sherman, of Youth With A Mission (YWAM) wrote:[26]

> "The worship of Baal was linked with the female goddess Ashtoreth and the use of the Asherah pole. Both these false gods were worshipped with lewd rites.
>
> One of the instructions given to Moses at the time of receiving the Ten Commandments was that the altars of despicable idols should be cut down and destroyed (Ex. 34:13). Likewise before the Spirit of the Lord came upon Gideon, to call the tribes of Israel to follow him, he was instructed to pull down the altar of Baal and cut down the Asherah, and, in an orderly manner, to build an altar to the Lord God on top of this stronghold.
>
> The Asherah pole, which was used for obscene worship, was made by man to resemble the female anatomy for his lustful satisfaction. Today we see the building up again of the modern version of the asherah through the multi-million dollar business of pornography, through videos and

26 Watchman Report 21 April, 1987

magazines such as Playboy and Penthouse now in colour photographic form of the female anatomy to enslave the passions of men. Pornography is born of lust; it thrives on lust (James 1:14). Pornography is of an evil heart (Mark 7:21). Research clearly demonstrates a direct link between pornography and bizarre anti-social behaviour involving sexual violence. Pornography is the theory, and rape the practice! N.S.W. has already had 300 cases of rape reported in the first two months of 1987!

These modern Asherah poles have been erected throughout the nation to destroy our nation's lifeblood, and it is time for us to rise up and pull them down. We need to make sure that our eyes, minds and hearts are not contaminated by this idol which God really hates."

If you have a pornography problem, you know what to do to break its chains of lust. Give your life to Christ and celebrate with a great bonfire.

3.4 FORNICATION (SEX OUTSIDE OF MARRIAGE)

On the subject of fornication and in particular sex before marriage, there are some satanic lies that must be exposed. It is a deception to say that sex before marriage gives a person a better chance of finding happiness by

(i) overcoming early shyness and clumsiness

(ii) increasing sexual skills and

(iii) affording experience in love and sex and thereby equipping young people with the know-how and experience to choose a permanent, compatible mate.

If sex was purely a physical act these theories may have some substance, but as the soul/heart and the emotions are also involved and we humans were designed to be one flesh (and one spirit) with one mate, the truth of the matter is that the *more* illicit sexual experience in which we indulge, the *less* chance we have of finding a permanent relationship within which God's plan for completeness, procreation of children and family security can flourish.

A trial marriage is no protection against FRIGIDITY. Many couples who have a "satisfactory" sex life outside of marriage and believe their trial has been successful find that things can change dramatically after the wedding (this is discussed more fully under the heading FRIGIDITY). To the question "What is the solution to the problem of lust in a woman?" a comedian answered "marriage". While this may be considered a disparaging comment on marriage, nevertheless it emphasises how things can change, not because marriage as an institution is the problem but because OUR soulish emotions are so often inspired by unclean forces and seek to undo God's perfect will for us.

(A) BRINGS DISHONOUR, GUILT AND HATRED

The more variety of sexual experience we have, the more confused we become, the easier it is to stop and start relationships with increasing numbers of the opposite sex, the more insecure and fearful we become, the more guilt-ridden and riddled with hopelessness, and as a result of all this, the more we HATE the opposite sex. I have never met an habitual fornicator who didn't claim to love women but in actual fact in his heart he HATED them for giving in to him and increasing his guilt.

The satisfaction of tasting the forbidden fruit of conquest without commitment turns to emptiness, disrespect, contempt and finally loathing. Not only is this the experience of life today with widespread wife and de facto bashings, but it was spelled out for us in the Bible with the tragic story of Amnon's rape of his beautiful sister *Tamar* (2 Sam. 13:11–15). To begin with he desired her more than anything. He deceived her, took her body and then hated her, and she was innocent in her heart throughout.

Likewise with prostitutes. Some are supposed to have "hearts of gold" but deep within they HATE the men who buy them. Australian actress Wendy Hughes researched her role as a prostitute in the film *"Nights on a Moving Train"* by interviewing street girls in Melbourne in 1987. She is recorded as saying, "I was amazed by their hardness, their ability to turn their smiles on and off at will, and their utter contempt for the men... They often hate every minute of their work—they absolutely despise their customers and speak about them in a most derogatory way..." [27]

27 Sunday Telegraph 13 March, 1988

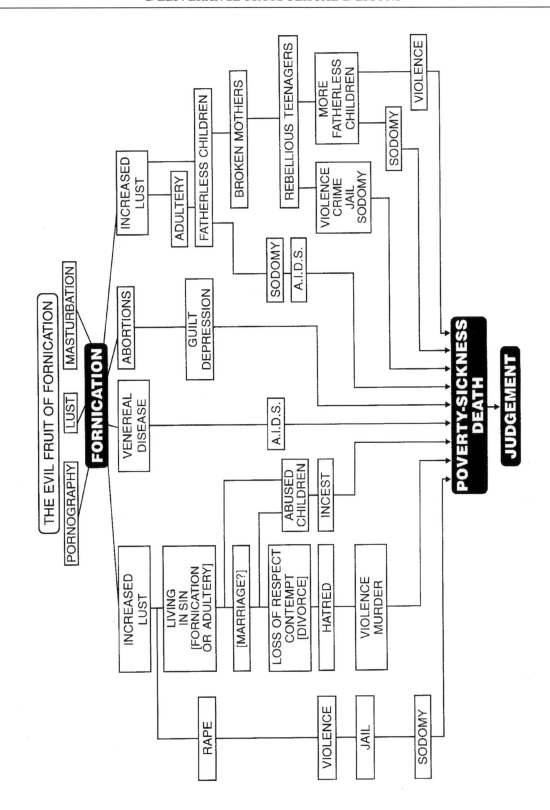

Many suppose that this hatred between fornicators is partly caused through contempt by the conqueror over the conquered—rather like a cowboy gun-slinger putting notches on his colt 45-mixed in with guilt and shame. *It is so much easier to blame and hate our partner in shame than to blame ourselves* for a deep-down guilty conscience that won't go away no matter how we try.

This is why so many de facto situations are prone to tragedy, with so many murder-suicides by de factos[28] following on "domestic" arguments, and child abuse and murder by men who "crack" under the weight of guilt and frustration of unclean living upon their consciences.

(B) BRINGS DIVORCE FOR THE MARRIEDS

Overcoming early shyness and clumsiness and increasing sexual skills is far better attempted with someone to whom we are FULLY committed and with whom we are one flesh and are bound by LOVE without guilt.

I have no doubt in my own heart that *the present rate of divorce amongst married people is a direct result of pre-marital fornication, recent or in the distant past.* Rather than providing a sound preparation it destroys the chances of two people making the necessary commitment to each other in their HEARTS.

To illustrate this let us look at a modern-day situation which is all too prevalent. A young man and a young woman are attracted to each other and have strong affection for each other but in the uncertain social climate of today they hesitate to marry, because this would mean a commitment which others have optimistically made before them, and failed to live up to. Therefore they are encouraged by popular opinion to live together in a trial "marriage" which enjoys the benefits of married life without the heavy responsibilities, e.g. sex without full commitment. They live reasonably happily for, say, six years and then they are persuaded to marry by parents and they do so to please them. After all, they reason that their "trial" has succeeded, and marriage would be good for children.

28 Daily Mirror 16 Jan. 1986

Disagreements and fights between the young couple now take on a new bitterness and within 12 months the marriage ends up in the Divorce Court. What went wrong? Is it, as the worldly-wise amateur philosophers tell us, that marriage is outdated and puts intolerable strain on young people? Satan would like everyone to think so, but the problem really started long before when they experienced sex without commitment.

This is even more true when, not only does a young man or woman indulge their passion for a lover BEFORE they marry each other but they experience passion with several different lovers before a marriage with someone way down the track of life.

Pastor Harold Dewberry explains that sexual intimacy involves a measure of soulish and physical bonding and this is what the Lord Jesus Christ meant when He taught that "the two become one flesh" (Matt. 19:5–6). Experiences of intimate and passionate pleasure are indelibly imprinted in the memory of mind and emotions, and are too easily replayed in the imagination of our hearts (Gen. 6:5, 8:21, Luke 1:51) throughout our lifetime.

These memories, although usually kept secret from one's spouse, are a constant source of division and opposition against a total and complete Godly bonding with one's life-long mate as "one flesh."

Thank God the curse of such memories and unclean bonding can be broken through the power of the risen Christ and a fresh beginning made.

Consider the experience of life itself. Some twenty years ago the divorce rate was growing but not nearly so horrific as today. At that time Australians were just beginning to catch on to the Hollywood disease of changing spouses whenever one's own wilfulness was thwarted. Hollywood presented a picture where beautiful women were not made to be a help meet (fit and proper) for man, but this design of God was turned around by the Movie Moguls so that they became goddesses to be adored and worshipped. The resultant material wealth and riches also meant independence for both male and female stars, and getting their own way at all limes became normal. Under those circumstances, clashes of will become intolerable, and division and destruction reign—until one can trade-in the old spouse for a new model—pending the next major frustration.

The truth of the matter is that when men and women have to stick together to survive the battle of life even for basic things such as bread on the table and clothes on their backs, then man fulfils his role as protector and provider, and woman is a help meet for man. One has only to think of the American pioneer families moving West, and family life in Victorian England, to confirm this. However, the influx of affluence and riches so often brings power, wilfulness, rebellion and selfishness beyond measure. How hard it is for a rich man to enter the Kingdom of God! (Mark 10:23–27)

Along with the poor example set by the "beautiful", the wealthy and the adored, and with this trade-in situation becoming more fashionable, there came a new prosperity whereby we no longer had to fight for survival, but we now fought to become millionaires (even unemployment benefits provide our daily bread!). Where is God in all this? It seems many have traded Him in also (as far as they are concerned) because like a faithful Father, He often thwarts their desire to indulge the flesh, to satisfy the lusts of the flesh, the lust of the eyes and the pride of life. So many of His creatures enjoy rebellion and uncleanness and playing the "power game" of the world that they exchange the love of God for gods of sex, money and power.

So in 1995 we find divorce reached epidemic proportions[29] in affluent nations but more than twenty years ago when the epidemic was beginning, the miserable humanistic philosophy being proclaimed to eager ears was that too many unsuitable people were being matched in marriage. The pseudo-wise men of the day told us the divorce rate was climbing because of (sexual) incompatibility.

Obviously one could find out one's future spouse's ATTITUDES on many things before marriage but the "old-fashioned" (i.e. Christian) standards prevented one discovering anything about SEXUAL compatibility beforehand. Therefore (said the pseudo-wise) trial marriage i.e. living together as de-facto man and wife, would remove this uncertainty and people could get married KNOWING what they were getting. The notion seemed so wise, so reasonable, so convincing and so attractive, but as the Word of God has warned us for nineteen centuries, it has proved to be a ***destructive deception.***

29 It is true that the divorce figures have been falling in Australia since 1986 according to surveys and the Bureau of Statistics (Daily Mirror 24/10/86, Sunday Telegraph 8/5/88). But that is only because more women are saying "I don't" and choosing other alternatives such as living in sin.

We do not need to be statisticians to know that in the area of trial marriages which are followed by subsequent legal marriages, there has been an explosion in the divorce rate.

The question is, why has this unexpected result occurred?

The key to the whole matter is that legal marriage means COMMITMENT. Hollywood movie stars from Hedy Lamarr to Loni Anderson (since married AND divorced) have expressed on television the now common view that marriage is just a piece of paper. *It is not a piece of paper, it is a covenant made between two people for life* (Mal. 2:14–16) and the piece of paper simply records the marriage covenant made at a point in time, for public, historical and legal purposes. God has designed marriage (among other things) as a framework for the right use of sexual intercourse, for *sex is the fullest expression of that commitment*. When we enter into sexual unity with another human being it ought not to be simply an expression of lust or an animal drive for satisfaction but it should give expression to a COMMITMENT of LOVE, unifying the two bodies as ONE, a fusing of both body and spirit. Therefore to indulge in sex before marriage is to put the cart before the horse and the two lives get off to a dangerous start. The percentages are ALREADY stacked against any such couple and unless there is total healing and cleansing through Christ's forgiveness I doubt that their lives can ever fulfil their highest potential.

When two people marry after having previous widespread sexual experience, either between themselves or with other parties, they are very prone to end up in the Divorce Court. Why? Simply because they cannot handle the one-flesh commitment. They have not been able to avoid rebellion and lust spirits, etc. entering their souls and they become unable to have a proper, i.e. God-designed relationship between them. It is not marriage that is the problem, it is FORNICATION (sex before marriage) that so twists and spoils so many young people that they enter into marriage without the moral integrity necessary in order to weather the inevitable storms.

(C) BRINGS LOSS OF RESPECT AND TRUST

As a deliverance minister I am called upon to do a degree of marriage counselling and my experience shows that trial marriages in no way increase a couple's chances of success together but rather the opposite. The erosion of respect for each other (hidden away in the heart) and the familiarity without a full sharing commitment is not overcome by a later legal marriage, which may then become a prison rather than a blessed, fulfilling unity.

The loss of respect and trust will be discussed under some of the other headings but for the moment please think about the following propositions:

(i) You can't stay in love with a mate you don't respect.

(ii) You can't continue to respect (admire) someone you don't trust.

Fornication destroys the human innocence upon which lifetime relationships can be built—relationships that lead one into **total** commitment to another because the other party is **trustworthy**. Only a fool would commit himself or herself to someone they do not TRUST. Perhaps one of the major reasons people are living together rather than marrying is because they do not trust either their de facto spouse or perhaps themselves: What a sad testimony this is to the work of satan in our lives. In effect they may be saying to their partner in sin "you'll do for now, until someone nicer, better, richer comes along!"

(D) BRINGS SHAME, REJECTION AND LONELINESS FOR THE UNMARRIEDS.

As we said before, modern philosophies on sex might be successful if we were only physical beings, but human beings are SPIRITUAL beings too, with soulish emotions! The apostle Paul warns us to *"flee youthful lusts, but pursue righteousness, faith, love (and) peace with those who call on the Lord out of a clean heart"* (2 Tim. 2:22) and the apostle Peter tells us to *"abstain from fleshly lusts which war against the soul"* (1 Peter 2:11). "Free" love and sexual "liberation'' demand a terrible price as spirits of lust and adultery build up within the soul, with their henchmen of rebellion and anger and all things pertaining to selfishness. The flesh, its lusts and our soulish emotions are inextricably bound up together—the Word of God says so and our emotions confirm its truth! For example RAPE normally causes greater damage psychologically than physically, according to film director Robert M. Young, whose daughter was raped in 1972. "Psychologically rape leaves a far deeper scar on the victim than the physical torment," Mr. Young is reported[30] to have said *"Rape is a violation of the SOUL, not just the body."*

Apart from the soulish emotional damage done to the victim of rape, we do ourselves damage when we consent to having a string of love affairs. To begin, there is the guilt which is inescapable. We may rationalize with our heads that fornication is not against the law (of men) and there is nothing wrong—all we need to do is to throw off our inhibitions which have been imposed on us by our parents, the previous generation, our religious training, etc.

What we forget is that it is against the moral law of GOD, and that when He made us He wrote His Laws on our HEARTS (Heb. 8:10)! It is possible to so continue to break God's Laws that our consciences are seared, i.e., ineffective (1 Tim. 4:2), but by that time we are in such a demonic mess, such a walking disaster, the successful pursuit and hope of happiness have long since fled. Only God through Jesus Christ can save you—and why should He? If you have ignored His Laws, written upon your heart—and ignored His Word (the Bible)—and ignored His Church (preachers, teachers and friends who have tried to guide you) you surely have only yourself to blame for the judgement that has come, and the judgement that will come, upon you.

However, the good news is that if this makes sense to you and there is still a guilt, a flicker of life in your conscience and heart, it is not too late to get right with God. Keep reading.

So it is not only your training, your parenting etc. that has given you a guilt complex, it is God who has written His Laws on your heart. That kind of guilt is a lot harder to get rid of! So even when we consent to fornicate with attractive people whom we like, the guilt and the emotional damage is birthed. When you go from lover to lover the cumulative effect is to lose all respect for the opposite sex and to make a life-long partnership with ONE particular person almost impossible. If you DO wed, the consequences are very likely to be adultery, hurts, anger, bitterness, hatred and

30 Daily Mirror 31 Dec. 1986

divorce.

Now, I am obliged to warn you, as a deliverance minister of twenty-two years experience, that the transfer of demons from soul to soul is often effected during lustful (unclean) behaviour and that ***any type of fornication is an open invitation to the powers of darkness to enter your soul*** and to twist you up emotionally and spiritually.

God did not set His moral laws in place for (His) fun, or to be a spoilsport, but in order to protect YOU, His precious creation, from the attention of your spiritual enemies. (Deut. 10:13, cf. Rom. 8:28)

This is the main reason people usually reject those who have had a lot of sexual experience from being potential life-long partners. There are exceptions, of course, amongst those who are already heavily demonised, but people with extensive sexual histories usually experience rejection and loneliness. Whether with consenting or non-consenting adults, ***each different sexual contact reduces respect and consideration for the opposite sex*** and also the ability to form a one-flesh unity as God intended. The apostle Paul warns us that ***"...he who joins himself to a prostitute becomes one body with her. For as it is written, The two shall become one flesh"*** (1 Cor. 6:16). If that is true of even a prostitute then it is true of all those who copulate together outside of the will and commandment of God.

This means a man can become one-flesh with many women but of course the cumulative effect of such conduct is to weaken and DESTROY the unity that God desires for a man and woman. It is designed to be a PERMANENT ONE-FLESH unity—not a collective string of half-baked relationships linked together by sexual gratification—and unclean, demonic linking of lust and animal spirits at that!

(E) BRINGS DEADLY DISEASE

No, I'm not talking about sexually transmitted diseases like herpes or syphilis or even A.I.D.S. I am referring to CANCER of the cervix and other diseases thought to have been eliminated:

PROMISCUITY, not the pill, may be to blame for many cases of cervical cancer, according to a leading gynaecologist.

Dr. Soo Keat Khoo, Associate Professor of Obstetrics and Gynaecology at Royal Brisbane Hospital, said there was strong evidence linking promiscuity and warts virus infection, which is in turn linked to cancer of the cervix.

In a report in the Medical Journal of Australia, Dr. Khoo said a recent study found "the risk of cervical cancer was highest in sexually active women who had used the pill for four to six years".

He said: "But the cervical cancer risk associated with the pill failed to become significant."

Controversy had linked the pill and cervical cancer but recent studies showed that this cancer was more likely to be related to sexual activity.[31]

Another report[32] two years later says that the number of sexual partners increases the cancer risk greatly:

"THE number of sexual partners is the single most important factor in the risk of contracting cervical cancer, according to a new study.

The risk of cervical cancer increased six-fold for women who had had seven or more sexual partners in a lifetime compared with those who had one or no partners .

The study, published in the Medical Journal of Australia, was carried out by the University of Sydney, the US National Cancer Institute and the Queensland Institute of Medical Research.

It studied 169 Australian-born women with confirmed carcinoma-in-situ (the infection which leads to cervical cancer) compared with 279 women without the carcinoma.

It found sexual risk factors were the number of partners, the age of first

31 Daily Mirror 31 Dec. 1986

32 Daily Telegraph 6 Feb. 1989

intercourse and exposure to venereal disease.

The authors found the risks were reduced slightly through a number of factors.

'We observed that the risk decreased as the period of breast feeding was prolonged (both in terms of the number of infants who were breast-fed and the duration of the breast feeding),' they said.

'We noted also reduced risks among women who utilised the rhythm method of contraception, although it is possible that these reduced risks may relate to unmeasured variable of lifestyle.'

Condoms and diaphragms have no significant protective effect."

The bottom line is that a later report indicates **the proportion of women under 35 with cervical cancer has almost tripled in the last 20 years.** This has been observed throughout the western world, due to the increase in the number of sex partners women were likely to have.[33]

Cancer is a peculiar deadly disease, insofar as it consists of rebellious body cells multiplying in a chaotic, wild and rebellious way against God's order and design. Its very nature reveals its sources of inspiration—spirits of death, destruction, infirmity and REBELLION. The first three spirits attend many diseases but cancer ALWAYS has a spirit of rebellion involved, and if you have accepted our explanation of Ephesians 2:1-3 in chapter 2, you will know that, unless you were born into a faithful Bible-believing Christian family, you, I, and everyone else was under the control of a **spirit of disobedience** BEFORE our conversion to Christ. Also, insofar as we still continued in some measure of (unintentional) rebellion AFTER our conversion, as we fall far short of Christ's perfection, it is self-evident that this spirit continues to have an evil influence in our lives. It is manifested more and more as we get older, both by our behaviour and on our skin through warts and moles etc., and sadly, sometimes with serious internal growths. Because of its inherited spiritual source as part of our original sin disease (Rom. 5:12) we are therefore ALL susceptible to cancer(s), but obviously the more our lifestyles are in rebellion against God through fornication, adultery and all forms of immorality the more speedily we open up ourselves to terrible suffering—and death.

33 Sunday Telegraph 5 March, 1989

The sexually transmitted diseases and cervical cancer bear stunning testimony to the truth of God's warnings.

Another report[34] says that:

> SEXUAL promiscuity in Australia is responsible for a resurgence of some diseases which were almost eradicated.
>
> Dr. Peter Stanley, visiting consultant at Fairfield Infectious Diseases Hospital, Melbourne, said such complaints as hepatitis A and gastric infection had re-emerged among promiscuous homosexuals and in heterosexuals.
>
> He said the re-emerging diseases provided a "pool" of infections which could spread to the rest of the community.
>
> The only answer to the increase in sexually transmitted diseases was for people at risk to reduce their sexual activity or become celibate.
>
> Dr. Stanley told a conference of the Royal Australasian College of Physicians in Perth that if patients showed symptoms of an unusual disease, doctors should question them about their social and sexual habits.
>
> He said: "With an increase in hygiene and a better standard of living, diseases like hepatitis A dropped right away in Australia.
>
> "Now the diseases are reappearing as being sexually transmitted."

Not only do we suffer traditional diseases such as **Syphilis** and **Gonorrhea** but now we have added **Herpes II, Chlamydia** and **A.I.D.S.**

At the same time there is a marked increase in cancer of the sexual organs, as we have seen with **cervical cancer in women** and now **testicular cancer in men**. A recent report (source unknown) reveals a staggering 300 per cent increase in cancer of the testicles of men between the ages of twenty (20) and forty (40) years of age.

However we should not forget that **most unclean spirits attacking our sexual nature lodge themselves in a man's prostate gland or a women's womb** and it is in

34 Daily Telegraph 6 May, 1983

these areas that we find a very high incidence of cancer or other infirmities.

(F) BRINGS DISADVANTAGED CHILDREN INTO THE WORLD.

We talked about the soaring birth-rates for illegitimate children in chapter 1 and it must be obvious that fornication often results in at least two evil, immediate consequences:

(i) **Abortion**. Even if one believes that abortion is sometimes justifiable in cases of rape or danger to the mother's life, the fact remains that interfering with God's creative processes and destroying a potential human being is a most serious moral action to take.

(ii) **Single parenthood**. Children born to single parents are greatly disadvantaged. A child born without the full parenting of a father and a mother can rarely receive the right male and female input into their lives, and if either male or female input into the life of a child is exaggerated above the other then identity warping is almost inevitable. It is this kind of character or identity warping that "creates" homosexuals (male and female), and so, in my view, heterosexuals cannot complain about homosexuals being responsible for the A.I.D.S. epidemic. Why? Because heterosexual fornication is largely responsible for so many fatherless children being brought into the world, who will eventually find themselves homosexual. Poetic or divine justice has travelled full cycle, and ALL fornicators must face the consequences of their day of reckoning. **As you sow so shall you reap** (Gal. 6:7-8).

There is always, ALWAYS, a price to pay for "sowing wild oats".

The U.S.A. is very conscious of its moral problem regarding fornication and adultery and recently was trying to promote a sense of sexual responsibility amongst its teenagers with slogans like:

"If you can't be a father, don't make a baby"

Likewise the Rev. Fred Nile wrote in his "Call to Australia" newsletter **"Australia**

needs strong fathers." Yes, indeed, we need strong, loving hands on the family situation, Godly, available fathers, not a land full of fatherless, emotionally twisted, wild, demonised children who terrorise the streets.

The Anglican Home Mission Society General Secretary, Canon Allan Whitham, wrote in his newsletter "CARE" that society had become less caring:

> "We pick up the pieces of broken lives at a huge personal, social and economic cost to us all," he said.

> "The victims of marriage breakdown are children. There are now 500,000 children living in poverty because of broken marriages and a corresponding 73 per cent increase in sole parents since 1974.

> "Laying the blame totally on governments for the homelessness of Australian children ignores fundamental attitudinal changes which have occurred at the very heart of our society since the 1970s.

> "There has been a tremendous emphasis on rights to the neglect of responsibilities.

> "Australian parents must realise that real love is not based on what you can get, but what you can give to enrich the lives of your children."

> **("CARE" 18th Apr. 1989)**

However Christ the Lord remains a way of escape who can transform any life given over to Him. The Word of God tells us He "visits the sins of the fathers upon the children unto the third and fourth generation OF THOSE WHO HATE HIM, but shows MERCY TO THOUSANDS of those who LOVE Him, and KEEP HIS COMMANDMENTS (Ex. 20:5–6).

Let us never forget King David's testimony to the goodness of the Lord—the one who sees (our needs) and provides (Gen. 14:22)—when he wrote:

> "I have been young, and now I am old; yet I have not seen the righteous forsaken, or his descendants begging bread."   **(Psalm 37:25).**

(G) DESTROYS HAPPINESS AND HUMAN BEINGS

It has been said that lascivious men who fornicate with many women are "great" lovers, suggesting they have more love (in their hearts) for women than other men, but of course, the reverse is true. If they truly loved a woman as they say they do, it is illogical to believe they can transfer that love to another woman, and another and another in quick succession. The truth of the matter is that having made their conquest they lose interest and respect for their latest victim. The game has been played and won. They have "proved" to their own vanity and ego whatever they wanted to prove, and satisfied their own insecurities, lusts and craving for victory and domination.

They have **not** proved that they are great lovers of women because they progressively become more and more INCAPABLE of truly loving a woman, incapable of commitment, incapable of being trusted and therefore incapable of truly caring, and anything else of lasting value. Theirs is a transitory world of fantasy, lust and vanity which is destructive and the woman who thinks she can change such a man is seriously deluded. Only Christ can change him TODAY. Alternatively life, sickness and death will change him TOMORROW, by destroying him.

Paul goes on to say:

> "Flee (from) fornication. Every other sin which a man does is outside the body, but the fornicator sins against his own body." **(1 Cor. 6:18)**

— and the same principle applies to the ladies, of course. Fornication (in all its breadth of meaning) is a unique sin—it strikes at our OWN FLESH and, of course, its savage penalties are manifested in the flesh, as well as the soul.

(H) DESTROYS UNBORN BABIES BY ABORTION

THE PROBLEM

From clinic bombings around the country to massive protests in Washington, from complex legal battles in the courts to rancorous debate in Congress, few issues in the USA over the past decades have roused such passions and proved so divisive as abortion.

The Australian Christian magazine LIGHT carried the following report in its May 1994 edition:

> Mother Teresa of Calcutta addressed the US National Prayer Breakfast on 3 February, attended by 3000 people including President and Mrs Clinton, Vice President and Mrs Gore and congressional leaders.
>
> Cal Thomas, journalist for the Denver Post and syndicated by the Los Angeles Times, wrote that the frail 83-year-old nun "delivered the most startling and bold proclamation of truth I have heard I in more than 30 years in Washington."
>
> He continued (in part): "Tying abortion to growing violence and murder in the streets, Mother Teresa said:
>
> 'By abortion, the mother does not learn to love, but kills even her own child to solve her problems. And by abortion, the father is told that he does not have to take any responsibility at all for the child he has brought into the world. If we accept that a mother can kill even her own child, how can we tell other people not to kill each other? Any country that accepts abortion is not teaching its people to love, but to use any violence to get what they want.'
>
> "At that line, most of those in attendance erupted in a standing ovation, something that rarely happens at these sedate events.
>
> "At the end, she pleaded for pregnant women who don't want their children, to give them to her:
>
> 'I am willing to accept any child who would be aborted and to give that child to a married couple who will love the child and be loved by the child.'
>
> "Mother Teresa said she has placed over 3000 children in adoptive homes from her Calcutta headquarters alone."

According to Senator Brian Harradine, more than 80,000 abortions were performed in Australia during 1987, which cost the Federal Government $6.4 million in Medicare payouts. The Senator also claimed the Federal Government was supporting research into the development of two new abortion-inducing drugs.

ABORTION SPIRITS

It is worth noting that an abortion introduces abortion spirits into a woman's soul[35]. And it doesn't matter whether the abortion is the direct result of a woman's rebellion against God or is directed by medical authorities to save the woman's life. I was speaking to my congregation several years ago about the removal of abortion spirits when one of the sweetest Christian sisters in my flock approached me after the service to confess a properly conducted medical abortion which saved her life. Briefly, the resultant ministry to her cleaned out some 200 abortion spirits. They were pretty weak and offered no resistance at all but she is better off without them. The incident simply confirmed that if the world wants to play sexual games, there is an enormous price to pay.

Let us reflect on the wonder of our creation by the Creator.

13. For You have formed my inwards parts; You wove me in my mother's womb.

14. I will praise You, for I am fearfully and wonderfully made; Marvellous are Your works, And that my soul knows very well.

15. My bones were not hidden from You, When I was made in secret, When I was woven in the lowest parts of the earth.

16. Your eyes saw my embryo being yet unformed.

(Psalm 139:13–16b).

ABORTION PILL DANGER

Do you remember the car sticker we referred to very early in this book? "ABORTION?

---

35 For more information on this point, see ***Ministering to Abortion's Aftermath*** by Bill Banks

ONE DEAD-ONE WOUNDED!"? Here is a report from the U.K. (Light mag.-May 1994)

Dr Margaret White, a medical doctor who is Vice-President of the UK Society for the Protection of the Unborn Child, has warned of the dangers of the controversial RU 486 abortion pill now being trialed in Australia.

Dr White said it is not only pro-lifers who oppose RU 486, which is marketed by the firm Roussel-Uclaf. Pro-abortion doctors have expressed concern about the possible short and long-term harm to women who take RU 486. The drug prevents the hormone progesterone from acting, and effectively kills the human embryo by starvation. But it acts on other parts of the body as well. Only follow-up studies over many years would show the full effect.

"In the short term RU 486, used in combination with prostaglandins, causes heavy bleeding, nausea and great pain in a significant number of women. Several have had heart attacks .

"RU 486 is bad for women, and fatal for their babies!" she said.

ABORTION DEATHS COVER-UP

Dr. White revealed that deaths from legal abortions in the UK are being covered up. "A question was asked in Parliament about the number of deaths in Scotland from legal abortion in a certain year," she said. "The answer came back, None.

"So the MP tried again, but this time asked a slightly different question: How many deaths last year in Scotland occurred within one month following a legal abortion?

"This time the answer was different: Seven. Each death was the result of a legal abortion, but was not recorded as such. One cause of death was stated as 'gangrene of the caecum'. This had occurred as a result of the suction method used for early abortions. The wall of the uterus and the adjacent bowel had been perforated by the suction machine.

"Two deaths were listed as due to anaesthesia complications, and two from clots. All seven deaths were the result of legal abortion operations, but the real cause was not stated on the death certificate. How many other such deaths are being covered up to make people believe that legal abortion is always safe?"

(I) CONCLUSION

What is the answer to all these disasters caused by FORNICATION? There is an answer for those who are still innocent and there is an answer for those who are nervous or emotional wrecks due to guilt and sin—Praise the Lord!

(i) For those who have tasted of the fruits and corrupt morality of the world in which we live there is offered the full salvation of our Lord Jesus Christ—a salvation of spirit, soul and body. A salvation which is able to cleanse the soul from every spirit of lust, anger, rebellion and guilt and to cleanse the body of all the diseases which are a consequence of our sinful lives. Those who yield up their selfishness to Christ become NEW CREATURES and a fresh start can be made which can see us transformed from vessels of wrath to vessels of honour in our Father's house (2 Tim. 2:20–22). It is not easy, because all that is unclean within us resists this change, but it can be done, indeed must be done if we are to be sincere disciples of the Lord.

(ii) For those who are as yet innocent of the fornication of the world, it will still be necessary for them to give their lives to Christ, but obviously the bondages of their souls will not carry anything like the sexual uncleanness of those who have regularly practiced fornication. They will have less complications when eventually making a one-flesh marriage commitment, all other things being equal.

The best advice one can give young people today is: no wedding ring?—no body! Which, interpreted, means marriage first, sex second. Obey the guidance of the Word of God—don't fornicate. WAIT! It is not as hard or difficult as it sounds. You can do it. Don't participate in sexual intercourse before marriage no matter how much you love each other, and no matter what other people say and do; otherwise you may weaken and eventually destroy the very relationship you seek to build and hold for a lifetime. Giving in to fornication leads to poverty, sickness and death, and after that the Judgement of God. Please remember that TRIAL MARRIAGES DON'T PROVE A THING, EXCEPT THAT YOU ARE A REBEL AGAINST GOD!

If you have already sinned in this regard it is not too late to right matters, because now you are aware of the problem you have created. Repent, and put things right before the Lord and He will heal the destructive component in your relationship. You may need deliverance ministry, but whatever the complexities are, if you obey the Lord He will enable YOU to make a Godly commitment to your loved one and to prosper you in your pursuit of happiness.

See what the prophet Jeremiah has to say:

JEREMIAH 7:3-11

V. 3 Thus says LORD of hosts, the God of Israel, "Amend your ways and your deeds, and I will let you dwell in this place.

6 "If you do not oppress the alien, the orphan, or the widow, and do not shed innocent blood in this place, nor walk after other gods to your own ruin,

7 "Then I will let you dwell in this place, in the land that I gave to your fathers forever and ever.

8 "Behold, you are trusting in deceptive words to no avail.

9 "Will you steal, murder, and commit adultery, and swear falsely, and offer sacrifices to Baal, and walk after other gods that you have not known,

10 "Then come and stand before Me in this house, which is called by My name, and say, 'We are delivered!'—that you may do all these abominations?"

We do well to heed the warning!

3.5 WITCHERY

(A) WE ARE ALL INFECTED

The first thing to understand is that the Bible says we are ALL tainted with a degree of witchery or witchcraft. Any non-Hebrew nation that can trace its history back prior to the coming of Jesus Christ will have records of spirit-worship and/or ancestor worship, and it is only the light of Christ that has enabled the gentile nations to shrug off spiritism and superstition, which is really witchcraft. Further, the Bible says we have all been born with a spirit of rebellion (original sin—Eph. 2:2), and that **rebellion is witchcraft** (1 Sam. 15:23). Please note that both the literal Hebrew and Greek[36] Old Testament scriptures say REBELLION IS WITCHCRAFT, not that rebellion is as the sin of witchcraft, as some nervous translators have suggested. The Word of God does not give us an approximation but a definitive equation, through the prophet Samuel:

— "REBELLION IS WITCHCRAFT" —

Christian marriage is a great bulwark against Rebellion/Witchcraft, and even non-Christian marriage is helpful or better than living in sin, but even so, every Christian carries on an unceasing spiritual warfare in the flesh against Rebellion/Witchcraft. Only by God's grace and making His Will our will can we become an Overcomer. In spite of the fact that a soundly converted Christian can experience an enormous improvement in personal attitudes and behaviour in comparison with earlier non-Christian habits and patterns of conduct, the average Christian is all too aware of how far he or she falls short of God's standards, and we all know something of how much we are bound up in the ways of this world.

Many Christians regularly conduct themselves in a way with which they themselves are disappointed—they appear to have bondages that intermittently or repeatedly trouble them and burden them with guilt, and they know the inward grieving (Eph. 4:30), the sadness of the Holy Spirit within them. How many Christian women have come for deliverance seeking help and bewailing the fact that they give their husbands a torrid time. Strangely the "worst" women seem to have the "best" husbands, whose

36 Septuagint

patience is sometimes quite remarkable, and vice-versa. Some women know they are spiteful, bossy, nagging and frigid, etc. but in spite of a work of grace commenced by the Lord within them they are unable to control the darkness in their hearts. This form of Rebellion/Witchcraft (henceforth R/W) is extremely common in women, and of course, men have their own areas of common difficulties such as lust, pride, unbelief, aggression, etc. It is important at this stage to remember that EVERYONE is affected and infected.

This is NOT an exercise in passing unloving and hypercritical judgement on you, or your loved ones or friends, nor is this information shared with the intention that YOU should be equipped with a "knowledge" that gives you power or an advantage over others, that you might laugh, mock or "put them down". Such activity would simply indicate that YOUR R/W condition is worse than those whom you criticise.

Once it is established that ALL have the spiritual heart/soul disease of R/W, it is simply a matter of observing HOW this disease is manifested in people's lives, because when we see the FORM it takes, THEN we can focus onto and particularise the problem. Of course, a more definitive assessment or diagnosis is necessary before we can know what ministries of the Lord Jesus Christ are to be brought to bear upon the problem(s).

The second thing to understand is that the mind-blowing consequences of the statement that Rebellion is Witchcraft mean MOST people are practicing witchcraft without realizing it, as they live lives that are not in accordance with Christ and the moral law of Christ. This, of course, explains the occult and witchcraft revival that began in the 1960s, and the only thing that prevents witchcraft becoming the national religion is the inherent understanding in people that it is evil and they will come to a bad end if they get too involved.

Witches are busy trying to tell us they only do "good" and cast "good spells", but witchcraft is an abomination to the Lord (Deut. 18:10–12) and those who practice white or black witchcraft are under the wrath of God. So too with rebellion (John 3:17–19, 36), for they are the same thing in the eyes of the Lord.

Thirdly, some women tend to use a more recognizable style of witchcraft by employing physical attraction and sensuality through cosmetic make-up (like the witch *Jezebel*—2 Kings 9:30) and body movements, etc. They exert a strong "drawing" power for men (and also men for women) because of their sensuality. Vulnerable people flock around them and strive for words to describe the magnetism experienced through their senses, usually through their eyes. The male victim sees the walk, the posing, the body movements all unconsciously or consciously calculated to "draw" the male, and any lust spirit within the female quickly searches out and links up with similar spirits within the victim.

If an affair ensues it is described in terms of "electricity" and "being turned on" and "the right chemistry," etc. How the world approves of such a liaison (all the world loves a lover, we are told). In the majority of cases it is simply unclean spirits in two people linking up and abusing the bodies they inhabit by provoking rebellion against God's moral law in order that their human lives may be destroyed and God's highest purposes for them be thwarted.

(B) CLERGY PROBLEMS

Whether you are a man or a woman you need to watch out for *sensual body movements*. Be discerning—look past the physical and perceive the spirit which is endeavouring to suck you in. You may find the so-called "tender trap" set for you will lead to disaster. Christian and non-Christian alike are unfair game for satan in his campaign to destroy. Author-psychologist Keith Miller writes:

> "I intended not even to mention this, because I do not feel that this is a general problem in trying to see life from Christ's perspective. But as I have been sitting here deciding, I have seen, against the white wall across my office, the haunted faces of several of my Christian friends, who have found themselves inexplicably trapped in tragic situations. I remember especially listening to one lovely Christian woman. Through tears and stunned with amazement, almost disbelief, she told me that she had committed adultery, although she had never thought it even a possibility for her. And during these past few years I have spent hours talking to men and women, ministers and laymen, who are deeply committed to Christ but who in one way or the other have told me the same story ... Any

time a man or woman sets up a continuing relationship with a member of the opposite sex in an unstructured situation in which they are together privately, the chances of some kind of sexual involvement not taking place would appear to be small. And the fact that the content of the discussion is 'Christianity' or 'prayer', seems to make almost no difference…"

"A Second Touch" (P101–102)

Christians are almost as vulnerable as non-Christians and we need to remember the powers of darkness will delight to use whatever influence they have in your life to pull down a child of God for the subsequent dishonour and shame brought to bear on the Name of Jesus. It is, indeed, sweet delight to them, but a bitter pill to taste for the one who calls Him Lord.

American evangelist, Dick Mills, whilst on a visit to Sydney during 1975, declared that ***satan has a woman in every Christian congregation whose mission it is to destroy the minister, whether she herself be consciously aware of it or not***. One may not be able to substantiate his statement with statistics, but the vast majority of ministers who have had charge of a congregation will nod their heads in silent agreement, perhaps thinking of the (narrow?) escape(s) within their own experience. And, sadly, some have fallen. It is usually the "best" Pastors—the warm-hearted, caring, affectionate men whose strengths become their weaknesses, who fall. We have read too often in the media (it usually makes international news, of course, for the world loves to gloat over the fall of a man of God) that Rev. so and so had resigned due to immoral conduct. Placed in a position where Mrs. Bloggs was in desperate need of comfort, counsel and strength, and a shoulder to cry on, the pastor finds his compassion turning to warmth and then affection and ultimately desire, particularly if the wife at home is unsympathetic, frigid or in rebellion. Satan weaves his web well and who else could engineer such a fall from grace? Perhaps the evidence will expose even the spirit of a lusty witch, continually drawing a man over a period of time in order to fulfil her mission.

However let me make it quite clear that this evil mission to destroy the clergyman will rarely be in the conscious mind of the lady involved. It is something that overtakes both the man and the woman as they relate to each other with the best of intentions. The Word of God warns us well when it says that when we want to do good, evil is present (Rom. 7:21). If, during this unconscious or soulish "drawing", there is anything in the man that "clicks" he could be in real trouble. Everyone needs to remember clergymen are MEN, and while living in the flesh they will be affected by its weaknesses and pollution. The Word of God recognizes this when discussing the frailties of the High Priests in the Old Testament dispensation. The writer to the Hebrews says:

> "For every High Priest taken out of men is appointed in regard to God on behalf of men, that he may offer both gifts and sacrifices for sins, being able to feel sympathy for those who are ignorant and led astray since he a/so is beset with weakness, and because of this he ought to offer sacrifices for his own sins as well as for those of the people."
> **(Hebrews 5:1–3 lit.)**

What is true for the Old Covenant High Priesthood is also true for today's ministers of the New Covenant.

Thanks be to God these are still days of Grace and a backslidden Christian, whether clergyman or layman, living in sin, can still call upon the Name of the Lord to be forgiven, restored and blessed. If your heart is heavy, burdened with anguish and you are in a miserable condition of guilt and condemnation because of your past and present sins, then take heart and act now. Sexual sins may be deadly and cost you your salvation (1 Cor. 6:9–10) but they are not unforgivable. You must repent quickly. The Lord still loves you, but who knows what hour your soul will be required of you, and it may be too late. Hear the words of the prophet Isaiah:

> "Seek the Lord while he may be found, call upon him while he is near; let the wicked forsake his way, and the unrighteous man his thoughts; let him return to the Lord, that he may have mercy on him, and to our God, for he will abundantly pardon. For my thoughts. are not your thoughts, neither are your ways my ways, says the Lord. For as the heavens are higher than the earth, so are my ways higher than your ways and my thoughts than your thoughts." **(Isaiah 55:6–9)**

O man and woman of God—the Bible is full of the weaknesses and sins of great men of God (David, Moses, Samson, Aaron etc.) and many were reconciled again to

God, the same as ANY sinner! Put it right NOW! Whatever steps are necessary for you to take to put your house in order, take them NOW. Time is running out. God's calendar is FAST drawing to a close for this Age and Judgement is upon us all in, and out of, the household of God (1 Peter 4:17).

The Lord is about to shake the Heaven and the earth (Heb. 12:25–29) and every UNFORGIVEN sin will be exposed to your everlasting shame, UNLESS you act NOW!

(C) THE CREATION OF A WOMAN'S LIBERATIONIST

Whereas many spirits of witches are extremely lusty, there are others at the opposite extreme whereby they are so jealous and possessive of the body they have inhabited that they react strongly to any physical touch by the opposite sex ("Hands off—she's mine" attitude). Some women have both lust and frigidity problems combined and their husbands find them quite unpredictable, while they themselves find their emotions and instincts torn, confused and inexplicable, which makes for frustration and anger on every side.

Sexual distortion has very destructive consequences—despair, anger, bitterness, hatred, death-wish and suicide often flow from the abuse of our sexual natures. It is interesting to note that the so-called "liberated" Scandinavian countries with their sexually permissive laws also led the world with their suicide rates. When lust or frigidity go together with these highly strung characteristics, I believe we are looking at a real, live spirit of a witch controlling a kingdom of satan within the human heart (soul).

These emotional problems (anger, hatred etc.) are very much part of the Women's Liberation movement, the philosophy of which is one of the most anti-Christian in the world today. But it is not altogether the ladies' fault. They were deceived into believing sexual promiscuity and licence was sexual freedom and no harm would befall them.

They did not understand that virginity before marriage is precious and that men tell lies when seeking to make a conquest. Men test girls out to see if they have moral character and value their bodies and virginity. They will play around with those who do not so highly value themselves, but they marry girls they can TRUST, if they can find one.

The truth is that even serious, family-minded men who are looking for a wife will severely test a woman's level of morality and are often secretly disappointed with a girl who says "yes" to sex before the wedding. Serious courtship is all about testing each other out to discover standards, habits and philosophies. Everybody wants someone they can love, respect and trust. At least, that is the ideal—however hard it may be to attain today.

So when a girl gives everything she's got BEFORE marriage she often finds the man's sweet talks are just empty promises.

"Perturbed" wrote in the Daily Mirror:[37]

> Don't always blame the woman. After all, it takes two to tango and very often the selfish and uncooperative attitude of the man in regards to birth control is the very reason she became pregnant in the first place. I should know as my boyfriend decided he'd had enough when I was six months pregnant and went overseas (with I might add the encouragement of his parents!). I He has contributed $10 towards his child's future.

It may have been he was only after sex. Alternatively the sweet-talk may have been genuine at the time, but when the girl does not measure up to the man's **secret moral standard**, she is dumped! (And all she did was give in to him, to please him!).

Stage 2 in the making of a Woman's Libber is achieved when she continues to try to please succeeding boy-friends by giving them her body.

Stage 3. She begins to realise she is pleasing THEM the wrong way and they are using HER! Hurt and bitterness enter her soul.

Stage 4. The trend continues, but now she is older and her defences are up. She plays the harlot, but selectively, and makes the men pay, one way or another. She is now an emotional time-bomb who hates men. The spirits of more than one witch now control her, and seek to control any man who is attracted to her body or is under

37 6 Jan. 1986

her authority.

Stage 5. Worldly ambition and professional standing now replace the disappearing and almost unattainable noble family goals as a means of satisfying one's personal needs of self-worth and esteem.

Stage 6. Because of her distrust and hatred of men in general, her sexual preference changes and she seeks comfort, love and eventually sexual experience from sympathetic girlfriends as well as men.

These stages are, of course, a generalisation, and may occur in a different order.

(D) STAGES OF A MODERN RELATIONSHIP

Special writer Richard Roeper gave a man's eye-and a somewhat cynical-view of the 15 stages of a modern relationship in the Daily Mirror.[38]

1 THE FIRST MEETING

YOU meet someone. She makes your glands do a drum solo. She likes you, too. Let the romance begin.

2 COURTSHIP

EVERY date is like a bad musical interlude in a schmaltzy made-for-TV-movie. You buy balloons together, you go to the zoo, you hold hands and you exchange greetings with kindly old vendors.

3 GETTING SERIOUS

YOU make an impromptu visit to her house, and you see her standing on the porch with a guy. You punch the guy. It turns out to be her cousin Norm, who is visiting from Queensland. You all go inside and have a big laugh. Norm, holding an ice pack to his jaw, decides to go to bed. Now it's just you and your girl. She's touched by your noble jealousy. You tell her that you can't stand the thought of her with anyone else. She says she feels the same way about you. All of a sudden, you have entered the land of commitment.

38 5 Nov. 1986

4 MOVING IN

YOU move into her place. Because you're so much in love, even moving day is fun and special.

5 THE HONEYMOON

YOU stay in bed together for one full week. Certain physical feats performed prompt you to call the people at the Guinness Book of Records.

6 REALITY

Her snoring wakes you up at 5am. You stumble into the bathroom, where you are immediately lost in a jungle of panty-hose. By mistake, you pick up her razor. She changes the blades as often as most people rotate their tyres. You cut your face to ribbons. You ask her to drive you to the emergency room, but she says she can't because she's too depressed. Depressed about what, you say. If you really love me, you wouldn't have to even ask, she says. Reality has set in.

7 NASTY HABITS

SHE eats only the yellow portions of the hard-boiled eggs, and puts the white parts back in the fridge. She loves soapie re-runs. Her contact lenses are tinted, and eyes that you thought were ocean blue are actually grey. You have at least twice as many bad habits and hidden secrets, or so she says.

8 LOATHING

THERE is a fine line between love and hate. Without knowing how or why, you've crossed it.

9 MOVING OUT

NOT really as much fun as moving in. You do all the work, while she sits on the sofa in her nightshirt, doing some serious pouting. The slick guy from down the hall drops by and says, "Moving out today? Hey, looks like I won the pool."

10 SEEING OTHER PEOPLE

INSTEAD of admitting it's all over, you say that you're just seeing other I people. Whenever you tell anyone that, they give you a sincere look and tell you they're very sorry. "We're seeing other people" is one of those phrases like "My cat died"—it automatically makes people feel sorry for you.

11 LAST DITCH EFFORT

YOU both decide that it's worth one more try, so you plan a get-away weekend. It doesn't work. She drives back home. You stay behind, because you are a man, strong, alone, tough, one with nature. For the rest of the weekend, you drink beer and sob, drink beer and sob.

12 OFFICIAL BREAK-UP

SHE comes over to pick up a few miscellaneous items. An argument ensues, and you call each other rotten names. She slams the door on her way out. You think of a really clever and mean thing to say to her, but it's too late. She's gone.

13 THE LAST TIME

SEVERAL weeks later, she shows up on your doorstep, and says she misses YOU. You have a great night together. Afterwards, she tells you that she's been dating her boss, whom she used to refer to as "the slime". She came over because she just had to make sure you were out of her system. She kisses you on the cheek and says goodbye.

14 THE END

IN an effort to win her back, you write her the letter of a lifetime. It comes back unopened, with the title of an Elvis Presley song written on the envelope: "Return to sender. Address unknown." You decide to kill yourself. You go to the chemist to buy a bagful of sleeping pills.

15 THE NEW ROMANCE

THE young woman behind the counter bears a startling resemblance to Rachel Ward. She tells you that she likes your tie. You ask her out. She says "yes". You don't buy sleeping pills. You walk outside. The sun is shining.

New hope with a new romance? Sounds good doesn't it? Unfortunately it is like the script writers of "Loveboat" who deal in fantasy and dreams where relationships gone sour can easily be exchanged for newer, happier ones.

However, the levels of demonisation and sin now present in our western society continue to accelerate, and all non-Christians have left is dreams and unreality to lift them out of the harsh realities of daily survival. Far from improving things, the sexual merry-go-round or regular exchanging of partners is often the equivalent of jumping out of the frying pan and into the fire, as domestic violence in de facto situations amply testifies.

It all adds up to a miserable, self-destructive merry-go-round or tread-mill which each participant must bring to a stop and turn around before it is too late. Jesus said REPENT (which means—change the direction of your life and purpose) or perish! (Luke 13:3–5). You can do it, with His help.

Clifford F. Boyd of South Australia has some very useful. things to say about the feminist movements:[39]

> Perhaps it is time to review exactly what the goals of the feminist movement are.
>
> The various "affirmative action" programs never have any "sunset clauses"—they never indicate at what point "equality" is deemed to have been achieved, therefore it must be assumed that these programs are designed to continue until feminists run everything.
>
> Indeed, if one is to believe Dr. Helen Caldicott's statement on the ABC's Talking Shop TV programme, when she says "We (women) have to get into politics... we have to take over", there can be little doubt that this is the ultimate objective.
>
> Feminists are, in fact, hell-bent on establishing a world-wide "matriarchy".
>
> But it is first necessary for them to destroy as many men and their families as possible.
>
> If there is domestic violence and child abuse in Australia, it is much more likely to occur within those loose adulterous relationships euphemistically termed "shacking up", "living together" or "de facto" than among Christian married couples and their children, yet it is precisely this traditional family group against which the campaign is primarily directed.
>
> The Christian religion is perceived as a "patriarchal" system, handed down from parent to child, and therefore the family group, which perpetuates

---

39 "The Australian" 20 July, 1988

it, must be destroyed.

It seems ironic that thoughtful, caring Australians will wax wrathful against abortion, prostitution, family breakdown and moral disintegration but allow the perpetrators of most of this national disgrace, the militant feminists, to get off scot-free.

Surely it's high time to call them to account?

It is not surprising then, that both classical and lesser forms of witchcraft have an emphasis on sexual rituals and **witchcraft and prostitution go hand in hand. The spirit of a witch** likes nothing better than to inhabit a sweet young thing well favoured in appearance through whom she can weave her destructive web about the lives of the men who come within range, and sexual abuse may well be the door through which "she" entered in strength. Sometimes after a few years of continued sexual abuse and misuse the face of the witch begins to show through with all her sin so that coarse men will cruelly comment "so-and-so would be alright (sexually) if a bag was put over her head." What foolish blindness—to be joined to and become one flesh—with a witch, with all her spiritual pollution, and expect that there should be no consequences to oneself—bag or no bag. It is safer to shake hands with a leper!

With startling frankness an internationally known beauty, film star and sex symbol was reported[40] as saying "I am a witch ... I have eerie premonitions ..." Such refreshing honesty when most people who have premonitions and psychic warnings of disaster etc. would claim to be gifted by God.

In conclusion, and so that we should not be accused in any way of deceiving people into thinking married people are free of problems, let us consider some symptoms of Rebellion/Witchcraft in marriage, remembering that these symptoms are common to Christian and non-Christian alike, only in the matter of Christians, it will be necessary (and probably more difficult) to look past the work of grace and into the blackness that lies hidden beneath.

The Word of God in Genesis tells us that a woman's role is to be a help meet (fit, proper) for man and John Bunyan wrote: "Women therefore, whenever they would

40 Sydney Sun 14 March, 1979

perk it or lord it over their husbands, ought to remember that both by creation and transgression, they are made to be in subjection to their own husbands."[41] John Bunyan's editor in the Victorian era however, was not content with this statement but added a pointed footnote:

> "Most married men find this to be an exceedingly difficult duty. There are few Eves but whose dominant passion is to rule a husband. Perhaps the only way to govern a wife is to lead her to think that she rules when in fact she is ruled."

I always thought that ploy was how women ruled their men!

Man is supposed to be submitted to Christ but is in rebellion, and woman is supposed to be submitted to man but is also in rebellion against him. Therefore any reversal of leadership roles between man and woman is a distinct warning signal that Rebellion/ Witchcraft is at work (1 Cor. 11:3). Evidence of frustration, resentment, bitterness, hatred, anger, rages, extremes of sexual interest (or disinterest), fear, anxiety, envy, jealousy, possessiveness, depression, etc. indeed what one would call today "a highly strung nature" is enough to indicate that deliverance is required.

Most 'highly strung' people become quite unreasonable when aroused for it is not a 'reasonable' warfare but spiritual, and obedience becomes impossible until self-control is first able to be exercised. The role of witchcraft or the spirit of a witch within a woman (Christian or non-Christian) is to destroy men—as many as possible before the Day of Judgment, and it is a "no-holds-barred" warfare, but perhaps it is as well to be reminded that men suffer from the disease of witchcraft as much as women.

Christina Ford, second wife of Henry Ford II is alleged to have philosophised:

"Time goes by and history repeats itself ... We women believe what men say. We tell them we understand. But the understanding woman eventually becomes the 'strega' (witch) at home..."[42]

Christina Ford's sad but perceptive comment may be the normal situation for multi-

41 John Bunyan-Complete Works Vol. II P. 438

42 Aust Women's Weekly 26 March, 1980

married people, but marriage itself is God's institution and provided we run it along HIS guidelines, and not ours, it is a great and blessed institution indeed.

(E) THE WORD OF GOD

The Word of God has much to say about the dangers of illicit sex, i.e. sex outside of God's regulations. Those involved in Deliverance ministry are discovering more and more that God's commandments are not simply set up to spoil our fun but to protect us from destruction. His commands are not simply that of the Creator exercising power over His creation but rather LOVE FOR His creation and we disobey at our own peril. We live in an age where we are being given understanding as to why God has commanded this and that, but the key to being a true child of God is still obedience when we do NOT understand. That is Faith or Trust. He speaks and we obey without arguing and wanting reasons, simply because we trust Him, for He knows the unseen dangers that beset us.

But when we pit our feeble understanding and intellects against Him and choose our own course that pleases us He is not mocked and we reap what we sow—as we are warned in the book of Proverbs:

> "For at the window of my house I have looked out through my lattice, and I have seen among the simple, I have perceived among the youths, a young man without sense, passing along the street near her corner, taking the road to her house in the twilight, in the evening, at the time of night and darkness.
>
> And lo, a woman meets him, dressed as a harlot, wily of heart. She is loud and wayward, her feet do not stay at home; now in the street, now in the market, and at every Corner she lies in wait. She seizes him and kisses him, and with impudent face she says to him: "I had to offer sacrifices, and today I have paid my vows; so now I have come out to meet you, to seek you eagerly, and I have found you. I have decked my couch with coverings, coloured spreads of Egyptian linen; I have perfumed my bed with myrrh, aloes, and cinnamon. Come, let us take our fill of love till

morning; let us delight ourselves with love. For my husband is not at home; he has gone on a long journey; he took a bag of money with him; at full moon he will come home."

With much seductive speech she persuades him; with her smooth talk she compels him. All at once he follows her, as an ox goes to the slaughter, or as a stag is caught fast till an arrow pierces its entrails; as a bird rushes into a snare; he does not know that it will cost him his life.

And now, O sons, listen to me, and be attentive to the words of my mouth. Let not your heart turn aside to her ways, do not stray into her paths; for many a victim has she laid low; yea, all her slain are a mighty host. Her house is the way to Sheol, going down to the chambers of death." **(Proverbs 7:6–12, 21–27)**

"For the lips of a loose woman drip honey, and her speech is smoother than oil; but in the end she is bitter as wormwood, sharp as a two-edged sword. Her feet go down to death; her steps follow the path to Sheol; she does not take heed to the path of life; her ways wander, and she does not know it." **(Proverbs 5:3–6)**

Refer also Proverbs 2:16–19; 5:18–23; 6:24–33.

This is the Word of God speaking the truth to every man and woman.

If you have followed after harlots, prostitutes or whores NOW is the time to get off the broad road that leads to destruction. Now is the time to find the narrow road—JESUS—who leads to life (Matt. 7:13–14). If you want to be forgiven for your sins and start afresh with Christ as your Lord, be encouraged—turn to Chapter Five now. You will find a simple but effective formula there for changing the direction of your life, and all the chains that satan has cast about you through immoral men or women—or whatever—will begin to snap. Even the loose (unclean) man or woman can receive mercy through the grace of our Lord Jesus, who died for you and me, for such was the woman caught in adultery. (John 8:1–12 KJV)

3.6 FRIGIDITY

I will probably lose a lot of friends for saying this but I want to go on record as saying that *frigidity in a woman is as destructive to a family situation as lust in a man*. One might also say that it is as common as lust and that when both "enemies" operate freely within a marriage, disaster is normal.

I know a housewife with three children who was very dependent on father figures, whether it was the local doctors or me, the local minister. Jane would often complain to get attention, and one day I caught up with her husband, the cause of many of her complaints.

He seemed a normal enough working man, struggling to provide for his family and enjoying a few beers down at the local Club. Both were baby Christians and soon Alan confided to me that he was starved of sex, which occurred about once every month or two. Jane was certainly not afraid of men (father figures) and it did not surprise me in the slightest when she confessed to adultery on one occasion. However, the next thing she was telling me was that Alan had been charged with sexual child abuse by a neighbour. She defended her husband vigorously and when she had finished, asked me who or what I believed. "I'm sorry", I said, "but I believe your neighbour". After a long pause she said very quietly, "Yes, so do I".

Assuming the charge to be true, should we lay all the blame on the frustrated Alan? Would the Lord lay it all on Alan?

Without minimising the horrendous crime or seeking to shift the major portion of blame from Alan, did not Jane's frigidity towards her husband lay the foundation for what followed? Unfulfilled sexual desire (even lust) within a marriage can so easily lead to other dishonest and defiling forms of expression.

Perhaps I am wrong. Perhaps I have heard of too many broken situations where lust and frigidity have destroyed men and women.

Another Christian family had the same tension between lust and frigidity, particularly after their children were born. After enjoying little or no sex for years the man was charged with sexually interfering with his daughter and was sent to jail. He drew closer to Christ in jail and upon his release sought to reconcile with his ex-wife and children.

They all hate the ground he walks on. He is despised while the mother is considered a "saint". However, unforgiveness has its own penalty. One daughter's marriage has broken up. Another tried to commit suicide and the son has been charged with car-stealing.

Without excusing the reprehensible nature of the man's wicked deeds upon a defenceless child, and his own flesh and blood at that, perhaps it could all have been avoided if frigidity had been overcome much earlier.

This word FRIGIDITY is more usually applied to women and ranges in degree from wives who have defensive headaches when their senses perceive their husbands are sending out amorous signals, to the other extreme where a woman cannot bear her husband to even physically touch her at all, now or ever.

In the former case the amorous signals from the husband usually stop abruptly when she says "I have a headache" which can be invented, imaginary, or real if brought about by the unwelcome prospect of yielding to her husband.

In the latter "don't touch me" category many frigid women truly love their husbands and it all seems very confusing, illogical and perplexing but of course the answer does not lie in the realm of logic but in the realm of the spirit, and we need to examine the *soulish* area for the answer.

Obviously many things can precipitate frigidity even before marriage. Sexual assault or rape can induce a great fear of men and fear of sexual intercourse. Also fear of childbirth can be an underlying cause. Some of the women who have come to our ministry for help are literally filled with various sex-related terrors. They have never married and will never marry until the terror is completely removed. Some have been molested as little girls (see "Incubi") and some have been subjected to incest or have had these problems passed down to them through their hereditary blood-line. What chance do they have for happy, healthy, normal lives of fulfilment unless they come to Christ Jesus for His cleansing, healing, restoring, delivering, renewing grace?

Some men are so lustful and perverted they would make any normal women frigid. American psychiatrist Dr. Greenberg wrote that call-girls and prostitutes were invariably frigid![43] They may have begun in lust, greed or need but they all became frigid. Perhaps it is the only way they could cope with their devilish business.

Others have been taken over by spirits of sodomy, lesbianism and homosexuality, some have become transvestites etc., all of which seek to overrule the normal sexual responses of a woman with their own particular distorted character.

Frigidity is often thought of as being prevalent amongst married women who seldom or never experience orgasm but this is basically a minor reason. It is more likely that she has never had an orgasm because she is frigid ("hurry up and get it over with") rather than she is frigid because she has never had an orgasm.

This may come as a surprise to you, and it has surprised many husbands to find the experience of an orgasm does NOT necessarily overcome the problem of frigidity, as many writers for immoral magazines would have us believe. The problem of GENUINE frigidity is not physical but spiritual, although many unfulfilled wives may SEEM frigid. It is this problem which caused the French poet Charles Baudelaire (1821–1867) to comment rather bitterly "A sweetheart is a bottle of wine, a wife is a wine bottle." But, praise God, it doesn't have to be that way.

However we are not as concerned about frigidity where the spiritual causes are easily discernible, but rather we wish to look at the most common and vexatious situation where a woman has participated in a fairly active or satisfactory sex life in the past but for some inexplicable (and for the husband, frustrating) reason, has become progressively more frigid over the years. Let us begin at the beginning and examine some fundamentals of our creation.

Does it not seem strange to you that in all the commandments of God except ONE we find satan opposes the will of God and seeks to induce men and women to break, deny and ignore such commandments. There is ONE commandment of God, however, that satan is very happy for men and women to obey because it not only gives glory to God as Creator, but because of the kingdoms of sin and death which now reign in the hearts of all mankind since ADAM and EVE (Romans 5:12), it increases satan's empire also.

---

43 "Girls of the Night"

The commandment we refer to was given to Noah and his sons as representatives of the human race when they alone survived the great Flood:

"Be fruitful and multiply ..." ! (Gen. 9:1,7)

This is the one commandment that mankind has had no difficulty in obeying because it suits satan's purposes also, for every human creature that is born is born with "original" sin (sin and death) transmitted down from Adam and Eve within their hearts. Hereditary unclean spirits of every kind, such as lust, can be passed down from generation to generation simply through normal childbirth, that is, by being born the *first* time, in the flesh (John 3:6–7).

Satan is happy for children to be born whether the motives for the union between man and woman are moral or immoral, love or lust, Divine or animal, because he knows that what is born once—of the desires of the flesh—are his anyway, for has not the Lord said *"You must be born again"* that is, born a *second*[44] time, of the Spirit, if we are to enter the Kingdom of God? (John 3:1–6).

This transference of kingdoms of unclean spirits from parents to children down through the generations gives us the key to understanding what goes on spiritually and emotionally in a woman's heart, which she herself may not understand; and that is her desire to bear children may not always be clean and pure, but the plan of satan to extend his own empire is mixed in with God-given instincts to procreate.

Sometimes this emotion (from the witchcraft kingdom within a woman's heart) to bear children does not have any righteous or Godly ingredient at all but is totally unclean, and I could quote many examples from our case-book. For example there are the young unmarried girls who want to have children so that they don't have to work but can receive financial support from the Government as unmarried mothers. Also the young mother whose marriage was breaking up and wanted to have another child before the final break because she said "I may not get another chance". This was a typical case of the spirit of a witch within her expressing its will to extend its influence by colonising itself in a potential new-born baby regardless of the welfare of that baby or of the mother herself. Totally illogical and totally spiritual in motive.

---

44 This is not to be confused with the notion of re-incarnation or repeated flesh births.

Then there are many women who will admit to wanting a man for only one thing, not lust but fertilisation. They want children and the easiest way to get them is through intercourse. Once the man has been used in this way he is discarded until he is required again for further extending of the SPIRITUAL empire of the witch i.e. the ruling spirit inspiring this motive from within the heart. Let us construct a very common life pattern of the modern non-Christian married woman.

A young girl meets the man of her dreams and begins to spring "the Tender Trap" wherein the man begins to chase her and the lass makes sure she is caught. At this point she is sweet and soft and responsive, and both of them present themselves at their best. The young man burns with passion, but marriage is financially impossible and the lass is not prepared to deny him. At this time of their lives the two lovers will do almost anything for each other.

Marriage follows and now that commitments have been exchanged and family security established the woman's "headaches" or whatever make an occasional appearance when the husband would like to have intercourse. A child is born, followed by more frequent "headaches" and disinterest by the wife for sexual intercourse. When a family reaches three or more children the wife may go through a period of post-natal depression for months after childbirth, especially if there have been some problems with the birth, and further childbirth will be difficult or is unlikely. Once the queen witch inside the woman's soul realises its colonising days are (nearly) over it gets very depressed. Tears and depression are the order of the day, and wifely submission to a husband doesn't figure in her plans at all.

This is all very confusing to the man, who may have read a book by Psychiatrist Anthony Pietropinto and writer Jacqueline Simenauer. They wrote:

> "Many men thought a wife should be a lady in the living room, an economist in the kitchen a*nd a slut in the bedroom.*
>
> *"Some were lucky enough to have found such a woman. Others apparently wound up with a* lady in the kitchen, a slut in the living room and an economist in the bedroom." [45]

45 "Beyond the Male Myth"

Eventually a hysterectomy is necessary to tidy up some gynaecological problems and the finality of it all is simply too much for queen witch. Again it's tears and depression in a final emotional torment which the medical profession calls "post-operative" depression. All that remains is for queen witch to dominate and rule the family she has produced for as long as the wife lives, seeking to control and add to her established colonies whenever possible.

It is at this time that the sexual relationship with the husband may die out altogether. He gets "the seven year itch" and finds himself another woman who understands his needs and is prepared to meet them, at least for a time while her own "Tender Trap" is being laid and then sprung. ***It is not that "the other woman" always consciously sets out to draw in the needy male***. As far as she is consciously concerned she is quite genuine in her sympathy and supportiveness. She just does not understand the forces within her own soul which are very likely to turn nasty on the unsuspecting male at a later stage, leading him to think he has gone from the frying pan into the fire.

Exactly when the husband is driven by his own desires or allows himself to be led into adultery depends upon his own self-control, moral standards and the prevailing circumstances. If his wife's headache stage was more than his lust could handle it could have been quite early in the marriage but in any event a potentially happy marriage has been destroyed due to the rebellious scheming of a witch spirit's possessive grip on its dwelling place, the wife's body.

What we have said here is, of course, a very ***broad generalisation*** only but the fact remains that spirits of witches can change from lust to frigidity very rapidly, which can be very confusing for anyone who does not understamd what is going on. For example, a queen witch can be very possessive about the body it inhabits. It often sees sexual intercourse as an intrusion into its empire, a surrender of the body it controls to another authority.

"My body is mine," says the witch through the wife—you (husband) keep away! It's/She's mine! I control her and she is yielded to me!" But the Bible says a woman should be in submission to her husband and one flesh with him, not with some unclean intruder. ***There is a choice to be made***. God's way or satan's? The Bible's guidance is clear for Christians, who should not be subject to or give way to unclean forces within them, but be led as true children of God by the Holy Spirit of Love and the Word of God.

It is necessary for the Christian to renounce all submission to unclean powers and to acknowledge and if necessary positively re-affirm their submission to God and the moral law of Christ.

This will mean that within marriage the husband is the head of the wife (1 Cor. 11 :3) and that wives will obey their husbands in all their righteous (not unclean) commands, although we hope that such commands will be in the form of loving and courteous requests, remembering that in the matter of their sexual relationship not only does the husband have authority over the wife's body but the **wife has authority over the husband's body**. To summarise this, either partner should feel free to approach the other or let the other know their sexual needs without fear of rejection. The apostle Paul puts it this way:

> Let the husband meet his obligations to the wife, and likewise also the wife to the husband. The wife does not have authority over her own body but the husband (does); and likewise also the husband does not have authority over his own body, but the wife (does). Do not deprive (refuse, reject) each other unless by agreement for a time, that you may have opportunity for prayer and come together again lest satan tempt you because of your lack of self-control. **(1 Cor. 7:3–5 lit.)**

The Christian spouse who suffers from frigidity should reflect on the disastrous consequence that can flow from a frustrated spouse, then burn these verses into her/his heart and re-affirm where her/his loyalties and commitments really lie. Are you loyal to the unclean in your soul or to the Word of God? Rejection, especially unwarranted rejection, is a terrible foe and must be eliminated from a Christian marriage.

The good news is that today there are a growing number of deliverarce ministries available to ensure victory in Jesus' Name for those who are determined to possess it.

3.7 INCUBI AND SUCCUBI

The discovery that the psychiatric conditions known as *incubi* (for females) and *succubi* (for males) are caused by unclean spirits and are therefore curable for all Christians was probably the greatest breakthrough granted to us by the Lord during 1975. We do not say this was a new discovery—just new for us! It provided a significant step forward into effective ministry for nearly everyone suffering from sexually distorted spirits. Frigidity, anger, criticism, confusion, rages, fear of men (in women), other fears, depression, frustration and nightmares seem to be included in the normal syndrome.

Incubi are invariably present in women when sexual experiences have occurred during childhood (such as molestation) through to early teenage (e.g. playing doctors, nurses and patients, with a sexual emphasis). Even masturbation at such an early age can open the door to these foul spirits and tremendously increases the grip of sexually distorted spirits upon the person breaking God's covenant in this way.

Therefore you can quickly see that although the words INCUBI and SUCCUBI are probably not well known in western civilisation, the symptoms which make up these conditions are very well known indeed for they are widely experienced. There are numerous references to these demons in Babylonian records.[46]

What do these words mean?

Incubus (singular) and Incubi (plural) is defined in the Concise Oxford Dictionary as an "Evil spirit supposed to descend on sleeping persons; nightmare; person, thing that oppresses like nightmare."

The International Webster is, I think, more detailed about INCUBUS: "Nightmare; an imaginary being or demon, formerly supposed to be the cause of a nightmare, and believed to have sexual intercourse with women in their sleep … and SUCCUBUS "A female demon fabled to have sexual intercourse with men in their sleep …"

"But," you ask, "how can that be? How can a spirit being have sex with a human being? It is impossible." Well, it is no joke to those who suffer such interference,

---

46 "Epilepsy in Babylonia" by M. Stol

and a full-time Deliverance minister will have many case histories to which to refer. I remember a South Australian woman who wrote that she was usually attacked with invisible sexual activity while in her laundry. I wanted to lead her to Christ so that we could get started into delivering her but, unbelievably, she chose to fight on in her own strength. (This spirit is sometimes accompanied by a spirit of stupidity.) The same thing happened more recently. A woman rang who opened her conversation with the words "The goblins have got me!"

She went on to describe how she was usually attacked between 4.00 a.m and 6.00 a.m (some people are attacked in the daytime as well) and attempted sex was accompanied by weird little people and animals chattering away. She was living in a de facto situation and didn't believe the Bible, both of which circumstances are fairly common with this condition.

As she began to parade her ignorance and mock the Bible I perceived I was talking to her unclean spirit, and after a little plain speaking from me she rang off with the comment "I'll stick with my goblins," confirming the discernment given me.

The Bible sheds some light on this condition way back in Genesis. It plainly teaches that "the **sons of God** came in to the **daughters of men** and they bore children to them" (Gen. 6:4). This was before the Flood and at a time of great evil on earth—perhaps even worse than today. The text indicates that spiritual creatures met and had intercourse with physical creatures. This situation was obviously separate from Noah and his family, and as they are the only men who could possibly be labelled sons of God at that time, the text cannot mean that Godly men had intercourse with ungodly women—there WERE no other Godly men. In addition the unclean union of creatures of spirit and flesh produced "mighty" men, apparently a reference to men of extraordinary stature (perhaps giants) and deeds, but again there is no suggestion that this refers to Noah and his sons.

So it is fairly clear that "the sons of God" mean "angels" in this context, and "the daughters of men" needs no explanation. This can only mean there was sexual activity between angels and women. Now, today, both the Bible and experience of life testify to this activity, although we know fallen angels today as ruling unclean spirits or demons.

"Prove it," you say. "How can you interpret fallen angels as ruling unclean spirits?" Well, angels are spirit beings (Heb. 1:13–14) and "fallen" suggests "unclean". Fallen angels may not be the only unclean spirits on earth (Rev. 12:9) but they certainly belong to that grouping. The Word of God also suggests that they are rulers and authorities (Eph. 6:12).

"Angels attracted to women?" you ask? Yes, and this may well be the main reason women are to cover their hair (their glory) when communicating with God. As soon as women pray or prophesy the angels are summoned round about them. In such circumstances the **Bible says they are to cover their glory (hair) with a symbol of being under the authority of a man "because of the angels."**[47] (1 Cor. 11:10)

The angels attending the ladies (whether good or evil would take too long to discuss here) are attracted to the ladies' hair, so the wearing of a head covering serves two purposes:

(i) The hair glory is hidden from view and removes temptation from the angels...

(ii) it shows the spirit world that the lady is not a vulnerable rebel against man and God, but is in submission to a man in authority over her, who is her protector against spirit, man and beast.

"But," you say, "that is ridiculous! Who wears a head-covering when praying today?" Well, some Bible-believing ladies do. More importantly the evidence available indicates that this kind of sexual molestation is widespread, although the vast majority of incidents are not reported officially to psychiatrists. However this is only one of the causes of INCUBI. We must not forget the physical molestation of those who never pray, by human beings who are child-abusers, molesters, paedophiles etc.

Being attacked by INCUBUS or SUCCUBUS can be a most frightening experience. You are minding your own business, perhaps in the privacy of your own room, and then suddenly sexual activity occurs. You feel it but you see nothing. Sorry to horrify you, but it happens—it is real and it is unclean, and therefore the risen Christ can save the sufferer from this degrading attention, praise the Lord!

47 If this subject quickens your interest it is more fully treated in *"Headcovering and Lady Pastor-Teachers"* available at www.impactchristianbooks.com/peter

Jack Smurl has an interesting story to tell. A reviewer for his book[48] describes what happened:

> Jack awoke one night to see a creature about three metres high, with a furry head, blinding red eyes and a pig-like snout. It slavered and clawed at the air with rake-like fingers, threatening to disembowel him.
>
> Alone in the house one day, Janet Smurl was nearly choked to death by invisible hands gripping her throat.
>
> Jack Smurl was raped for the second time by a succubus. He was shocked awake by the form of a voluptuous young woman on top of him, riding him in the position of sexual domination. Despite her beauty, her eyes were a sickly neon green. Beside him, Janet was in a deep, psychic sleep.
>
> He found he was unable to move or speak. He could only watch as the demon performed and then vanished.

There are some people, of course, who like this ghostly intimacy, just as there are those who like adultery or homosexuality, etc. "It was very strange", recorded one young lass,[49] but I began to realise that I was enjoying what was happening to me. Soon I started finding myself waiting for him."

It is self-evident that such obvious manifestations of unclean spirits lie at the very heart of spiritism and witchcraft, but the good news is that the deliverance ministry of Christ always relieves the situation, sometimes quite speedily.

Praise God for His great Salvation!

---

48 "The Haunting: One Family's Nightmare."

49 "News of the World" 26 March, 1978.

3.8 INCEST

Incest is sexual activity within a family group, but not between the husband and wife. As such it is becoming a problem of epidemic proportions in our sexually orientated society as lusty humans look for sexual relief and satisfaction when their spouses are not available.

The frigidity and/or unavailability of a wife will often drive a man to look lustfully upon his maturing young daughter(s) and should he engage in sexual intercourse with a daughter he is guilty of fornication, adultery AND incest. One man who had been jailed for incest with his daughter told me, without any trace of shifting full blame from himself, that his wife had denied him his conjugal rights over a long period.

Sexual activity between brothers and sisters, indeed anyone of blood relationship, is also incest. It usually follows that the emotional and mental problems of each person engaged in incest, because of their existing close blood relationship, are severely compounded in any offspring, causing all manner of mental and emotional illness.

The Bible says the **soul is in the blood** (Lev. 17:11,14) and as the soul "contains" the unclean spirits residing in a person it is likely that offspring from incestuous relationships will get a double dose! For example if a family has carried a hereditary problem of fear down through two or three generations, and two members engage in incest, it is highly probable any offspring will be doubly bound up in fear, and insanity is not uncommon. The Church of England's "Book of Common Prayer (1662)" lists a table of kindred and affinity in order to prevent people entering into an unsuitable marriage with inherent incestual dangers on the basis of Leviticus chapter 18:6–17. I remind you again that the Word of God says **any conduct which defiles us (makes us unclean) is inspired by an unclean spirit**. (Eph. 6:12, etc.).

Incest is obviously a major part of the present Child Abuse problem in the world today. The problem has reached epidemic proportions, and the damage being done to children and young people is horrendous and irreparable (without Christ's deliverance and healing) this side of the grave. The lifelong damage may include a range of unclean spirits which produce manifestations of a highly strung, emotionally unstable character, such as fear, terror, frigidity, hatred (of the offending sex), inferiority, criticism, paranoia, insecurity, incubi, succubi, domination, etc. which, as you can see, are all closely related to the **witchcraft kingdom**. Thank God for the Cross of Calvary, by which we can be set free!

3.9 BE(A)STIALLTY

I use this word in the sense of human beings having depraved sexual activity with animals or beasts. I am sorry to have to include this section in this publication because I can think of no other human conduct more depraved than this. However, its existence illustrates my point about animal spirits. A man or woman is not normally attracted sexually to an animal, but an animal spirit in a man may well be so lustfully attracted.

Rape or sexual assault will often result in the accused being labelled an "animal"[50] or a "beast," which accusation is almost certainly true in the spiritual sense.

Therefore I judge that rape or similar sexual offences, even though committed by human beings against other human beings (and not animals) are, in fact, spiritual bestiality.

Lust itself is animalistic, is it not? And when "ordinary" lust degenerates into more and more animalistic (or snaky) conduct, the greater the level of demonisation experienced and the greater the need for Christ's deliverance.

Enough said.

3.10 SATYRIASIS

Satyriasis is defined by Webster's International Dictionary as an uncontrollable sexual appetite in males (the counterpart of nymphomania in females). It is derived from the word "satyr", a Greek and Roman term for a deity or demon which has the form of a half-man and half-goat, a goat being symbolic of a rebellious, lusty animal. In the adaptation of Isaiah 13:21–22 and 34:14 by the Book of Revelation the language is quoted from the Septuagint version of the Old Testament and the word **demons**

---

50 Apologies to Animal Rights lobbyists who quite rightly point out that calling rapists animals or beasts is insulting to the animal world (as we physically know it).

is used (Rev. 18:2 R.V.). What does this mean to you and me? In simple language, excessive lust is demonic. Let me go further and say the Word of God tells us **all lust is demonic** (Eph. 6:12, James 3:15) but I purpose here to look only at **extreme lust** or **satyriasis**.

A businessman came to my study one day (by appointment) accompanied by his attractive wife. He stated his problem very simply— "I want to screw every woman I see." Unfortunately that man could not carry out the counselling he received that day, but his problem was, and is, not uncommon. According to the "Murder Casebook" series, before the 1960s the United States had thrown up just one or two serial killers in a decade. Then, however their numbers began to increase: Six in the sixties; 17 in the seventies; 25 between 1980 and 1984. The evidence seems to indicate that most serial killers suffer from excessive sexual appetite and/or demonic influence. Let us take a look at a few case histories:[51]

John George Haigh was accused and found guilty of the Acid Bath murders in Sussex, England and was executed August 10, 1949 after admitting to four murders. He said "I experienced no remorse after killing, for I know that I was led by a superior force."

Lennie Lawson took captive five Sydney models into the Australian bush and raped two of them. His death sentence was commuted to life imprisonment in 1954. On release from jail eight years later he then raped and murdered another young model and shot dead a schoolgirl. He is a classic case of someone who seems benign and harmless on the outside but dangerous when roused. No wonder he fooled the psychiatrists into recommending early release. One would need the gift of "discerning of spirits" (1 Cor. 12:10) to know whether his demons had departed or not. And why would they leave? Hide perhaps, but not leave.

Albert De Salvo-The Boston Strangler: Thirteen women died in his two-year reign of terror and many others were also raped, or seduced from 1962–1963, perhaps as many as 2000. Regarding his sexual appetite he said. "It ain't that I'm better than any other bum, it's just that I'm a physical freak... but lots of broads don't like it if you're too sexy—my wife don't."

51 Courtesy "Murder Casebook" published by Marshall Cavendish.

De Salvo had nothing to boast about. What he should have said, of course, was that he was more demon-possessed than other men. He began his sexual experiences at the early age of about seven and quickly gained a reputation amongst both men (homosexuals) and girls. However when he married, his, relentless, insatiable sex drive eventually disgusted his wife.

"Society right from the beginning started to make me an animal... that's why I started all the killing." When he talked about the stranglings, he often used the third person in English grammar "he" of himself, as if **he had been a powerless observer of what was happening**... and the catalyst at each murder seemed to be when the woman turned her back on him, provoking rejection and hatred .

"I'm a sick person. I know that. How could a normal guy do what I did? ... **It was like another guy inside me!**"

De Salvo's defence attorney Lee Bailey focused on the unusual nature of the man, and pleaded that he should be kept alive for research purposes saying science and many other sick people could benefit from an in-depth psychiatric study of De Salvo's mind and actions. "Albert De Salvo should be the subject of a research grant," he said.

Well, I can save the city of Boston perhaps millions of dollars in grants by simply referring researchers to the Bible—Mark 5:1–20. The story of the demon-possessed man with the Legion is all one needs to know in order to apply the right and only solution, through Jesus Christ our Lord. There are only two proper responses—MERCY and JUSTICE. If the ministry of deliverance (mercy) is refused, then justice must be applied (Gen. 9:5–6). We should also remember God's forgiveness does not necessarily mean that God's justice on earth is nullified. It may be that murderers should receive both God's forgiveness and Eternal Life, AND ALSO pay the consequences on earth for their crimes.

David Berkowitz—The son of Sam killer terrorized New York in 1976 and 1977. With no obvious motive, he shot 13 people before his arrest. He claimed that supernatural voices had commanded him to kill, but the court judged him sane and sentenced him to 365 years.

Peter Sutcliffe—The Yorkshire Ripper murdered 13 women, after having sex with some of them, between October 30, 1975 and November, 1980.

Peter Sutcliffe was a grave-digger at Bingley Cemetery for nearly three years. He developed a macabre sense of humour during his time there, mainly as a way of playing down the gruesome nature of the job. On one occasion he pretended to be a corpse, lying down on a slab with a shroud over himself, making moaning noises when his workmates appeared.

He used to boast to friends he had removed gold and jewellery from corpses. At his trial, Sutcliffe also claimed he had heard the voice of "God" while he was working at the cemetery. As he was digging a grave, he heard a voice coming from the top of a hill. He had followed the echoing and mumbling to a cross-shaped headstone. The voice then instructed him to go out on to the streets and kill prostitutes. But, as it turned out, not all Sutcliffe's victims were prostitutes.

"My desire to kill prostitutes was getting stronger than ever and took me over completely," he said. "They are all in my brain, reminding me of the beast I am. Just thinking of them reminds me what a monster I am."

Three eminent psychiatrists diagnosed Peter Sutcliffe as suffering from paranoid schizophrenia.

Jeremy Bamber—The White House Farm murderer of 1985 killed his adoptive parents, his sister and her two children in order to get his hands on the family inheritance. He was alleged to have had an exceptionally strong sexual appetite and lived in the "fast lane." His philosophy, as described by a court witness, was that Bamber never believed murder was a crime. He believed morality and conscience were only for the weak. Perhaps this is a good example of how lust destroys a moral conscience and when it degenerates further into satyriasis, the committing of murder does not present a moral problem. It is as Jesus said, you let one unclean spirit into your house (mind and soul) and seven others even worse will follow! (Matt. 12:45).

David John Birnie[52] was arrested and charged with four counts of sex murders in Perth. When police investigated the house involved they found four graves, twenty-three photographs of necrophilia, stacks of pornographic books, several videos, chains

52 Daily Mirror 17 July, 1989.

and ropes. The ordinary brick house had become a place of horror.

Birnie's mother spoke to reporters of her son's obsession with sex. "He was always desperate to get girls", she is quoted as saying, and Birnie's brother told of his fury when he was deprived. "He's just got to have sex," he said. "If he can't get it, he cracks up."

SUMMARY

Now a man is a prime suspect in ***forty-eight sex deaths*** of women over seven years in the Green River murders which began near Seattle in 1982. A raid on the suspect's home uncovered 1800 video tapes, police uniforms and badges and twenty-nine firearms.[53]

What a sorry, sordid tale of woe, human misery and cruelty has been this chronicle under the heading of satyriasis! Perhaps now we will all believe the Word of God when it tells us to abstain from fleshly lusts which war against the SOUL (1 Peter 2:11)!

There are, of course, millions of men throughout the world that are enslaved by a sexual appetite that no wife could satisfy. They began their conquests usually at a very young age and quickly grow to hate all women. Any woman who requires respect and honour, and thwarts their slightest whim is a bitch to be insulted, profaned, and an object of hatred and potential violence.

Who said demon-possession is rare?

3.11 TRANSVESTISM

Another area of sexual distortion which must cause concern to anyone with a shred of compassion is the despairing plight of human beings who do not know whether they want to be a man or a woman. I am not now referring to those who shout the charge of "sexist!" into the faces of those who believe that God made men to be men and women to be women, or Women's Libbers or homosexual or lesbian groups in

53 Reported in the Sunday Telegraph, November 16, 1986

particular, but to those individuals who have experienced such a massive confusion of mind and/or heart that they genuinely do not know to which sex they would prefer to belong, and consequently make enquiries regarding having a sex-change operation performed on themselves.

(A) SCHIZOPHRENIA

When cases of multiple personalities occur within one human being in our society it has often been viewed as *"emotional instability"*, *schizophrenia* or *insanity* but today at least, an awareness of the spiritual realm is growing and even atheists and agnostics are recognizing the probability of demonisation for cases of *multiple personality disorder* (MPD).

If the scientific world, with its widespread unbelief of the things that are INVISIBLE can face up to the question of spiritual causes of complex emotional problems, then one would expect the universal Church ought to be able to give the lead in helping these unfortunate people.

Is there a distinction between transvestites and homosexuals? Obviously the two conditions overlap but the Word of God does distinguish between sodomites (homosexuals) and effeminates (1 Cor. 6:9). Certainly they are serious unclean conditions to have but they are not irreversible (Eph. 2:4–10, 1 Cor. 6:11–12), as we shall see.

There can be very close relationship between spirits of schizophrenia and confusion with transvestism. Only recently, when Verlie called out spirits of transvestism at one of our Deliverance and Restoration meetings, a young man who was receiving ministry for schizophrenia reacted. For the next two weeks he was into his mother's wardrobe and insisted on wearing her nightdresses, skirts and jumpers everywhere. He was shown the warning of the Word of God:

> "A woman shall not wear man's clothing, nor shall a man put on a woman's clothing, for whoever does these things is an abomination to the LORD your God". **(Deut. 22:5)**

and also warned that he was making a fool of himself, but such was his confusion and compulsion that he could not, or would not, wear normal clothes while the transvestite spirits were being expelled. Then, as suddenly as he began, he ceased, and his speech also become normal again, praise the Lord!

For "macho" type men such as footballers to wear women's clothing at a party or celebration is considered a formula for certain success. Gales of laughter erupt at the sight of such "he-men" made up as women, but if you listen to the laughter you will not need much discernment to detect demonic uncleanness. When I was a young boy it was known as dirty laughter. But now I am older and wiser I know it to be *demonic* laughter.

(B) SEX CHANGE OPERATIONS?

A broken man came to me because his favourite daughter was contemplating a sex change. However, she was alarmingly inconsistent, having apparently three personalities. "Norma" reflected her own human spirit, "Norman" expressed the very strong male[54] spirit that had entered her soul, and when yet another unisex-styled spirit was in control of her personality, she answered only to "Norm". This girl was under great pressure from Norman to have a sex-change operation and become a "man". However Norma and Norm were not at all happy about this and the poor girl's soul was a real battleground between her human spirit and the two unclean spirits.

If she does have the operation I suspect she will become like another tragic case who came to me after one such operation—still changing backwards and forwards between male and female, confused and suicidal. Operations may change the outer casing but will never remove the indwelling spirits which are causing all the confusion, distortion and torment. God made everything good but satan is the great distorter and corrupter. Thank God that through Christ the good can be restored to each and every one of us, i.e., YOU!—and the foul intruders eliminated from our souls and lives.

Recently we used the above "key" to great effect. We had a number of homosexual

---

54 Not a HUMAN male spirit from someone deceased, as the re-incarnationists might teach, but a MALE CREATION or ELEMENTAL spirit from the demonic world. See Chap. 2 and Book 4 for further discussion.

conditions in a Sunday group Deliverance and Restoration meeting and my wife Verlie, who is our main deliverance minister, took a young man's name, changed it to its corresponding feminine name and cast the intruder out in Jesus Name! Let us say the sufferer's name was Joseph. Verlie then commanded out the spirit of Josephine, with dramatic results.

The message is this. We humans may get things distorted and fouled up through drugs and the misuse of science but God doesn't make mistakes. *If the body is clearly male then there will be a male human spirit buried in the soul somewhere*. All other spirits (except the Holy Spirit in Christians) are unclean and removable in Jesus' Name! *The same applies to a person who clearly has a female body. Somewhere in the soul will !be buried the original female human spirit,* and all other spirits, no matter how strong and dominating, will be unclean intruders and therefore removable in Jesus' Name!

In cases where satan has been allowed to so distort the human creative process that even the body is a mixture of male and female and there is some medical doubt regarding the sex of the person, let us remember that God is able to re-create and restore to health all of satan's evil destructiveness of His creation. Gifts of healings and deliverance; discerning of spirits, and words of knowledge and prophecy, etc. are all available weapons to the Christian minister so that restoration can be achieved to the Glory of God. With God, nothing is impossible! It may take time but victory is possible through Christ the Lord!

Cases of physically mixed sexual bodies could become more and more prevalent as the sins sown by the fathers and mothers back to the third and fourth generation are reaped in today's children, together with the continual tampering of science into genetics, fertilisation and the cumulative effects of drugs, administered in good faith, eventually reap a harvest of devastation.

The bottom line is that if a person has a man's body (Cecil) but a woman's emotions and instinct (Cecilia), he may feel faced with a need to have a medical operation to change his body into a woman's body, believing that "nature" has made a mistake and needs to be corrected.

However medical science is limited in what it can do, and there is a much better solution available. Instead of cutting up the human body and trying to re-shape it into the likeness of the opposite sex, why not seek God and through His anointed ministers, have the dominant female unclean spirit(s) removed? So, anyone suffering from transvestism who wants to get free of it has two options before them. They can:

(i) have a SEX CHANGE operation, whereby your body is surgically changed in order to be compatible with the gender of the ruling (unclean) spirit in your soul,

OR

(ii) give yourself to the Creator, the Lord Jesus Christ. He will make your body and your soul a temple of His Spirit (1 Cor. 3:16–17) and begin to put right all that burdens you. LET us all submit to a deliverance ministry program, so that the Lord can remove all our ruling spirits. Our human spirit, which has been helpless for years, can become strong and take its rightful place in our soul and body, in partnership with the Spirit of God (Rom. 8:9—16).

Solution (i) above is "man's" way—and the pollution remains. Solution (ii) is your Creator's way, according to His Word, and the **pollution is removed**.

Spiritual surgery can be a lot easier than medical surgery. It is for rich or poor, and is God's solution to the problem, as against man's.

Thank God our hope is in the Lord!

The New Testament Scriptures are not joking when they teach us that Christ Jesus is our only Hope (1 Peter 1:13, cf. Psalm 39:7, 71:5).

In all these many sad and hideous circumstances and no matter how satan may seek to devour the creation of God, Jesus Christ is Lord and is able to answer the cries of His people far more abundantly than all that we ask or think (Eph. 3:20).

(C) SY ROGERS' TESTIMONY

The question the transvestite or transsexual person is going to ask is "Does it really work? I mean, can Christ really set me free? Are there any recorded cases of a transvestite becoming normal?" The answer is yes. Sy Rogers has testified to the world that:

> "although physically a man, I felt I was really a woman trapped in the wrong body. I desperately desired to change my outward sex, conforming my body to what I believed I was mentally and emotionally".

He has since helped thousands of others.

Sy goes on to say that he tried to live out his childhood fantasy of becoming a woman in hopes of being truly loved at last. He attended the Metropolitan Community Church in Honolulu which welcomes homosexuals and portrays a God who blesses homosexuality rather than condemns it.

> "Like many homosexuals whose hearts are not calloused", says Sy, "I was looking for a spiritual salve for my convicted conscience and at M. C. C. I found a religion which conveniently approved my sexual preference. I was deceived, as were my friends, yet I knew something couldn't be right when I could freely attend church socials "in drag", dressed as a woman. My friends became Hawaii's first male homosexual couple to be married, and I was one of their best men. To think we believed that God could bless this abomination!

> In the spring of 1977, I completed my Naval tour of active duty and returned to the security of my native Midwest. I'll never forget the look on my parents' faces as I stepped off the plane—a burned out, used up case at age 21. I watched their shoulders sag as shame enveloped their faces. I must have been a pathetic sight.

> A few months after I was home, I received a letter from my gay friends— the 'married couple' in Hawaii. They told me they were no longer homosexuals. They said they were Christians now, and that the teachings of MCC were lies. They still loved each other, though not in a homosexual way; and they no longer lived together. 'What traitors!' I thought.

Sy Rogers' story continues ...

> "After a crisis point in my life, I finally told my parents what they had long

feared was true: I was unhappy living as a man and desired to have a sex change operation. I began psychotherapy sessions in my pursuit of 'The Operation.' A battery of tests, including a chromosome test, proved that my gender identity confection was not the result of some bizarre genetic mistake. However, having done my research into transsexuality; I was able to give my psychiatrists the "right answers."

They officially diagnosed me as a transsexual, suitable for sex reassignment surgery. I was to undergo continued therapy and later have surgery at Baltimore's Johns Hopkins Hospital, which was famous for such operations. My parents, pushed beyond their ability to cope, resigned themselves to losing me. I believed a sex change was my last-ditch effort at finding happiness, and I was willing to sacrifice everything to achieve my goal. With my bags packed and my bottle of prescribed female hormones in hand, I was on my way at last!

"Powder and paint, to make us what we ain't…" The chant I'd heard from the drag queen prostitutes echoed through my mind. Staring into the mirror through a drug-induced haze, I saw what I had become: not just a liar, but the embodiment of a lie. I'd come to understand the art of illusion handed down from Babylon to Hollywood. While living and working as a woman for a year and a half, I had a good office position with a contracting firm near Washington, D.C. Achieving much-desired acceptance in my role as a woman, I was considered attractive and was riding the crest of popularity on the party circuit."

After John Hopkins Hospital had announced that they would not be proceeding with any more sex change operations because that was not the answer, Sy experienced being Born Again in Christ…

It was during Christmas vacation that everything came to a head. My heart had been beating more and more irregularly and my chest pains intensified. Finally one night, I dropped to the floor, clutching my chest. I couldn't breathe right, and was beginning to black out. Terrified, I cried out to God, begging Him to spare me. "Please don't take me like this!"

I pleaded with Him, "Let me live to know You first." The crushing pain began to subside. Shaken, I saw my desperate need to get right with God. But how? I turned to the Bible, knowing I'd find the answer.

"Come now, and let us reason together, says the Lord. Though your sins are as scarlet, they will be as white as snow; though they are red like crimson, they will be like wool. If you consent and obey, you will eat the best of the land; but if you refuse and rebel, you will be devoured by the sword. Truly, the mouth of the Lord has spoken." (Isa. 1:18–20)

As I read this Scripture, I broke. Bitterness, guilt, and shame for the lost years of my life poured out of me as I wept at the foot of my bed. I admitted my failure and guilt before God as I cried out to Him, "God, I cannot change what I am, but I'm willing to be changed.

I know You have the power. Make me the man You want me to be!" To be pleasing to God, to be loved and not rejected by Him that was all I wanted. As I placed my life into His hands, trusting Him, the "old me" died, and the "new me" was born! The Twilight Zone existence was over.

My spiritual regeneration was evident immediately. Overnight I'd been set free from immorality and drug addiction.[55] **The bleeding sores in my oesophagus (an apparent result of drug abuse) healed in one day! As I discovered the intense, intimate love of God for ME, I was set free from that consuming drive which had held me a slave to perversion.**

There were some rough times too, following my conversion. Seeking to establish myself in fellowship, I attended different churches I and found some people had a hard time relating to me. Though I dressed in men's clothing and had short hair, the residue of my old life—effeminate mannerisms, high voice, and the results of female hormones—caused many people to mistake me for a girl. At first I was crushed with humiliation, but I was more determined to live for God.

I did go through times of heavy temptation in many forms. However, I learned that Satan could only tempt me ... he couldn't force me to give

---

55 That is from SLAVERY to immorality and drug addiction. The temptations remained, but the POWER to overcome indwells Sy.

in, so with God's grace, I didn't. As I grew stronger and spent time in the Word, the Lord severed my past relationships and associations. It was time to move on. During the summer following my surrender to Jesus, I began to work with a Christian ministry, and joined a church where I was warmly accepted into fellowship with other believers.

Nine months after my conversion, I experienced the energizing power of the Holy Spirit. During this three-hour experience, the Lord revealed to one of my prayer partners that she would become my wife. Never saying a word to me concerning what the Lord had shown her, she waited on Him to bring it to pass. About one year later, I became aware of God's direction for our lives. At first I baulked at the idea of marriage. Inner fears and deep-rooted feelings of inadequacy surfaced. But as Karen and I developed a beautiful friendship in the two years before our marriage, God brought healing to all these areas of my life.

God has blessed us with the precious gift of honest, open communication, with Jesus and with each other. We've discovered many strengths and weaknesses, and see ourselves without masks. Today, my wife end I work together in full-time Christian service. Our marriage is NOT proof of my freedom from sexual perversion, but it is one of the most beautiful evidences of my new life and growing relationship with Christ ...

Being my own toughest critic, I sometimes have difficulty seeing the changes God has brought about in my life. I understand now that I may never live up to society's unrealistic standard for being "a man." But then I'm reminded that I no longer live according to the corrupted values of this dying world. I follow Jesus! He is my example of masculinity, my ultimate standard and goal for manliness."

In an interview with ON BEING Magazine[56] many years after Sy's testimony was first published, he was able to confirm the lasting nature of his change and also something of the Lord's processes in dealing with him gently. Here are some of his **answers to questions:**

56 August '88.

God didn't zap me into a heterosexual lifestyle over-night. But He did begin the process of healing the underlying motivations which contributed to my gay identity.

He also gave me power to say 'no' to homosexual desires and urges until the healing work was complete. I've been out of the gay lifestyle eight years and have been very happily married for five. That's not proof I'm not gay, but it is evidence of a new life that is available to me in the Lord.

Q. You say you didn't change into a heterosexual overnight. A lot of Christians probably wished you had.

A. Because Christians are so uncomfortable with homosexuality, the fact that people aren't made 'straight' at the altar disturbs them. Their attitude is: "You say you're redeemed? Then you shouldn't struggle with homosexuality any more." It's like a switch is supposed to be flipped.

It doesn't happen.

A homosexual identity takes years and many ingredients to develop. God is gentle; He puts the pieces back together slowly. It takes three ingredients to heal someone in overcoming homosexuality: God, the person's cooperative will, and the nurturing of the body.

Q. I wonder if generally the church has a shallow understanding of sin as behaviour, and has failed to understand it's also a power that enslaves.

A. I agree. And it takes the supernatural power of God to break that power over us. When I was in the gay life I used to blame God: "How dare you tell me I'm doomed to hell for being gay when I didn't choose to be this way?" I didn't understand the good news that He enables us to change.

The problem is that the church isn't mature enough to deal with dirty diapers. New babies aren't potty trained overnight. But when people come out of a situation of life-dominating sin Christians expect some microwave fix.

There is just so much wisdom in Sy's answers. Christians have NOT generally understood the enslaving nature, indeed the SPIRITUAL bondage of sin, and have been fed such exaggeration in the past about instant cures they have little understanding of the long and gentle processes by which God overthrows demonic strongholds, and then restores, step by step, the new creature He is moulding.

Sy's full story of the grace of God is available from Last Days Ministries, Box 40 Lindales TX 75771-0040 or Mount Hope Incorporated, Box 1511 Hagerstown MD 21740, U.S.A., where, at the time of writing, Sy and his wife Karen are on staff.

From my reading of Sy's testimony the specific ministry of deliverance by casting out demons was not exercised by any human agency but they were removed in some measure by the sovereign intervention of God. Now that the Church is beginning to understand and use the deliverance ministry of Christ we can expect deliverances similar to Sy's to be multiplied many times over in the future, and with ever-increasing depth and effectiveness.

PRAISE THE LORD!

3.12 HOMOSEXUALITY

Let us say at the outset, before anyone with a homosexual nature gets offended unnecessarily, this book has been written to set people free from all kinds of bondages. Our purpose is to save and to cleanse, not condemn. It is to give hope and direction, not to hurt.

(A) IDENTIFYING THE PROBLEM

Homo-sexual simply means same-sexual and therefore commonly means sexual activity between two or more men OR two or more women (lesbians). A lesbian is simply a female homosexual.

Having spoken of the problem of transvestites and their demonisation which manifests itself through a *"multiple personalities" syndrome*, it must be obvious that the same spiritual principle applies to homosexuality although the type or content of the demonisation may be different.

The first homosexual we had the privilege of helping was a fourth year medical student. When **sodomy spirits** came out of him, they were very noisy, screaming the place down, so we tape recorded the deliverance session. Later the same year (c. 1973) the Anglican Diocese of Sydney held its Synod (Parliament) and considered the homosexual question. I took my cassette tape and player into that Synod debate, hoping to contribute, but by the grace of God, I could not catch the Archbishop's eye and was not given the opportunity to speak or play the tape for Synod.

As I reflect on the scene there were many homosexuals in attendance in the public gallery and the effect of the deliverance tape on them could have been even more dramatic than on the staid and traditional clergy present. In those days most clergy seemed to think the demons of which the New Testament speaks had somehow disappeared from the face of the earth.

Wishful thinking indeed!

(B) NATURAL OR UN-NATURAL?

It is quite wrong to believe that God made homosexuals the way they are—He did not! When God made the creation it was good (Gen. 1:10, 12,18,21,25,31) but when mankind rebelled against God every living thing became polluted by satan (Rom. 5:12, 8:20–21, Jer. 17:9), whose name means "adversary."

I have no desire to frighten, hurt or offend anyone, only to help, but it is time for some basic truths to be grasped. Homosexuality is NOT natural nor normal in God's Creation design, but is a part of the pollution of this earth.

I am sure you are aware that the homosexual lobby has successfully "convinced" governments (in Australia, at least) that the homosexual disposition is normal and is simply a matter of "sexual preference" because that is the way God made them. Sounds reasonable, right, fair and even good—if you don't think about the facts too much and if you don't know the mind of your Creator Christ.

THE BASIC TRUTHS OR FACTS THAT NEED TO BE CLEARLY UNDERSTOOD ARE:

(i)   God the Creator has given to mankind (which He has created in His image) the privilege and the power to produce other human beings, also made in His image (Gen. 1:26–28, 9:1, 17:3–7, 33:5) for the continuation of the human race.

(ii)   This privilege and power to create life is entrusted to the human race and is to be used according to the moral law of God and His Christ (Matt. 15:16–20).

(iii) Used according to the will of God this gift brings great blessing to mankind (Psalms 127:3–128:4).

(iv)   Abuse of this privilege and power brings the three-fold curse of poverty, sickness and death, to be followed by Judgement and the second death[57] (Rev. 2:11, 20:6,14, 21:8) and all that means.

(v)   Used within God's laws, normal (un-perverted) sexual intercourse between a man and a woman bonds them together as one flesh, one unit (Matt. 19:4–6). This flesh unity involves the soul of each, deeply affecting the mind and the emotions (1 Peter 2:11).

(vi)   Through sex the seed of man enters the woman, and through the working of God's natural laws, may germinate the seed of the woman, to create the beginning of a new life.

(vii) In this way the human race is continued, as God commanded "Be fruitful and multiply..." (Gen. 9:1).

(viii) However the destructive plan of the evil one (satan) is to bring men and women into disobedience, that they might self-destruct and come under

---

57 The Second death is discussed in Chapter 4

the wrath of their Creator God (Rev. 21:8).

(ix) Through the activity of demons, men engage in sex with men, and women with women (Rom. 1:18, 26–29).

(x) This dispensing of the need of a woman by a man calls into question why God bothered to create woman in the first place? Homosexual conduct by men is the greatest attack on women and womanhood. If normal and acceptable it makes them irrelevant, except for procreation.

(xi) Man's life-giving seed is deposited into the anus of other men, to die in a futile attempt to find a female egg to fertilise (so much for homosexuality being "natural"). Procreation is impossible, and therefore this form of sex is clearly contrary to God's creation order and will.

(xii) When the male seed dies in the anus it dies in the midst of human excrement. The Bible has a four-letter word for this waste filth. The world also has a four-letter word (expletive) for it, which it uses to "suitably" express disaster, but we'll stick with the Bible's word. The male life-giving, creative seed supplied by God dies in a mess of DUNG. Anal sex (sodomy) is a perversion and a defiant act against the God who made us.

(xiii) Is it any wonder that such sexual behaviour is an abomination to God (Lev. 20:13)? Is it any wonder that a whole range of diseases attend such abuse of God's design and will?

(C) CAUSES

I would like to make it quite clear at the beginning of this section that I recognise homosexually inclined people have been very largely discriminated against, persecuted, and treated quite cruelly, not for their own sins, but for the sins of their fathers. Therefore, when we identify that homosexuality (sodomy) is inspired by an unclean spirit[58] we do so in the context of the following facts:

1. Unclean spirits can be removed by the same Power which raised Christ from the dead.

2. A homosexual may be no more demonised than others with problems of heterosexual lust, gluttony, anger, fear, greed, violence, depression, self-pity, drugs, alcohol etc. etc., and therefore should be approached with the same love of Christ as any other sinner.

Obviously for a man to have female characteristics to the point where he is sexually attracted to other men suggests that an invasion of his soul by a controlling female-style spirit has taken place. Similarly, when a woman is sexually attracted to other women in the manner of a male, it is safe to assume her soul (the instincts and emotions) has been invaded by a controlling male-style spirit. These are the basic principles but, of course, things can get much more complicated.

Depending on the strength of the invading spirit(s), a person may find themselves slightly homosexual, bi-sexual or may completely "lose" their natural instincts because their own God-given sexuality is obliterated by the strong, unclean intruder, which then imposes its own foul cravings on the unfortunate sufferer.

How is this caused? Well, if we were to cover ALL the possible causes in terms of human conditions, environment and behaviour, that question would require a fairly complex answer, because we know that unclean spirits enter the human soul at every opportunity presented to them. However, here are some main causes in brief:

(i) A SINGLE PARENT

A very common method—probably the most common for male homosexuals—is simply the childhood lack of an EFFECTIVE father, resulting in mother domination. There is nothing new in recognising this causal situation, but it may be helpful to

---

58 This does not deny or contradict scientific evidence relating to chromosomes, etc. Every natural effect has a spiritual cause (Gen. 1, Eph. 6:12).

understand it is the very need for the mother to be both mother AND father to the youngster that opens the door to homosexual spirits. **Single parenthood** poses a particularly grave danger to children because they receive their personalities from their parents' souls and their souls need to be "fed" and nurtured by BOTH a man AND a woman. If they come only under the nurturing of the soulishness of a woman, then the spiritual transferences from the soul of the mother to the soul of the son will be DOUBLE what they normally would be. Where there is an effective fatherhood operating, the father's personality (which flows from what is in HIS soul), would not only approximately HALVE the transferences from the mother but also balance out any such transferences with a contribution from his own soul, *thus preventing an exaggerated transference of femininity from the mother.*

Historical experience also shows that it has been the immoral HETEROSEXUAL males (especially) who by their siring of fatherless children (whether they carelessly sowed a few "wild oats" before marriage or later deserted their wives and children) are responsible for breeding a race of mother dominated lads who easily became bisexual or homosexual in their sexual natures.

Let us not forget that various armies of soldiers have sowed many wild oats in the foreign countries they either occupied or were passing through during World War II, and now a generation later we are reaping what they sowed in full measure. *Fornication and adultery by heterosexuals has produced hordes of young men* without the blessing of a balanced family life with its components of love, security and responsible commitment to each other, and who in turn were unable to provide masculinity for THEIR children.

However, the wrath of God may be reaped in full measure as the homosexual community now passes the death penalty in the form of A.I.D.S. back to the promiscuous heterosexual section of the population which caused the problem in the first place. Were it not for the coming judgement of God upon ALL flesh in the foreseeable future one could conceive the grim possibility of both groups being wiped out and being survived only by chaste and virtuous persons committed to monogamous family life.

However, *none of us have any say in our parenthood* and little say in the matter of our upbringing, so we can thank God that even if our lives begin as a disaster, through no direct fault of either parent OR child, He is able and willing to straighten us out, praise His Holy Name!

(ii) IDOLATRY-CAUSED BY FALSE, RELIGIOUS SPIRITS

In addition the Bible, which is far more penetrating than any book on psychology, informs us that almost ALL of us are subject to infection by homosexuality because its ROOT cause is IDOLATRY. When we really get down to it *IDOLATRY is the root cause of ALL mankind's problems* (Romans 1:18–25):

> "Therefore God gave them up in the lusts of their hearts to uncleanness, to the dishonouring of their bodies among themselves. They changed the truth of God into the lie (of other gods) and worshipped and served the creature (man, birds, animals or reptiles—v. 23, or creation such as the moon, sun etc.) rather than He who created (all things) who is blessed forever—amen!" (Rom. 1:24–25 lit.)

The nations today ignore Almighty God (who can ONLY be communicated with through the Lord Jesus Christ (John 3:36, 5:23, 14:6, Galatians 3:13–14, 1 Peter 3:18) and follow after other gods and their prophets. Even we in Western "Christian" countries are so flabby about our Christian heritage that 95% of the population (and therefore the Government of the day) acknowledge other faiths, gods and prophets as valid, equal to or better than the Christian faith of our fathers. It should not surprise us then, that the apostle Paul declares in the opening section of his letter to the Romans that Almighty *God GIVES US UP* as a people to dishonourable passions (Romans 1:26) and to a base mind and improper conduct (Romans 1:28), and that our minds become darkened (Romans 1:21).

As we turn to other gods, satanic KINGDOMS of unclean spirits pour into the mind and soul, and our soulish natures become distorted, *men lusting after men, and women after women* (Romans 1:26–27). This distortion of the human soul, the apostle Paul describes as "being FILLED with all unrighteousness, wickedness, covetousness, evil; FULL of envy, murder, strife, deceit (guile), malignity (Romans 1:29). Please note, that although these kingdoms infect homosexuals THEY ARE NOT CONFINED TO

HOMOSEXUALS but infect ALL the immoral and idolaters—i.e. ALL who fail to honour or give thanks to Almighty God through Jesus Christ (Romans 1:21) e.g. fornicators, adulterers etc. We will examine this text by means of a chart in 4.6.

(iii) HETEROSEXUAL WOMANISING

Homosexuality can also occur when a promiscuous male womaniser reaches the end of his consuming interest with the female body, because he has experienced many of them, and has done just about everything that can be done to the point of nausea and hate. In his constant search for innovation and sexual satisfaction he finds, usually to his horror, that his big "macho man" image begins to be overruled by homosexual lusts. Similarly female prostitutes often become lesbians.

What has happened in the spiritual realm is simply that ***the unclean spirit of heterosexual lust has invited in other spirits even worse than itself***, in order to consolidate satan's kingdom in the soul even more (Matthew 12:43–45). This biblical principle means that the homosexual condition can arise in any demonised person, ***and especially where other types of lust spirits have preceded it.***

To summarise our answer to the question "How is this homosexual condition caused?" we have put forward the following major possibilities:

> (i) Lack of an effective father-figure (for male children)
>
> (ii) Hereditary idolatry (Romans 1:20–32)
>
> (iii) Promiscuous heterosexual activity

(D) ANSWERS

What can we do after the damage is done? Well, you have heard it before and I'll say it again. Christ is the answer! But before you tell me that some homosexuals have tried Christianity and it didn't help much, let me explain where I believe some homosexuals have misunderstood. I said Christ is the answer, NOT conversion to Christ. Conversion is basically a turning point, when we turn ***away from*** sin and the old life to Christ and a new life. Conversion is only the beginning. *It is essential but it is not the END, only the BEGINNING.* It is Christ who delivers us after our conversion that we all need, especially where heavy sexual bondages of ANY kind are in evidence in our lives.

(i) FAILURE OF THE CHURCHES

I believe the Churches have failed to minister effectively to homosexuals basically because we have not understood the problem nor the Bible's solution, and we have been theologically hazy:

1. Notwithstanding the fact many battle-hardened Christians believe all things are possible with God, "success" with healing homosexuals has been so rare and disillusioning that we wonder where things went wrong. (Perhaps they can't be helped? Oh well we'll show them love anyway.) This in spite of 1 Cor. 6:9–11 which clearly illustrates that some Christians were EX-homosexuals, and those who still practice are outside the Kingdom of God. When conversion prayers and standard follow-up fail, we sometimes give up and blame the other party because we don't know what else to do.

2. The greatest error lies in accepting the proposition that Christians cannot have a demon or an unclean spirit. This is based on the more fundamental mistake of believing that upon conversion all converts are automatically FILLED with the Holy Spirit and if we are FILLED with the Spirit of God, we obviously cannot have an unclean spirit. This latter proposition is being taught today with monotonous regularity, no doubt in the hope that if it is repeated often enough, some will believe it. However if it is believed (and, thank God it is not) it spells a life of torment, guilt, defeat and finally destruction for those Christians who would otherwise, if properly counseled, seek a powerful deliverance from their slavery and a genuine fullness of the Holy Spirit of God.

3. Another common mistake amongst Christian homosexuals is to argue

that Jesus never spoke against homosexuality. Paul did, but Jesus didn't. This is to misunderstand the role of Jesus in bridging the Old and New Covenants. He spoke to an Old Testament situation and set the foundations for the New. Hence when the Holy Spirit came after Jesus' resurrection, He was to lead Jesus' disciples into all truth (John 16:13), teach them all things (John 14:26) because during Jesus' time with them, they were unable to receive all He wanted to share with them (John 16:12). Much was to come later.

With His coming, the Lord Jesus Christ set a new direction, and it is His apostles who explain the fine details for us. They put the flesh on the bones.

To deny the writings of the Apostles as the Word of God is to therefore distort the whole of the New Testament.

Before conversion to Christ a male homosexual usually blames society for all the feeling of guilt, frustration, loneliness, distortion and destructive anger. He could allow himself to be persuaded that "they" (society) were responsible and that once "moral persecution" was eliminated he could live happily ever after, doing his own thing in a pluralistic non-condemnatory world.

However, when the Holy Spirit is invited in, the human conscience is pricked even further and battle flares within the soul. He discovers his main frustration and oppression does not come from outside of himself (society) but from **within** and in the majority of cases, conversion and the receiving of God's Spirit does not provide **automatic** deliverance and victory against homosexual spirits, neither does ongoing 'normal' Christian involvement. Assurances that Jesus is sufficient for every need begin to have a rather hollow sound to him and doubts creep in. The desperate choices that appear to lie before such sufferers are:

1. Admit failure as a Christian and fall back into the world.

2. Fight on by maintaining sexual celibacy, hopefully resisting the enormous pressure of lusts within.

3. Join a "Christian" church where homosexuality is not regarded as a sin but as

an acceptable expression of love.

If he is faithful to the New Testament teaching of the Word of God, choice No. 3 is automatically eliminated as a blind alley to hell, and if he finds his dark urges becoming overwhelmingly and agonisingly dominant, choice No. 2 becomes impossible.

Don Grant, who joined a Monastic Order for a season, testifies to the ineffectiveness of a monastery life-style in enabling monks and brothers overcome homosexual lusts and live celibate lives. He writes,

> "During my stay with the Order I observed many of the brethren, and discussed with them their many reasons for joining the Order, as some had obviously joined at a very early age, mostly early-to mid-twenties.

> "All without exception came from 'High Church' backgrounds. Many had been servers and choir-boys and most of them liked to dress up in robes (transvestism?). Many of them practised dressing up in women's clothes during and after puberty. Quite a number had some form of sexual activity with their priest or some other church official (choir-master, senior server or some other dignitary).

> "All without exception, who admitted to these sorts of aberrations, confessed to feelings of deep guilt and contrition and all knew it was wrong in the sight of God. The ratio of those serving in the Order who were homosexually inclined, was about 80%. Of the rest 50% admitted to having had some form of sexual contact with other boys in their early life. They seemed to be saying "God has made us like this and so long as we serve Him, in a life of good works and attend confession and mass every day, all will be well." Others believed it was laid on them TO OVERCOME the temptations by seeking to live a life of prayer and service to God in order to expiate their feelings of guilt. To go into a monastic situation seemed a better alternative to struggling against temptation outside, knowing full well there were many others in the BROTHERHOOD doing the same thing and for the same reasons.

"It was a feeling of being accepted with love and understanding that drew so many to a monastic vocation. There they could also indulge their love of DRESSING UP to their hearts' content. During closed days (no visitors) the more effeminate would indulge in 'CAMPING IT UP' and that sort of behaviour. It seemed to the others that was a good way of letting off steam, so we all 'turned a blind eye.'"[59]

Why do people with serious sexual problems seek a monastic Christian life-style? It is quite obvious really. It is the same reason that people like working for high-ranking church leaders. They may not articulate it, or even think it consciously, but subconsciously they sense "I have problems which only God can help me with. I need help from God and those close to Him. The closer I am to those who are close to Him, the more help I am likely to get. The more victory I will have over this uncleanness in my life!"

The result of this thinking is that people with problems, especially sexual problems, join secluded monastic Orders to get victory, to get help from all the other devout brethren who are also seeking to get close to God.

The intentions may be good but what is a common result? One finds oneself surrounded by people with the same or similar problems. It is not help they get but temptation from many sides, and false comfort from being one among so many.

(ii) THE ANSWER

Does this leave choice No. 1 as the alternative? Thank God the answer is NO! For all the promises of God are YES in Christ (2 Cor. 1:20). Jesus is the Great Deliverer—praise the Lord—and not only for sexual problems, but for the fearful, confused, violent, bitter, sorrowful, rejected, unloved, arrogant, domineering, greedy, cursed by the occult and crushed in spirit. Indeed, our Lord Jesus Christ bled and died on the Cross to set free all those in bondage to the enemies of God and mankind.

Christian Deliverance ministers have all the basic discernment they need from

59 Personal letter to me, printed with permission

Romans 1:18–31 in order to cast out demons from homosexuals who come to them for help in Jesus' Name. ***It is the ONLY thorough way to get free.***

Now the good Lord offers us all the opportunity to be members of His Kingdom (the Kingdom of God), forgiveness of sins and a full salvation which includes the REMOVAL of our POLLUTION. It's a whole NEW LIFE—

IF WE REALLY WANT IT!

Mark Pierpont wrote:

"I have truly come out now, I have come out from the hell I was living. I have come out of the gay closet. And that's what it was—a closet … a dark, closed-in, cluttered, confusing life-style-from which there is only one exit. That exit is Jesus and He has set me free."[60]

Let us give Sy Rogers the last word: "Today I am happy and heterosexual, never in a million years thought it would be possible."[61]

Praise the Name of the Lord!

3.13 PEDOPHILIA (PEDERASTY)

A recent report in a Sydney newspaper[62] covered the killing of Gordon Lindsay Kerr, 67, who was found dead with multiple axe wounds to his head and a garden hatchet embedded in his buttocks. His killer, who pleaded guilty to manslaughter, later told police he had wanted to make "him bleed from the arse the same way I did."

Police found the killer curled up in the foetal position on a neighbour's porch, crying and mumbling about the "bad man."

The killer's defence counsel, Mr Graham Thomas, said his client was sexually abused by Kerr between the ages of five and fourteen in the central Victorian town of

60 "How I Came Out" For further reading "Pursuing Sexual Wholeness" by A. Comiskey.

61 In NSW we also have Living Waters, c/o Christian Life Centre, 188 Young Street, Waterloo 2017.

62 "The Australian", 2 August, 1996.

Kyneton. Mr Thomas said Kerr had reaped the whirlwind of his actions. "This is not a vigilante killing ... this is a disturbed man confronting his demon."

There are no winners, only losers, with this kind of demonic sexual activity.

CHILD SEXUAL ASSAULT - No Excuses - Never - Ever!

So begins a NSW Child Protection Council (henceforth NSW CPC) information pamphlet in wide circulation throughout hospitals and clinics. The problem has been hidden throughout history but NOW, in THIS day, it is being exposed in developed societies as ENORMOUS.

According to the above report —

"A national study conducted in the United States in 1981 found that in approximately 90 percent of child sexual assault cases the offenders were male and 90 percent of victims female. Australian studies reinforce this finding.

An incest phone-in conducted in Sydney in 1984 found 99 percent of offenders were male and 99 percent of victims female. A similar phone-in conducted in Adelaide in 1983 recorded that 97 percent of offenders were male and 90 percent of victims female. Tables from both the Sydney and Adelaide phone-ins also provide some useful insights into the relationship of victims to offenders."

DEFINITION

I understand Pederasty (Paederasty) to mean homosexual activity between a male adult and a male adolescent. This is different from the term Pedophilia (Paedophilia) which may be extended to cover the abuse of little girls and boys, and is therefore a broader term.

The NSW CPC pamphlet goes on to say:

"Child sexual assault occurs when an adult or someone bigger than a child uses his power or authority over the child and takes advantage of the child's trust and respect to involve the child in sexual activity. Child sexual assault does not refer only to sexual intercourse, although sexual intercourse is often involved. Child sexual assault includes fondling genitals, masturbation, oral sex, vaginal or anal penetration by a finger, penis, or any other object. It may also include exhibitionism and suggestive behaviour. In all cases, the offender has more power than the child and misuses that power to take advantage of the child.

False impressions

Until quite recently, child sexual assault was hardly ever discussed. The silence which surrounded this subject not only made it difficult for the facts to emerge but also allowed false impressions to go unchallenged. Now that the silence has been broken, people are becoming more aware of the facts and many old, mistaken ideas are disappearing. For example, most people now realise that "stranger danger" is only a small part of the problem and that approximately 85 percent of cases of child sexual assault involve the child's relatives, family friends, or someone known and trusted by the child.

Another false impression is that child sexual assault happens only in poor or "problem" families. In fact it happens in all types of families, rich or poor, large or small, well educated or not.

Many people also believe that child sexual assault is just another form of child *physical* abuse when in fact there are some important differences between the two. With child *physical* abuse, both men and women commit the offence although women, who are usually the ones who spend the most times with children, are slightly in the majority. With child *sexual* assault, on the other, hand, it is overwhelmingly men who commit the offence, even though women are the ones who spend most time with children."

This article makes clear that pedophilia is a predominantly male problem. There is such an enormous gap in understanding between men and women regarding their sexual desires and instincts. Most men do not understand women and most women do not understand men, and each what makes the other "tick".

If young mothers had the slightest idea of what the prophet Jeremiah meant when he spoke for the Lord, saying:

> The heart is deceitful above all things, and is desperately wicked; who can know it? (Jer. 17:9)

— they would never allow their little children to run around naked on a public beach. They enjoy their picnic and outing completely unaware of the effect the nakedness of the children may be having upon watching demonised males. All the nonsense about their children enjoying fun in the natural completely overlooks the spiritually polluted state of the human (male) heart. We will never know how many pedophiles have been stirred up to commit ugly and serious offences by such "innocent" activity.

RESPONSES

There are two ways to view the crime of sexual assault on children. We can be:

(i) utterly disgusted that such perverted behaviour should be directed towards and upon defenceless children, and desire the heaviest penalties against offenders, even death,

or

(ii) sense compassion that human beings can be so heavily demonised, either (a) because of their own childhood experiences with the perverted, or (b) they were born with such demons by means of generational (ancestral) baggage loaded onto them at conception. The bottom line here is that "there, but for the grace of God, go I."

The Old Testament law by which Israel had to live as an example of a model, righteous society under God, made no bones about it at all. The answer was simple. Anyone who was stupid enough to give in to the control of perverting spirits inspiring a whole range of acts of fornication was to be put to death (Lev. 20:10–16).

This not only showed the seriousness with which God viewed the abuse of His gifts of sexuality, procreation and creation design, but also prevented unclean spirits being passed down and infecting the next generation, both adults AND children.

In the New Testament the good Lord offers a **wonderful solution**—the ministry of deliverance—made possible through the Victory of the blood sacrifice of the Son of God on the Cross. This not only enables us to get free of a horrible, foul, controlling, unclean spirit and live a normal life under God's blessing, but it also lifts from us the fear of God's judgement. Obviously, **failure to avail oneself of the Lord's grace** in deliverance still results in the first and the second death (Rev. 20:6,14).

SOME STATISTICS

The prevalence of child sexual abuse through the Roman Catholic Church is quite distressing. Whereas 90 percent of child sexual abuse is by men on little girls it would seem that the Roman Catholic church has a very serious problem—probably making up most of the 10 percent where men sexually abuse boys. The facts and figures now emerging are only "the tip of the iceberg":

From "Sins of the Fathers" documentary by COMPASS (14 July '96)

1. 600 priests reported for sexual abuse in the U.S.A. in the last 10 years.

2. Fr. James Porter found guilty of 46 charges of sexual molestation.

3. Canon lawyer Fr. Thomas Doyle, with two other researchers, reported on the problem to the Bishops Conference in 1985. The Report was "buried" for 10 years.

4. 3000 priests estimated to be sex abusers of minors, out of 50,000 presently serving in the U.S.A., says therapist and author Richard Sipe, a former priest.

The support group for victims of sexual abuse by clergy, Broken Rites, was set up in Victoria as recently as 1992. Already it claims to have more than **1000 reports** of sexual abuse and estimates that **15 percent of Roman Catholic clergy** are the subject of current complaints. That is one in every seven clergy!

Victim Mark Cade suffered similarly at the hands of the Christian Brothers in South Melbourne. He testifies to being gang-raped by four brothers, along with twenty other victims who have made sworn statements on similar abuses, with at least another thirty victims on the sidelines.

PROTECTION RACKET

Following on the tragedy in Canada where 18 Roman Catholic priests were alleged to have been involved in sexual offences against young boys during the 1970s, we in Australia have been shocked to learn of secret pedophile rings operating in business, diplomatic and Roman Catholic priestly circles, all under the protection of bribed police.

The original shameful 1973 "hush-up" in Canada at least appears to have been done to protect the reputation of the Church at large, and the good work of thousands of true God-fearing servants of the Lord. Not so in Australia. The evil of pedophilia thrived here so that corrupt police officers could collect filthy lucre (Titus 1:11).

If there is no excuse—NEVER—for the pedophile, with all his problems, where does that leave the bribe-taker who protects him? Thank God for the forgiveness of sins through Christ!

FAILURE OF CATHOLICISM

An example of the failure of both Church and State to protect children in their care is the case of Father Gerald Ridsdale. He is alleged to have assaulted over ***200 children*** over ***20 years***. The complaints began in 1975 and the then Bishop said to those in the know that he would handle it, which seems to have involved shifting the problem (Ridsdale) from one location to another. Twenty years later he was sentenced to 18 years jail in 1994, the judge commenting:

> "In seeking to sate your perverted lust it seems no victim was too frail or
> vulnerable . . . Your acts of debauchery were wicked and appalling . . ."

It seems that Roman Catholicism has been quite unable to administer a careful screening and vetting of its full-time workers. Given that the priesthood is always going to attract applicants who have little or no interest in heterosexual sex and therefore marriage, there seems to have been little understanding in the past that other abnormal lusts (euphemistically called "sexual preferences") might infiltrate their ranks.

With almost no **sexuality screening, discerning of spirits** and **follow-up deliverance ministry where necessary** (1 Cor. 12:10) the noble notion of celibacy in the cause of Christ (1 Cor. 7:1–9) has turned into a farce.

It is an enormous shame that so many Roman Catholic clergy who suffer from pedophilia have not availed themselves of the Victory of the Cross (Isa. 53:5, Matt. 8:17, Col. 2:14–15, Rom. 6:6, 1 John 3:8), and the ministry Christ offers to them (Acts 10:38).

So near, and yet so far!

How is it possible that the Church, i.e. the biggest church denomination in the world, has failed? Pedophilia is obviously a curse but surely a TRUE church can deal with curses (from the devil) and turn them around into a blessing? (Psalm 109:27–28). It should be able to:

(i) support the WRATH of God upon UNrepentant pedophiles

OR

(ii) bring the POWER of God upon REPENTANT pedophiles, and deliver them from their uncleanness.

It is an indictment upon any church if it has moved so far away from the powerful, effective but simple conduct and ministries of the early disciples/ apostles of Christ in meeting human need that it does not even occur to its leadership to apply common New Testament ministry solutions, such as deliverance.

The counsel seems to have been "Tut, tut, you've been a naughty priest but never mind. (I remember my priestly days … God help me!) We'll move you a couple of hundred miles west but you must be good from now on. Let's get your Confession and

Penance started..."

After their Confession would it not be more biblical to insist they enter a Deliverance and Restoration program or alternatively be reported to the Police? If they refuse God's mercy ministry then only His righteousness (justice) remains. The D.& R. program is, of course, for ministering a FULL SALVATION to the offenders, in accordance with the Great Commission our Lord commanded His Church to carry out to the end of the Age (Matt. 10:8 with 28:20).

HOPE FOR THE VICTIMS

The good news is that pedophilia by pseudo-servants of Christ has not prevented at least some childhood victims from finding the Risen Lord and true Christianity. Victims Claude Distefano who was sexually assaulted as an altar boy by Father Michael Glennon, currently serving 9 years jail, and Bob Harrison both found Christ, healing and new life in a Pentecostal and Baptist church respectively. Bob had been sexually abused two or three times a week for all the years he was in a Christian Brother's orphanage in Western Australia. He is one of about 300 victims suing the Church and the Christian Brothers. Such claims have resulted in some Insurance Companies pulling out of their policies indemnifying the Church against damages.

FEAR OF THE CHURCH UNFOUNDED AND UNNECESSARY

There is absolutely no need to fear the Church of Rome; the worst anyone can do is to kill the body (Matt. 10:28) and the Pope has no say in who will enter the Kingdom of Heaven and who will end up in Hades. The keys given to the apostle Peter (Matt. 16:19) refer to his UNREPEATABLE privilege in opening up the nations to the outpouring of the Holy Spirit. First Israel (Acts 2:38–41), then the Samaritans (Acts 8:14–17) and finally the gentiles (Acts 10:44–45). What the good Lord has opened, no man can close. Judgement belongs to the Lord (John 3:18–21,5:22, Rev. 20:11–15).

Perhaps some people allowed themselves to be bribed partly because they did not want to harm the Church but rather gain favour with the church, and God. It never seems to occur to people that they have nothing to fear or gain from a corrupt church. What should clearly be understood is that corruption is corruption and that a corrupt church or individual is neither to be feared nor helped except by means of true repentance (change of heart and direction).

God is God, awesome, holy, righteous and just. It is the corrupt who need to be afraid.

The truth of the matter is that the Roman Catholic Church is not the only true church, but by its fruit it has shown itself to be a ravenous wolf that devours the sheep. It should be pointed out the claim that Peter was the Rock on which Jesus would build His Church is extremely shaky. Whereas the questionable Latin and Aramaic translations of the New Testament may support such a claim, the original Greek text, considered by scholars of all theological persuasions to be the text inspired by the Holy Spirit, ***makes a distinct contrast between the Rock and Peter (a little stone)***.

I live next to two very caring, conscientious Christian nuns whom I believe love the Lord, but my advice to any troubled Christians in the Church of Rome, from pew-warmers to Archbishops, is to get out, repent and start afresh like Claude Distefano and Bob Harrison while there is still time. The good Lord will deal with the Vatican in due time as she sits on the seven hills of Rome[63] (Rev. 17:1–9, 18:1–10, 16–20) but as for YOU, come out of her (2 Cor. 6:17–7:1) — or suffer with her.

There is so much more that could be said, thanks to the excellent ABC Four Corners documentary by reporter Sally Neighbour, ***"Twice Betrayed"***, a major source of our Australian statistics, but it is important to say we ALL have our demons, some worse than others, but for pedophilia there is NO EXCUSE-NEVER-EVER! Just as Adam blamed Eve and Eve blamed the serpent, each human trying to unload the blame for the first sin, THEY BOTH FAILED. ***All three participants were held accountable in the judgement of God*** (Gen. 3:11–19).

One additional point needs to be made before concluding with some of the

---

[63] As this complete destruction of Rome is recorded towards the end of the Book of Revelation, and just before the marriage between the Bride and the Lamb of God, it is clearly still to come in the future. As we are also nearing the close of the Church Age, it cannot be far away.

consequences of child sexual assault. Governments and their committees and councils (such as the NSWCPC) do an excellent job in gathering data and relevant statistics, analysing behavioural patterns and issuing the appropriate warnings for parents, guardians and children to note and beware.

However, as is normal with scientific method and human logic, little or no place is given to spiritual factors or the Word of God and true Christian morality. At the beginning of this topic the NSWCPC informed us about FALSE IMPRESSIONS.

Also under that heading they wrote:

> "Although the false impressions are gradually being replaced by the facts, some mistaken ideas still remain. Many people continue to believe that offenders must be "sick" or "perverted", even though all evidence shows that very ordinary men, often 'pillars of the community', are often involved. People seem to feel more comfortable if they can dismiss the vast majority of those who sexually assault children as "sick"—just as, until recently, people found it easier to dismiss them as "strangers". The problem about clinging to false impressions is that they hide the truth and make effective solutions difficult to find."

If you can follow the logic of that, you are doing better than I. I think it is saying that because pedophiles are often "ordinary" or otherwise "respected" men they are not sick or perverted. Apparently only abnormal nobodies can be called sick or perverted, according to the NSWCPC. The truth is that every human being is sick with sin and death according to the Word of God (Rom. 5:12) and we cannot measure the level of demonisation in a person from outward appearances. If we could do so, the release of prisoners from jail, or mental patients from hospitals would pose no problem at all. You can find out more about *causes* and *solutions* in the Word of God (cf. Matt. 10:7–8).

CONSEQUENCES OF SEXUAL CHILD ABUSE

The immeasurably serious consequences of sexual child abuse cannot be overstated!

1. The resultant demonisation and emotional scars of the victims may *be carried into the next generation* where the victims of yesterday become the abusers of today.

   The television documentary entitled "The Choirmaster" focuses on a long-running Anglican pedophile, and records the fears of one of the choirmaster's victims. He expresses the fear that having been a victim he might one day become a predator, an abuser.

   I say to all with such fears, search out the Bible believing churches and get into a Deliverance ministry or program and allow the Holy Spirit to search you in the inward parts, over a period of time. Let the Holy Spirit dig deep —and remove — all the spiritual pollution that has invaded you (Psalm 139:23–24, Matt. 15:10–20).

The two choices that lie before you are:

   (i) get rid of your demons through the ministry of Christ.

OR

   (ii) risk becoming an abuser and passing some of your demons on to your victims.

2. The *loss of trust in the clergy* (especially Roman Catholic) and their relationship and ministry to young people.

3. Suspicions when ANY Christian minister befriends or is kind to young boys and girls. If we act like caring Christian people *we can be viewed as probable evil pedophiles* with ulterior motives. Our spiritual interest is thus gravely compromised. Parents have every right to be highly suspicious.

4. Many abused will never trust Christ's servants ever again and will view Christianity as a fraud, not realizing they have been assaulted by **FALSE brethren** (Gal. 2:4) who will themselves face the wrath of God if they do not genuinely repent. If victims can shake off the deception of a large denomination claiming to be the one and only true church they may yet discover Christ Jesus and His healing grace. As Jesus said "**By their fruits you shall know them**"—whether men are true disciples, or ravenous wolves in sheep's clothing (Matt. 7:15–20).

5. Unrepentant sexual abusers will face the wrath of God.

Whereas many people might defend fornication which is either heterosexual (different-sexual—a man and a woman) or homosexual, our western societies have yet to become so totally evil and demonised as to approve of pedophilia or pederasty. The bottom line is that **all these problems in the sexual area are spiritual and require spiritual solutions** if both the first (natural) and second (spiritual) death[64] of which the Word of God warns is to be avoided.

POEM BY A CHILD MOLESTER

"I am the slayer of the soul
destroyer of the dream
the nightmares that occur
and wake you with their screams
I am the end of innocence
the planting of the fear
that eats away inside your mind
and kills you year by year"

There are no prizes for discerning the inspiration of an unclean spirit here. Do not be deceived—it really is a matter of life and death—sooner or later. No one who practices unacceptable sexual habits (fornicators, adulterers, effeminates and sodomites) will inherit the Kingdom of God (1 Cor. 6:9–10).

64 Rev. 2:11, 20:6 & 14, 21:8.

The good news is that just as Jesus warned His hearers that despised tax collectors and harlots would enter the Kingdom of God in front of the religious leaders (chief priests and elders) of the day, so also today's harlots (representing all sexually immoral people) may still enter the Kingdom of God, perhaps before some of OUR religious leaders, IF they repent and believe (accept) God's way of cleansing and righteousness (Matt. 6:33, 21:28–32).

After the many public revelations of paedophilia in the media the Nelson Bay Baptist church (and many others) displayed the following on its public notice board:

"Even when the Church lets you down, JESUS NEVER FAILS!"

3.14 FUTURE TRENDS

The picture for the future of western civilisation, indeed the world, does not look very bright. Sexual conduct is clearly on a downward slide into deeper depravity in most societies, but of course, the Christian doesn't have to follow down the broad road that leads to destruction just because everybody else does.[65] Even the "weak" Christian should have some idea of what is right and wrong in the eyes of the Lord. In any case, with the rule of Antichrist becoming more and more evident in the world every day, this is no time to stay a weak Christian. The time has come for EVERY Christian to renew his or her commitment to the Lord Jesus Christ and His Kingdom, which is coming soon.

Television and Video Recorders have for some time made the viewing of salacious films remarkably easy and the Video Rental shops report excellent trade in the hiring of explicit sex movies. The Australian Federal (socialist) Government has shown its alignment with the spirit of Antichrist by opening the doors of Australia to allow a flood of pornographic material to be imported. The A.C.T.[66] Classification of Publications Ordinance (1983) brought amendments to the Customs law and created a new X classification, designed for films that are too hot for the cinemas to handle.[67] The

---

65 Matthew 7: 13–14. These precious verses caused me to be "born again" in 1959.

66 Australian Capital Territory, i.e. the Federal territory surrounding Canberra-Australia's capital.

67 Sun-Herald Feb. 19, '84 Leone Lamont.

State Governments are expected to fall in line with the Federal decision, indeed the A.C.T. and South Australia have already done so.

In this chapter we have discussed briefly a long list of unclean sexual manifestations and, no doubt, there are others that could have been included, but ***our purpose is only to show the CAUSE of sexual uncleanness, that is, unclean spirits***. We ought also to recognise that as fornication becomes even more widespread in our society and more blatant and shameless we can expect the "age of consent" to be removed. This would be a logical regression of attitudes. Obviously if sex before marriage is considered harmless and acceptable by the fornicators then who is going to set age-limits? Children will be permitted to and even encouraged to fornicate as soon as they are able—the only restrictions being imposed by their physical ability. Pedophiles have already pushed their case for sex with children as being harmless and worthwhile on Sydney television news unsuccessfully thus far.

The days are coming when only those who love the Godhead will endeavour to live moral lives. People will be "good" because they love the Godhead and have received the Holy Spirit, NOT because they are "law-abiding" atheists or agnostics, because there won't be any laws, except perhaps against the Christians. There are moves afoot even now to outlaw corporal punishment for children—not only in the schools, but in the homes. Imagine—governments legislating to make illegal the rights of a parent to spank his or her children—when they deem it necessary—such is the demonic wisdom of this world. No-one questions the need to prevent and discourage and in some cases punish sadistic child-bashers, but to use them as an excuse for legislating against the family laws of God is ridiculous (Prov. 19:18,22:15,23:13–14,29:15,17). Soon we will have a lawless society where people can do what they want, provided it is anti-Christian. The two kingdoms will soon be operating openly on earth—the Kingdom of Christ growing and including all those who shun the opposing kingdom of darkness with all its ugliness. Those in the Kingdom of God will be undergoing cleansing and deliverance as part of their preparation for the coming of the Bridegroom. They will be keeping the Covenant ratified by the blood of Jesus Christ, while those in the kingdom of darkness will be doing their own thing, which will be the things inspired by the unclean spirits which dominate them. God's people will get cleaner and satan's children will get more and more spiritually polluted, and when the days of grace are over, during which time God's forgiveness was available, it will be impossible to change kingdoms (Rev. 22:10–11).

Which Kingdom do YOU want to belong to? Because if you are in satan's kingdom the time to change is NOW!

What we must do is show you HOW (with God's help because He ENABLES us) YOU CAN HAVE THE POWER to change direction and GET YOUR LIFE RIGHT WITH HIM! But first we should understand *the extraordinary and wonderful part that the wrath of God plays in our lives on earth.* For example, if you are in the porn business as a pornographer, you may be interested in the following letter from psychologist Dr John Court, which was printed in the May 1994 edition of LIGHT magazine:

EARTHQUAKE DESTROYS PORN

Your readers may be interested in an article by Perucci Ferraiuolo in Christianity Today (7 March '94, p.57) about the big Los Angeles earthquake in January.

The article says (in part): The quake was centred in the cities of Northridge, Chatsworth and Canoga Park, which are home to nearly all of California's 3-billion-dollar-a-year soft and hard porn video industry.

Everyone of the primary porn studios and distributors, a total of around 70, suffered damage. The headquarters of the largest, VCA Pictures, collapsed, destroying equipment and master copies of several films. At least for the moment, high level porn studio executives and models are edgy.

An executive at World Modeling, a San Fernando Valley agency supplying actors to the porn industry, says clients are backing away from X-rated acting as a result of the cataclysm.

"Our clients have a definite lack of motivation," says the agent for porn actors, who requested anonymity. "It's put the fear of God in them." .

"It seems as though the earthquake forced these people to get honest," says Pastor Jack Hayford of Van Nuys. "It has stirred many to the deepest points of introspection. If just one of them is turned away from the filth they're involved in, it is a major victory."

Hayford, along with Hollywood Presbyterian Pastor Lloyd Ogilvie and Los Angeles Cardinal Roger Mahony, have sent a letter to the California legislature, asking lawmakers to draft a bill eliminating child pornography.

(Dr) John Court
Altadena, Los Angeles, USA

4
THE WRATH OF GOD— FACT OR FICTION?

INTRODUCTION

This particular subject has come very much to the fore during the 1980s mainly due to the A.I.D.S. (Acquired Immune Deficiency Syndrome) epidemic, now accelerating world-wide.

In addition the number of disasters world-wide is escalating all the time. The African disasters continue. The United Nations naturally hoped that when the famines in Ethiopia and Somalia abated that would be the end of it but now Rwanda and other nations have violence and catastrophic famines, with diseases such as cholera (and Ebola) causing deaths on an unprecedented scale. Even if media reports are exaggerated, the deaths run into hundreds of thousands, perhaps millions.

Even if the United Nations was able to slow the tragedy, which nation(s) will be next?

Australia has had its horrendous bush-fires and now earthquakes. America has had its floods and earthquakes but very few people are asking why and then listening for the true answers!

A.I.D.S. of course, is a world-wide disaster affecting both western cultures and undeveloped nations.

Malcolm Maclure of the School of Public Health at Harvard University wrote: *"Imagine full 747 jumbo jets crashing daily throughout 1990 and you grasp the possible scale of the A.I.D.S. epidemic to come. Each day in 1985, 1000 more Americans were given tickets (the virus). A new sexual partner is not just one new*

contact, but indirect contact with 10 or 100 or 1000 ex-partners of the ex-partners of the ex-partners of your new partner. "(Newsweek, Sept. 2 1985).

A study released in April 1990 by the U.S. Government's Centre for Disease Control shows that **one in four New York men aged between 25 and 44 is now infected with AIDS**, and that the infection rate in New York city is the highest in the world.

The study includes a survey of New York hospitals which shows that 8 per cent of patients have tested positive for AIDS. The highest rate of infection—among males aged 25 to 44—was 24 per cent. Of women in the same age group, 8.1 per cent have tested positive for the human immuno deficiency virus, or HIV, which causes AIDS.

The overall US rate of HIV infection is 2.2 per cent and the rate for adult men is 4 per cent. **"There was no hospital in the nation that did not have HIV cases,"** the study says. Author of the study Dr. Timothy Dondero says data shows an increase in HIV infection nation-wide.

A.I.D.S. has been called "the wrath of God syndrome" with good reason, because no matter how much academics, intellectuals and even some church leaders attempt to play down or ridicule the concept of the wrath of God upon sinners, their arguments always seem to ring so hollow and vain in the face of the reality of the dreaded disease itself. Added to that is the witness of God deep within our spirit or conscience that tells us differently. An opinion poll conducted by the West German magazine BUNTE in August, 1985 revealed that nearly half of all West Germans regarded A.I.D.S. as a punishment for promiscuity, and this is but a sample of public opinion everywhere, even among homosexuals.

A little later in 1987 there was evidence to show that the A.I.D.S. debate had swung things around, and media influence debunking the disease as the wrath of God had made an impact. More recently the Sunday Telegraph reported on 5th March 1989 that a panel convened by Adelaide's Roman Catholic Archbishop Leonard Faulkner to speak on his behalf made a submission to the Australian Government which said:

> "We affirm at the beginning of this submission that we reject any notion that AIDS is a divine retribution upon people".

Psychologist Patrick Heaven of the Riverina-Murray Institute of Higher Learning at

Wagga questioned 178 people of various ages and educational levels and had his findings published in the Medical Journal of Australia in September, 1987.

God was "blamed" by only 11 per cent who agreed with the statement that "Nothing can stop A.I.D.S.—it is a curse from God," and 20 per cent were unsure. Perhaps if the question had simply been "Is it a curse from God?" more people would have agreed, because every sickness is a curse, but sometimes medical "cures" are found, thus temporarily halting the curse until such time as newer diseases break forth. I do not doubt that at least a measure of cure may be found for the A.I.D.S. virus (the Human Immune Deficiency Virus — H.I.V.) and when this happens it will be replaced by something else. This is the history of disease and medicine, is it not?

The leprosy of the Old Testament was considered an unclean, defiling disease imposed by God as a judgement against those who broke the moral law of God (Lev. 14:19, Num. 12:9–10, 2 Kings 5:27, 2 Chron. 26:19–21) and seems to have been replaced by cancer, and now A.I.D.S. in our own day. It is interesting to note that the Word of God talks about healing the sick and CLEANSING lepers. Why? Simply because *lepers are not only in need of physical healing but also moral cleansing from sin.* The moral cleansing from sin and sins sets up the physical healing of the body so lepers are spoken of as being CLEANSED (Mark 1:40–45, Matt. 10:8) as distinct from other diseases which are healed.

All three—leprosy, cancer and A.I.D.S.—are a curse upon mankind for which the medical profession has still not found any answer. Why? Curses cannot be effectually broken by medicine and they continue their slow, destructive work to create future problems, until they are broken by recourse to Almighty God through the Lord Jesus Christ.

The bottom line is that in Dr. Patrick Heaven's survey, a huge sixty-nine per cent of people appear to have lost sight of God's involvement in the human race.

4.1 THE EFFECT OF DISASTER

Disasters usually bring out the best and the worst in people, as the recent Newcastle earthquake demonstrated.

There were acts of unselfishness, superhuman effort and great courage as people fought collapsed buildings with their bare hands to help the injured and save lives. There was also some hint of looting, which the media report as a fairly common occurrence throughout the world at such disasters.

Apart from these two effects, a minister of religion involved in the funerals of those killed in the earthquake was shown on the television news as asking the question ***"What are you trying to say to us Lord?"***

What a good question! Many people are too afraid or hurt to ask it. The same question was being asked by Cardinal Sin in the Philippines as Mount Pinatubo continued its destruction during July, 1991. Cardinal Jamie Sin of Manila was reported as confessing that God is sending a message through all the disasters and freely admitted that he did not know what the message was.

"On bended knee, let us ask God what He is telling us through these calamities", he said.[68] Sometimes we are afraid to ask a question because we do not want to know the answer. If we discover the answer it may mean a radical and revolutionary change in our life-style, perhaps something that would shatter us even more than an earthquake. A married man may have to leave his mistress (de-facto) and return to his wife and children. An undetected sex murderer may have to turn himself in to the Police. A wife and mother may have to cease her secret affair. A homosexual may have to live the celibate life. Drastic changes are required of individuals when they start asking, "Why? why me?"

---

68 Sunday Telegraph 7 July, 1991.

I write as one who loves and cares about God's Filipino people and I can answer part of that question for Cardinal Sin. Many of his people worship in churches filled with idols. There are horrendous graven or carved images of "things in Heaven above" contrary to the clear command of God (Exod. 20:3–6). Also bribery extorted by government officials seems part of the normal cultural economy (Prov. 29:4).

For Cardinal Sin to even begin to see the wrath of God turned aside from the nation, he must first put his own house in order, and see it cleansed from all idolatry and bribery (Isa. 33: 15–16, Amos 5:12). .

4.2 TRAGEDIES CAN HAPPEN TO ANYONE

The human tendency is to view someone who has suffered a tragedy as "probably deserving it". We have a sense of natural or poetic justice, so we believe good things happen to good people and bad things happen to bad people. If a man with a long criminal record goes to jail for something he did not do, many people are quite happy about it, believing that he must have committed other serious crimes for which he was NOT apprehended and that poetic justice has caught up with him. While this attitude may be defensible, what is NOT defensible is the belief that goes hand in hand with this, that is, it won't happen to ME! I won't experience disaster because I don't deserve to!

Jesus made this very clear. He said his hearers were not to look at the tragedies that happened to some Galileans or eighteen people in Siloam as indications that they "were worse sinners than others ... because they suffered thus? I tell you, No; *but unless you repent you will ALL likewise perish*" (Luke 13:1–5).

So you see, whatever happens to a few of us (e.g. sudden death) will happen to us all one day, and if we die without repentance towards God and faith in our Lord Jesus Christ then we doubly perish. We perish for this life, and for the next Life also.

Courage is one response to disaster, looting is another, but the one thing God really wants from us is repentance, which means a change of direction in our lives from selfish pleasure-seeking indulgence to serving and obeying Him. As Jesus said, unless we repent, we will all likewise perish.

4.3 THE CAUSE OF TRAGEDIES

" keep the Commandments of the Lord, and His Statutes which I am commanding you today *FOR YOUR GOOD!*" (Deut. 10:13)

There are so many disasters happening in the world today. Some can be blamed on human error but many of them are described in legal terms as "acts of God". That is to say, they are not considered as (directly) the result of human activity.

In 1989 a Jumbo airliner blew up over Lockerbie, Scotland, killing 270 people. At the memorial funeral service the preacher said, "Some will ask why did this happen, and the answer is that God only knows." Everywhere the cry goes up, "Why did God allow this, why did God allow that: If He is a God of love why did not God protect me—Why?"

It is strange how people get things back to front, especially spiritual things. Amidst all the disasters and crises in the world today, people are asking where is God? That in itself is not a bad question but all too often it is asked with an accusing spirit, seeking to blame God for all the problems. The next (logical) step in this kind of thinking is to say that there is no God, because if there was one, He would DO something to help us.

All this is totally back to front. No wonder the Bible says "The fool has said in his heart, 'There is no God'!" (Psalms 14:1–3, 53:1–4, cf. 10:1–4).

Disasters are not evidence that God does not exist. They are evidence that satan does exist! If therefore satan and his army exist (and the Bible is therefore correct in this matter) it follows that the Bible is also correct in assuming and declaring the reality of God.

Why then the disasters? A very brief explanation is given in that poster many Christian churches have displayed outside their buildings. Very simply, it reads— "If God seems far away, guess who moved!"

What more is there to say? If a nation, society, community moves away from God, satan will supply disasters upon disasters. Alternatively if we (Australians) clean up our act, with the Lord's help we may yet become again "a delightful land" (Mal. 3:12, Isa. 62:4).

It was from our Universities that the ***"God is dead" movement*** arose in the middle sixties, largely because our students were flouting (Christian) conventions and standards and appearing to get away with it. The philosophy became, "Look! I can take drugs, enjoy the 'experience' and no harm has come to me. Where is your God? I can sleep with whoever I like, follow the desires of my flesh and no harm has come to me! Where is your God? I can indulge in perversion and nothing has happened to me. Where is your God?" Etc. etc.

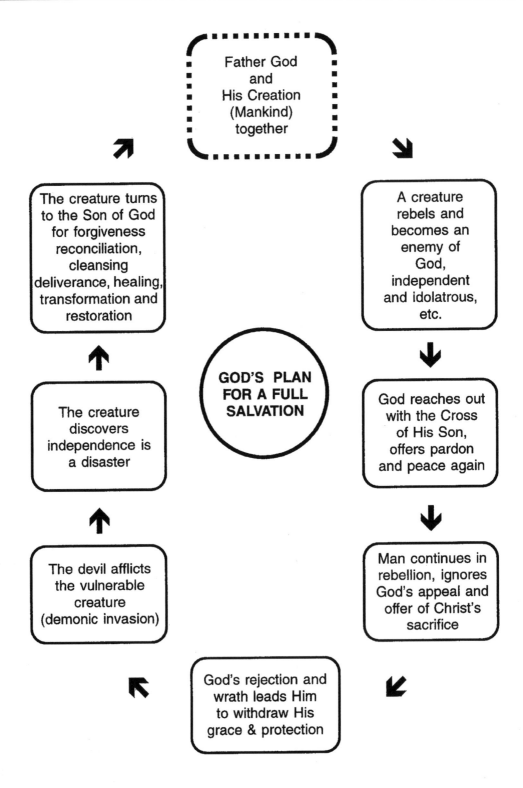

"Your God must be dead. Ha, ha, ha, ha!"

Fifteen years later, after many of His prophets, preachers and witnesses had cried out in the Name of the Lord, God's patience ran out. He has withdrawn His grace from many sinners. This is how He exercises His wrath—He simply withdraws Himself and His protection and lets us reap what we have sowed (Rom. 1:18–32, Gal. 6:7–8). (We will say more about this in 4.6).

So now the cry goes up from those who refuse to acknowledge the rule or even the existence of Almighty God. "There can be no God," they cry, "for if there were a God, He would not allow the wars, killings and diseases, not to mention poverty and starvation now upon the earth!"

So there you are. With some people there is no reasoning. They say there is no God when, in the patience of God He does not (immediately) punish them for their sins. Again they say there is no God when they ARE punished!

Oh foolish Australians (and Americans), who has bewitched you, whose ancestors dedicated your land to Almighty God? (cf. Gal. 3:1).

The answer is that God's protection of any of us is not automatic. Let me say that again—loud and clear: **God's protection of you or me IS NOT AUTOMATIC!**

It is available; it is to be applied by men and women of FAITH **but it is NOT to be presumed upon.** It is the height of stupidity to fail to apply (for) His protection BEFORE disasters happen, and then blame Him afterwards for our own failure.

What is the source of human tragedy? Or, to put it another way, where does evil come from?

Do we "blame" God for A.I.D.S.? Should we blame satan? What is going on? Well, in the first place we should not "blame" God for anything, in the sense that we (the creatures) accuse God (the Creator). With satan, it does not matter if we blame or accuse him for everything, but with the God who made us, it is better to ask if He is responsible, rather than "blame" Him.

Because we know God is Sovereign over all things and nothing can happen without His permission we usually divide God's Will into two areas, that of His ACTIVE Will and that of His PERMISSIVE or PASSIVE Will. This latter area of His Permissive Will we usually see as that area which God allows satan to do his dirty work, within limits that God imposes (1 Cor. 10:13).

From the Bible we have seen that the human race is not waging war against blood and flesh, that is, physical enemies, but against spiritual enemies called rulers and authorities etc., as we discussed in Chapter 2. We also learn that satan is the one who desires to destroy and hurt the human race (Job 1–2, John 10:10) and that he has his fallen angels to serve him in the task (Rev. 12:9). The fact that the Bible also says God sends evil spirits (1 Sam. 16:14,23) and destroying angels (Psa. 78:49) should not be a problem since it is God who gives satan permission to do anything, and satan then sends his unclean spirits on their missions to hurt us.

In all the circumstances it is better to blame satan for all the hurts of mankind since he is DIRECTLY responsible, rather than say God is responsible, UNLESS one perceives that God is ACTIVELY involved in judgement. This needs great care lest we humans be found judging others before their time, because even the Wrath of God is a consequence of God's Permissive Will as the apostle Paul plainly declares (Romans 1:18–32).

The following table illustrates four possible views on the source of DISASTERS:

THE SOURCES OF DISASTERS ARE:

1. NOT GOD BUT MAN

JER. 17:9	WICKED HEART
MATT. 15:18–20	DEFILED HEART
JOHN 2:24–25	JESUS KNEW...
ROM. 7:18–19	SIN IN PAUL

2. NOT GOD BUT THE DEVIL

JAS. 1 :13–16	TEMPTER
REV. 12:10	ACCUSER
1 PET. 5:8–9	DEVOURER

JOB 1:12, 2:6	LIMITED
1 COR. 10:13	LOSER

3. GOD'S PERMISSIVE WILL

DEUT. 31:17	HIDES HIS FACE
ROM. 1:24,26,28	GIVES THEM UP! (FORSAKES)

4. GOD'S ACTIVE WILL

EZEK. 11:11–12	JUDGEMENTS
LEV. 26:3-46	

Keep in mind we are often punished BY our sins rather than FOR our sins (Num. 32:23).

Be very careful NOT to BLAME GOD for what mankind or the devil does.

4.4 THE FEAR OF GOD

A generation ago many people knew that the Word of God says the **wages of sin is death** (Rom. 6:23). Today it seems only a small percentage of people who move in Christian circles have heard this truth. Why? Because with the onslaught of Humanism and Hedonism we now have a society that has very largely dispensed with God and His Christ and we have been lulled into losing our fear of God. Most people believe that even if there is a God they will receive automatic mercy because God loves everyone, regardless, or that their good works will earn them a place in the Kingdom of God.

Neither notion is true, of course. Jesus is the Way, the Truth and the Life and NO ONE comes to the Father except through Him (John 14:6) and the Wrath of God rests upon all who do not believe in or obey the Son of God (John 3:36, 1 Cor. 16:22). Also anyone hoping to get into Heaven by good works, that is, simply keeping the Law of God, is under a curse (Gal. 3:10)—surprised? **Jesus is the WAY**—believe it!

The fear of the Lord is the beginning of wisdom! (Prov. 1:7, 9:10, 15:33). There are many people, especially in the media, trying to deny the need to fear the Lord but we

DO need to fear Him. We will not hear His voice clearly unless we have the sense to FEAR Him first.

Dr. Heaven, whose survey we used earlier, deplores the Grim Reaper advertisement that has been used to warn people against A.I.D.S., accusing the Government of using scare tactics. *"Clearly there is a need for instructive and educational programs that educate rather than terrify the population,"* he is reported as saying.[69]

Peter Robinson, in his Candid Comment column wrote:

> "The crude rednecks of the National Party and others like to fall back on the theory that AIDS is nothing less than God's retribution for what are euphemistically called "unnatural practices." Hence the smearing of some anti-A.I.D.S. campaigns which stress the variety of ways in which the disease can be transmitted as being unduly influenced by the homosexual community ... There should be no room for country bumpkin prejudices or religious nutcases in this situation."[70]

Mr. Robinson's comments are a typical media attack on those who are seeking to uphold the righteousness of God. There are also other people in influential media positions that one might suspect as God-haters rather than God-fearers (2 Tim. 3:1–5).

IS EDUCATION THE ANSWER?

The truth of the matter is that we, as a society, must begin to get alarmed. The fear of God is the strongest possible motivation to help people straighten out their lives and keep the moral laws of God; and the fear of A.I.D.S. is the jolt that many people need to re-evaluate the truth that *as we sow, so shall we reap* (Gal. 6:7–8). The human race needs jolting—we don't need people telling us the answer is in education, and supposedly show us how to sin but still escape the wrath of God. What kind of stupidity is that? Education may trim the problem for a season but we are the most educated generation of all time, and we are going to be decimated by disease if

69 Daily Telegraph 21 Sept. 1987

70 Sun Herald 6 Aug. 1989

we do not begin to experience a little healthy fear, and change our lives accordingly.

One wonders about the future when leaders talk about education being the answer. I suppose that it is the best answer they can come up with, but what do they mean? Do they mean that the answer lies in the kind of education that:

(i) enables people to continue in sexual immorality without paying the price? Such education being centred on "safe" sex, use of condoms, various sex techniques etc.

(ii) seeks to differentiate between areas of sexual activity which are prone to infection, as against other types of sexual activity which do not appear (yet) to be risky?

(iii) gives better understanding of our biological and physical make-up, all of which is about as helpful as a packet of band-aids.

I heard one university student on my car radio explaining how A.I.D.S. began in the homosexual community "by chance" and how it could have happened anywhere. They were just unlucky. If you believe that, don't bother reading this book any further—it won't help you. However, I suppose when it comes down to it you only have the two options or choices. It is either the Wrath of God, or bad luck. One option is true, and one is a lie.

The Bible says there is no such thing as luck, but that we need to fear the Lord before we can even begin to have real wisdom. We don't want to get to the place where we have gone too far and God WILL NOT hear us:

"Then shall they call upon me (wisdom), but I will not answer; they shall seek me early, but they shall not find me: for that they hated knowledge, and did not choose the fear of the Lord: They would have none of my counsel: they despised all my reproof. Therefore shall they eat of the fruit of their own way, and be filled with their own devices." (Prov. 1:28–31)

So when we hate the knowledge and wisdom of God, and do not choose the fear of the Lord, we get what we deserve. If only those who talk about education being the answer would mean educating those at risk with the requirements and moral laws of

God, then we would get somewhere. ***An education that teaches people how to sin and get away with it is a waste of public money***. An education that teaches people how to live as God meant us to live will always succeed because it gets to the heart of the problems and gives real meaning for this life as well as for eternity.

4.5 WHY THE WRATH OF GOD?

"They provoked the Lord to anger with their doings, and a plague broke out among them". (Psalm 106:29)

(A) GOD FORSAKEN

We have already touched on this in our earlier comments. Here are some extracts from the Word of God, which speak for themselves:

22 "Now the generation to come, your sons who rise up after you and the foreigner who comes from a distant land, when they see the plagues of the land and the diseases with which the LORD has afflicted it, will say,"

23 "All its land is brimstone and salt, a burning waste, unsown and unproductive, and no grass grows in it, like the overthrow of Sodom and Gomorrah, Admah and Zeboiim, which the LORD overthrew in His anger and in His wrath."

24 "And all the nations shall say, why has the LORD done thus to this land? Why this great outburst of anger?"

25 "Then men shall say, Because they ***forsook the Covenant*** of the LORD, the God of their fathers, which He made with them when He brought them out of the land of Egypt".

26 "And ***they went and served other gods*** and worshipped them, gods whom they have not known and whom He had not allotted to them".

27 "Therefore the anger of the LORD burned against that land, to bring upon it every curse which is written in this book". (Deut.29:22–27)

So you see, it was prophesied to Israel what would happen to them IF they:

> (i) forsook the Covenant of the LORD
>
> (ii) served other gods

Here are some more scriptures telling us why the LORD forsook His people Israel, and indeed ALL the nations of the earth, for He is the Creator of ALL mankind:

> ***"Thus says the Lord, YOU have forsaken Me, therefore I have left YOU"*** (2 Chron. 12:5–12).

> The Lord is with you while you are with Him, and if you seek Him, He will be found by you; but if you forsake Him, He will forsake you (2 Chron. 12:2).

> "And the Spirit of God clothed Himself with Zechariah, the son of Jehoiada the priest; and he stood above the people and said to them, Thus saith God, Why do you transgress the commandments of the LORD, that you cannot prosper? Because you have forsaken the LORD, He has also forsaken you'" (2 Chron. 24:20).

If we forsake Him, He eventually forsakes us—it is as simple as that. But the good news is that by the grace of God there is a way back:

> "If My people who are called by My Name (Christians) will humble themselves and PRAY, and SEEK My face, and TURN from their wicked ways then will I HEAR from heaven and will FORGIVE their sin and will HEAL their land" (2 Chron. 7:14).

Even at the end of the World, not just the end of THIS Age, when the earth lies stinking under its moral and physical pollution, the cause of all the disasters will again be the human race's failure to keep the Covenant Laws of God:

> "THE EARTH LIES POLLUTED UNDER ITS INHABITANTS; FOR THEY HAVE TRANSGRESSED THE LAWS, VIOLATED THE STATUTES, BROKEN THE EVERLASTING COVENANT.

Therefore a curse devours the earth, and its inhabitants suffer for their guilt; therefore the inhabitants of the earth are scorched, and few men are left" (Isaiah 24:5–6).

Thank God I am forgiven for my sins through Jesus Christ My Lord!

(B) THE CURSE OF UNBELIEF

In the New Testament of our Lord Jesus Christ the level of BELIEF that is acceptable to God means "to TRUST IN." There is intellectual belief, of course, which requires no commitment at all, but heart belief, the kind where we put our trust in someone or something, costs us something, usually a commitment of some kind, or places us in some kind of risk.

When you were little you probably got into some kind of scrape from which you had to be rescued by your father. Perhaps you climbed a cupboard or a tree and couldn't get down. So you cried out for help and your father arrived. When he told you to jump into his arms you had a decision to make. Could you trust him to catch you? He would certainly try but could he do it? The alternative was to stay up in the tree forever. So you mustered your faith (trust), took-careful aim, and jumped.

Now, your father could have jumped to one side and let you fall flat on your face and say, "There! Maybe that will teach you a lesson not to climb trees any more!" But he didn't—and you knew he wouldn't because he loved you and cared about you. Now if your father, who was a sinner, could be trusted to catch you and save you from harm, how much more will your heavenly Father save those who ask Him? (cf. Luke 11:9–13, Matt. 7:7–11).

Somebody once said "To love is to trust (believe in)" and it is certainly true that in marriage, if trust is damaged and not repaired speedily, love will also become a casualty. It would be difficult, if not impossible, to continue to love indefinitely someone whom you could not trust, except perhaps they be your own flesh and blood.

So then, to believe in God (and have the kind of faith that God requires) means to **put your trust in Him**, and this gives us a basis upon which love can grow and from which obedience can flow.

Disobedience to the Commandments of the Lord is usually undergirded by the fact that people simply don't believe there is a God who exists and who requires obedience. If one does not believe He exists, a motivation to obey Him is removed and disobedience automatically follows. If one is an agnostic (without knowledge of God; don't know), one's motivation to follow behavioural patterns which are said to be God's laws is seriously impaired. Agnostics end up keeping the moral laws they like and not worrying about keeping the moral laws they don't like. The bottom line is they please themselves and hope that if there really is a God He will applaud them for whatever they did right and ignore the failures. What it boils down to is that *our ability to OBEY God runs directly parallel with our belief (trust) in Him, because BELIEF MOTIVATES us.* With our BELIEF and knowledge comes a holy FEAR of God, which is right and healthy (Psalm 19:9). Some people prefer to use words like "reverence" and "awe", but I think we need all three words to describe a right attitude to Him. Fear and faith help to keep us obedient to Him, and unbelief, which obviously destroys our holy fear, motivates us into disobedience, which leads us into idolatry, that is, replacing Almighty God with gods of our own making. That is why Paul explains that homosexuality and other deadly sins spring from idolatry, which in turn springs from a failure to acknowledge that our Creator exists, and give Him thanks (Rom. 1:18–32).

We will be looking more closely at the results of our ingratitude and unbelief in the next section, but for the moment let us establish that *UNBELIEF is a foundation sin and can be considered the sin of sins.*

The Rev. Charles Spurgeon preached "*The Sin of Unbelief*" on Jan. 14, 1855 at New Park Street Chapel, Southwark. In this message he said:

> "I affirm, and the word declares it, unbelief is a sin. It is the quintessence of guilt; the mixture of the venom of all crimes; I affirm, and the Word declares it, unbelief is a sin. It is the dregs of the wine of Gomorrah; it is the A1 sin, the master-piece of satan, the chief work of the devil...
>
> *It is the parent of every other iniquity ...*
>
> "Surely with rational and unprejudiced persons, it cannot require any rea-

soning to prove it. Is it not a sin for a creature to doubt the word of its Maker? Is it not a crime and an insult to dare to deny His words? Is it not the very summit of arrogance and extremity of pride for a son of Adam to say, even in his heart, 'God I doubt thy grace; God I doubt thy love, God I doubt thy power?'

"Oh! Sirs believe me, could ye roll all sins into one mass could you take murder, and blasphemy, and lust, adultery, and fornication, and everything that is vile and unite them all into one vast globe of black corruption, they would not equal even then the sin of unbelief. This is the monarch sin, this **can be considered the sin of sins**."

To which I add two scriptures:

"And **without faith it is IMPOSSIBLE to please Him**. For it is necessary that whoever approaches God believes that He exists, and He becomes a rewarder to those who seek Him" (Heb. 11 :6).

"**For whatever is not of faith is sin**" (Rom. 14:23).

Now why would God judge the sin of unbelief as worse than murder and rape, etc.? Why does the Word of God say we cannot please God if we do not have faith (trust) in Him, and all our actions that do not have the ingredient of faith in Him are sinful?

We learn the answer from the first letter of John. We read that those who say they know God but DISOBEY His commandments are LIARS (1 John 2:4). We learn that those who deny that Jesus is the Christ are also LIARS (1 John 2:22) but worst of all we learn that those who DO NOT BELIEVE God's testimony (by Word and Spirit) about His Son have made (called) **GOD A LIAR** (1 John 5:9–11).

It is one thing to have God call us a liar—that is bad enough—but it is even worse for us to call God a liar!

That is what UNBELIEF does! **Every unbeliever in Jesus Christ is calling God a liar!**

Martin Luther said "to believe in God is to go down on your knees", and he also coined the phrase "sola fidei" which means "by faith alone" indicating the means by which we are saved from the judgement to come.

> "For God so loved the world, that he gave His only begotten Son, that **whoever believes (puts their trust) in Him, should NOT perish,** but have everlasting life" (John 3:16).

Here are some more facts about UNBELIEF from the Word of God.

UNBELIEF:

- ✫ can be mixed with seed (little) faith (Matt. 17:20, Mark 9:24).
- ✫ causes backsliding (Heb. 3:12).
- ✫ prevents the Lord doing miracles (Matt. 13:58).
- ✫ brings the rebuke of the Lord (Mark 16:14).
- ✫ makes man's heart evil (Heb. 3:12).
- ✫ causes us to be rejected by God

    (Luke 12:46, Rom. 11:20, Heb. 3:19, Rev. 21:8).

So we can see that the great sin is UNBELIEF regarding the Son of God. NOT murder, nor rape, nor child abuse, nor some other horrendous crime but UNBELIEF! The sort of unbelief you can find in your nice, middle-class solid citizen as much as amongst the criminals or immoral people of this world. This may explain why A.I.D.S. is spreading far afield from homosexuals and heterosexually promiscuous people. It will eventually affect the WHOLE of society, even nations, not because of their sexual activity (only) but because of their unbelief. It will throw immense strains on us all, on economies and resources, even if we never catch the H.I.V. virus ourselves. Our lives will inevitably be changed for the worse because there is *so much unbelief in the world*, and eventually it will be unbelief that causes many to reject God's offer of a pardon, and results in them being cast into the Lake of Fire forever.

If you are in any doubt at all about the relationship between belief and obedience, unbelief and disobedience, then perhaps Jesus' words may clarify this for you and at the same time underline that unbelief and disobedience do indeed incur the curse of the wrath of God. *"He who BELIEVES in the Son has eternal life; but he who DISOBEYS the Son will not see life, **but the WRATH OF GOD remains upon him**."* (John 3:36).

Clearly the wrath of God is upon EVERYONE who does not BELIEVE in (to the point of OBEYING) the Lord Jesus Christ.

(C) OTHER COMMON CURSES

(i) Not Loving the Lord Jesus Christ

The apostle Paul says much the same thing in different words:

"If anyone does not love the Lord Jesus Christ, let him be ***accursed***" (1 Cor. 16:22).

Again we are reminded of the closeness of the relationship between love and faith (trust) in someone, especially the Lord Jesus Christ.

(ii) Good Works Without Christ

If these scriptures from the Word of God surprise you it is probably because you thought that "doing unto others as you would have them do unto you" was the way to get a pass mark with God. It is certainly an important law and principle for Christians to love their neighbour as themselves, but even more important than that is the first Commandment—to love God with all our heart, mind, soul and strength.

Keeping the second Commandment—to love our neighbour as ourselves will not, by itself, get us a pass mark, as Paul makes clear:

". . . all who rely on works of the law (of God) are under a ***curse***" (Gal. 3:10).

(iii) Humanism, Socialism and Idolatry

Indeed, being descendants of Adam and Eve we were all born under the curse of sin and death (Gen. 3:15–19, Rom. 5:12) and unbelief does not solve the problem. Some people seem to think that denying the existence of God will get them out of trouble. They think that believing in God means that you are answerable to Him, but if you do NOT believe in God, somehow you are no longer accountable to Him, even if He really exists.

Nothing could be further from the truth. The prophet Jeremiah makes this plain:

V.5 Thus says the LORD, "Cursed is the man who trusts in mankind and makes flesh his strength.

6 "For he will be like a bush in the desert and will not see when prosperity comes, but will live in stony wastes in the wilderness, a land of salt without inhabitant.

7 "Blessed is the man who trusts in the LORD and whose trust is the LORD.

8 "For he will be like a tree planted by the water, that extends its roots by a stream and will not fear when the heat comes; but its leaves will be green, and it will not be anxious in a year of drought nor cease to yield fruit" (Jer. 17:5–8).

Man always has a God of some kind. If it is not a spiritual being or sun or moon or stars or beast, and there is no acknowledgement of any other creature as being superior, then *that man has elevated himself to be the superior being in creation*. He has made himself God, accountable to no one, except perhaps other men. This is the teaching of HUMANISM, the religion of atheists and agnostics which has been such a curse upon eastern Europe for forty years under the labels of Communism and Socialism.

(iv) The Occult

People who dabble in the Occult or any form of Idolatry are under yet another curse (Deut. 18:9–14). This includes all kinds of FORTUNE-TELLING.

(v) Blood-shed

Last but not least there is the curse of bloodshed or shed blood upon a land. Some nations have such a history of murder and blood-letting that it is no wonder they are paying for it now. Bosnia? Some African states?

The Word of God says that blood which is shed cries out for vengeance to God against the guilty (Gen. 4:10, Heb. 12:24, Rev. 6:9–11), that righteous blood must be answered for (Luke 11:47–57), that murderers are burdened with "blood-guiltiness" and that the shedding of blood defiles (pollutes) the land (Num. 35:29–33).

So God says to the nations:

> "As I live", says the LORD God, "I have no pleasure in the death of the wicked, but that the wicked turn from his wickedness and live. Turn, turn from your evil ways! For why should you die…" (Ezek. 33:11).

> " ... Repent, and turn from all your transgressions, so that iniquity will not be your ruin. Cast away from you all the transgressions which you have committed, and get yourselves a new heart and a new spirit. For why should you die . . . For I have no pleasure in the death of one who dies", says the LORD God."

> "Therefore turn and live!" (Ezek. 18:30–32).

The next chapter will show you *how to turn your life around and get a new heart!*

There are other common curses such as failing to return thanks with tithes and offerings for all God's goodness to us (Mal. 3:8–18, Ezek. 36:28–30) and hating Israel (Num. 24:5,9) etc.

But having established that these mistakes, such as unbelief in the Lord Jesus, bring upon us the wrath and curse of God, let us remind ourselves that the sacrifice of Christ on the Cross for us, *when He took all our curses upon Himself, enables us to have every curse upon OUR lives broken, through Him* (Gal. 3:10–14). That is why it is so important that our unbelief be replaced by faith (trust) in Him, for this is what our Father in Heaven requires of us if we are to break free of the Wrath of God and move into His blessing. (John 3:17–18)

4.6 HOW DOES THE WRATH OF GOD WORK?

We touched on this when commenting on the Active and Permissive Will of God, and the role of satan and his unclean spirits. There is a very clear passage of scripture on this, written by the apostle Paul. He says that the Wrath of God is revealed from heaven against all ungodliness and wickedness of men (Rom. 1:18, Eph. 5:5–6). First they fell into idolatry and then homosexuality (Romans 1:20–27). Because of their idolatry God *gave them up* in their lusts to:

(i) dishonouring their bodies among themselves (v. 24)

(ii) dishonourable passions (v. 26)

(iii) a base mind (v. 28)

(iv) improper conduct (v. 28) Here is the passage of scripture in full:

18 For the Wrath of God is revealed from heaven against all ungodliness and unrighteousness of men who suppress the truth in unrighteousness.

19 because that which is known about God is evident to them.

20 For since the creation of the world His invisible attributes, His eternal power and divine nature, have been clearly seen, being understood through what has been made, so that they are without excuse.

21 For even though they knew God, they did not honour Him as God, or give thanks: but they became futile in their speculations, and their foolish heart was darkened.

22 Professing to be wise, they became fools,

23 and exchanged the glory of the incorruptible God for an image in the form of corruptible man and of birds and four-footed animals and crawling creatures.

24 Therefore God gave them over in the lusts of their hearts to impurity, that their bodies might be dishonoured among them.

25 For they exchanged the truth of God for a lie, and worshipped and served the creature rather than the Creator, who is blessed forever. Amen. (Romans 1:18–25)

(a)   **PAUL'S REVELATION ON SIN AND WRATH**
ROMANS CHAPTER ONE

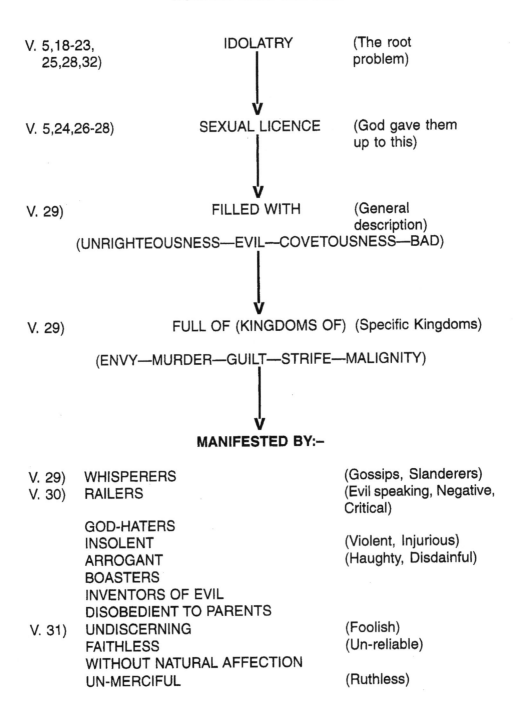

V. 5,18-23,   IDOLATRY   (The root
25,28,32)   problem)

V. 5,24,26-28)   SEXUAL LICENCE   (God gave them
                                          up to this)

V. 29)   FILLED WITH   (General
                                        description)

(UNRIGHTEOUSNESS—EVIL—COVETOUSNESS—BAD)

V. 29)   FULL OF (KINGDOMS OF) (Specific Kingdoms)

(ENVY—MURDER—GUILT—STRIFE—MALIGNITY)

MANIFESTED BY:–

V. 29)   WHISPERERS   (Gossips, Slanderers)
V. 30)   RAILERS   (Evil speaking, Negative,
                                        Critical)
          GOD-HATERS
          INSOLENT   (Violent, Injurious)
          ARROGANT   (Haughty, Disdainful)
          BOASTERS
          INVENTORS OF EVIL
          DISOBEDIENT TO PARENTS
V. 31)   UNDISCERNING   (Foolish)
          FAITHLESS   (Un-reliable)
          WITHOUT NATURAL AFFECTION
          UN-MERCIFUL   (Ruthless)

How does God's wrath work itself into our lives? According to the apostle Paul, He simply responds to our idolatry at other gods by WITHDRAWING from our lives. HE GIVES US UP. He says "If you want to serve other gods you can have them. I'll remove my hand of grace and protection and guidance from you because that's what you want. Let us see how your choice of gods works out. Let us see the reward you reap from your worship of sex, money, power and yourself. So He withdraws and leaves us to the merciless attention of the powers of darkness which seek to destroy us. His simple withdrawal from our lives, because we have made it clear that He is not wanted, is in effect the exercise of His wrath against a rebellious people, because we immediately begin to self-destruct.

When we become aware that we are self-destructing, only then do many of us cry out to the God who really is God, for help. We are like a rebellious little child who refuses to follow after our mother, but keep her dangling, waiting, while we pursue our own interests. However, should we look around and find that mother has gone, and we are left to fend for ourselves in a strange, uncertain world, we rush around trying to find our lost mother, crying our eyes out with alarm. Just about the only way God can get the attention of many of us is to withdraw and leave us to pursue our interests (gods) for awhile.

He withdraws His grace, His protection, indeed, He withdraws Himself from our lives.

The truth is there is a limit to God's long-suffering patience for an idolatrous and rebellious people and if they insist on serving other gods He finally takes His hand of blessing away and gives them up into the cruelty of the demonic gods they insist on serving and following, i.e. **gods of sex, money, greed, gluttony, ideology, politics, violence, luck and the occult etc**. (Rom. 1:21–32). The chart illustrates how the apostle Paul sees our degeneration from idolatry to total wickedness, deserving the wrath of God, as revealed in chapter one of his letter to the Romans, already quoted.

> "For speaking loud boasts of foolishness they lure with the lusts of the flesh those who have barely escaped from those living in error. They promise them freedom but are themselves slaves of corruption; for whatever defeats/controls a man, to that he is enslaved." (2 Peter 2:18–19)

(B) GOD'S GRACE

We normally understand that **God's grace means His undeserved favour towards mankind**, and that it works towards us in two ways:

(i) **Special grace**, where His Spirit brings forgiveness and Salvation to a "lost sheep" and they are born again and re-enter the Kingdom of God.

(ii) **Common grace**, where God upholds and sustains the world (Ages) by His Word of power (Heb. 1:1–3). He provides for all His Creation (Job 38–41) and gives rain to fall on the just and the unjust (Matt. 5:45)—for Christian and non-Christian alike.

This latter common grace is all part of His protecting, sustaining hand upon the Creation He has made, while restraining the devil from totally destroying mankind, made in the image of God. Day and night satan keeps asking for our blood (Job 1:9–11, 2:4–5, Rev. 12:10) and God keeps on restraining him, even though we don't deserve it.

However, when we forsake the Lord, He eventually forsakes us. He gives us up to the gods we follow and we discover, too late, how vicious and cruel they are, and how blinded and stupid we have been.

As we mentioned before (4.3) back in the 1950s, after a decade of unprecedented prosperity, Australians began to take their blessings for granted and turn to the religion of Socialism. University campuses pushed the "God is dead" philosophy and pro-Marxist violent demonstrations took place. Sexual immorality boomed with the free love, alternative-society, hippie culture. People began living in sin quite openly, and homosexuality began its fight for acceptance as a normal alternative.

Although all this was opposed by the Christian Church and moral groups, the media jumped onto the bandwagon and pushed hard for minority rights, quite oblivious to the destructive nature of what they were doing. *Anything novel, or a new story with a crusade flavour, and hang the consequences* seems to have been the trend.

With such one-sided media attention (and let's face it, many people think that a righteous, peaceful society makes for boring newspapers), Christians found themselves struggling to hold the line in a largely easy-going and uninformed society. We observed with alarm as Christian standards tumbled, and in all of that God seemed silent.

People were hopping from bed to bed, and apart from some risk of Venereal Disease, they were getting away with it. The Church sounded warnings of the consequences, promptly labelled "doom and gloom", and was ignored. Homosexuals were busy doing their thing—and nothing happened, or seemed to be happening from heaven. In 1972–3 The Anglican Church in Sydney produced a Report on Homosexuality which was unacceptable to the Homosexual lobby and they promptly produced a Retort to the Report which said, in part:

> "it pays no regard whatever to contemporary experience. Had it done so, it would have had to explain why France and Italy, neither of which have outlawed homosexuals for over 150 years are not threatened with the imminent visitation of fire and brimstone so confidently predicted on p. 31 of the Report".

You can see its appeal to experience. In other words they are saying, "What we are doing has been done for a long time in other nations and we are all still here. No harm has come to us. Where are the terrible consequences you warned us of? Where is your God? Where is His Judgement?"

In the long-suffering mercy and goodness of God, He gave them yet another seven (7) years to repent and change the direction of their lives before He withdrew His protection and finally gave them up as a group.

A. I. D. S. HAD ARRIVED!

4.7 REBUKES LEAD TO JUDGEMENT

> "For the land has become defiled, therefore I have visited its punishment upon it, so the land has spewed out its inhabitants" (Levit. 18:25).

So spoke the Lord when directing Moses on His law on sexual matters for Israel, and pointing to the abominations and fate of Israel's predecessors. Even before this Pharaoh had found himself and his nation on the receiving end of the Lord's rebuke.

Egypt had her own gods in those days and apparently Pharaoh and his captains thought that their gods were superior to the God of Israel. It took ten (10) severe rebukes as Pharaoh thought he could do battle with Almighty God and win. He lost every time.

You may remember how God demanded through His servant Moses that Pharaoh release their Hebrew slaves from their servitude to Egypt. "Let My people go" was Moses' message to Pharaoh and nine times he agreed after Moses did mighty signs and wonders as a warning, and nine times he reneged. Finally on a tenth occasion God sent the Destroyer to visit every home not covered by the blood of a lamb, and take the life of every first-born. The Hebrew homes were marked (covered) with the blood of the lamb, known throughout all future generations as the **Passover Lamb** because the Destroyer was not permitted to enter and take the life of the first-born but passed over harmlessly.

The Egyptian homes were not protected, and they suffered greatly. Even Pharaoh lost his son, the heir to his throne, and so he finally conceded defeat. He discovered that the God of the Hebrews was really God and he released them at last.

After the release he even reneged again and sent his army after the Hebrews to destroy them—and so he lost his army also. It seems incredible that men should be so stupid as to challenge and fight God, and of course only demonised men, bound and inspired by the powers of darkness, would even think of it.

Today we are again receiving rebukes from the Lord, but democratic governments seem powerless to act, being afraid of committing political suicide by offending their electorates.

The Hebrew Newsletter "MAOZ" had this to say regarding the way the Homosexual lobby has hijacked governments and their measures to combat the A.I.D.S. disaster:

> "The most ironic twist in this whole issue is the fact that because of the loud political clout of the homosexual community, the local governing bodies have been completely neutralized in acting as a government is supposed to act: to protect its innocent citizens against real danger. Instead the government is being mobilized to **even aid the spread of AIDS**".

It is not difficult to understand the dilemma of Governments and political parties who depend upon the democratic vote to retain political power. The homosexual lobby carries with it up to ten percent of the voting population—enough to topple any government in the West. So the political choices appear to be to either:

> (i) Take stringent measures to contain and control the spread of A.I.D.S. by registering known H.I.V. carriers and restricting their activities, with its inherent risk of losing government,

OR

> (ii) allow the homosexual community and other A.I.D.S. sufferers to regulate themselves, dying in their thousands, and keep government while putting the whole community at risk.

The governments of western nations are not the only ones facing insurmountable problems. Likewise totalitarian governments are crashing all around the world as starving people get sick of living on propaganda and overthrow the false religion of communism and its Marxist god.

How are these for rebukes from the Lord today?

- Famine and malnutrition (starvation) - Ezekiel 36:29-36
- Poverty
- Negative hygiene & disease
- Cancers
- Unemployment
- Savage weather, storms, heat-waves etc.,
- Overbreeding
- Lawless children from 8 years of age
- Wars (Religious)
- Sun-induced diseases
- Pollution (various) of land, water and air
- Floods
- Earthquakes
- Plagues (A.I.D.S.) Diabetes, Hepatitis etc.

If indeed all these are rebukes from the Lord, and aimed at getting our attention because of our wickedness, *we cannot be far away from the time when He judges the nations at the end of this Age.*

> "Let him who glories glory in this, that he understands and knows Me, that I am the LORD who practices steadfast love, justice and righteousness in the earth: for in these things I delight, says the LORD" (Jer. 9:24).

4.8 REBUKES ARE DESIGNED TO HELP US

Yes, there is a very positive side to a rebuke from the Lord. Let us consider for a moment how we would like to die. Would you like to die suddenly, without knowing what hit you, or would you prefer to die with some prior warning beforehand?

Most of us, I think, would like to die suddenly so that the fear of the actual experience was not experienced, but perhaps some of us, whose family and business affairs are not up-to-date, would like some time to order our estate, make certain arrangements for family and friends, and generally take care of loose ends. Some of us who have been neglecting our spiritual life and our relationship with God would want to make our peace with Him. **That is a loose end that must not be left untied or to chance in any way.**

I reckon it to be a fearful and terrible thing to have uncertainty about one's future after death. The Bible clearly says that **he who has the Son has life; he that does not have the Son (Jesus) does NOT have life** (1 John 5:11–12, cf. 1 John 4:13–16). Clearly we can know our future by our relationship with the Son, because we know we have the Son when the Spirit of Christ dwells within us (Rom. 8:9).

For Christians, generally speaking, a sudden death is most attractive, because they already have peace with God and know where they are going.

Praise The Lord!

At first sight sudden death might also appeal to a non-Christian practising homosexual, for example, but he doesn't realise his human spirit will be transported to Hades to burn there, awaiting the Great Judgement at the end of time, and the

Lake of Fire. So God in his mercy pulls back his protection and allows the devil to bring terminal disease to the one practising unclean rebellion, in order to bring them to repentance, and LIFE!

Now, I understand there are few things more moving to the human soul than to see a human being dying from A.I.D.S. My wife Verlie is not only a top Deliverance Minister, she is also a trained nurse with more than 30 years' experience and she tells me that no matter how one might be repelled by homosexuality, and acknowledge that homosexuals with A.I.D.S. are simply reaping the rewards of their own folly and rebellion, it is virtually impossible not to have compassion for them when caring for them. And this is right, especially for those who call themselves "Christian".

However, their present sad plight is nothing compared with being cast into the fires of Hades. The first death (physical) can never be considered as disastrous as the Second Death (spiritual) when some will be cast into the Lake of Fire forever (Rev. 19:20, 20:10–15, 21:8).

The bottom line is that ALL short, terminal illnesses give humans the opportunity, a last ditch desperate opportunity, to escape the Second Death, to make one's peace with the true God and Creator, through the forgiveness of sins made available to each one of us by the Cross of our Lord Jesus Christ.

We all have to die the first death sooner or later. **None of us has to die the Second Death!** God could end the life of a sinner suddenly and give him no last chance, but A.I.D.S. and other terminal diseases do provide each one of us, in the mercy of God, a time of sober reflection about eternal things and our coming meeting with the God Who made us, and Who loves us, and wants to spare us, pardon us, if only we will give Him the grounds to do so.

Do you remember the Word of the Lord?

> "Turn! Turn! Turn from your wickedness! Why will you die?" Says the Lord. "The Lord has no pleasure in the death of a sinner." "Cast away from you all the transgressions which you have committed against Me, and get yourselves a new heart and a new spirit" says the Lord God. "So turn and live!" (Ezek. 18:31–32, 33:11).

So you can see that the Lord LOVES us, LOVES YOU, and even when the Lord takes the restraints off the devil, and withdraws His common grace and protection from us because of our wickedness, even then He does so with the ultimate purpose of bringing us to our Godly senses and saving us. Praise the Name of the Lord! Let us not be numbered amongst those who have no hope in Jesus Christ, and grieve! (1 Thess. 4:13).

4.9 JESUS DELIVERS US FROM THE WRATH OF GOD

We know from the Bible that the Wrath of God is often ministered to us by sickness. God withdraws from us and the devil is allowed to afflict us (Job 2:1-7). Leprosy is clearly an instrument of rebuke (Lev. 14:19, Num. 12:9-10, 2 Kings 5:27, 2 Chron. 26:19–21), but even when we are being chastised the Son of God is available to heal all who are oppressed of the devil (Acts 10:38). Let us look at this latter scripture more closely:

1. " ... God anointed Jesus of Nazareth

2. with the Holy Spirit

3. and power

4. Who went about doing good

5. and curing

6. ALL those who were being oppressed

7. by the devil

8. because God was with Him"

Isn't that an absolutely marvellous Word from the Lord—for YOU! Did you know that Jesus Christ is the same today? Yes, the Bible says so: "**Jesus Christ the same, yesterday, today and forever**" (Heb. 13:8). Whichever way you look at it, what Jesus did in 30–33 A.D. during His earthly mission, He is available and willing to do today through His anointed disciples.

There are many, many scriptures in the Word of God which describe how the Lord Jesus delivers us from the clutches of the devil (which quite often is an expression of the Wrath of God) but perhaps the best-known one is the Gospel verse, so-called because it summarises the Gospel message so well:

1. "For God so loved the World

2. That He gave His only begotten Son

3. That everyone who believes (trusts in) Him

4. should NOT PERISH

5. but have everlasting life" (John 3:16)

When the Lord Jesus Christ delivers us from the oppression of the devil, and from perishing, He delivers us from what God the Father has permitted us to experience, that we might turn to His Son for mercy. So the wrath of God is designed to end in mercy and reconciliation.

Getting down to essentials, the Word of God promises His protection in almost all dangerous circumstances PROVIDED we:

a) Turn away from our sins (**repent**) (Luke 13:3–5)

b) Put our trust in the Lord Jesus Christ (**believe**) (Acts 16:31)

c) Fear God and keep His commandments (**obey**) (John 3:36, Eccles. 12:13, cf. Psa. 19:9, Isa. 48:17–18)

These principles will also mean that we should:

(i) Live according to the New Testament of our Lord Jesus Christ.

(ii) Put on the Gospel armour daily (Eph. 6:10–18).

(iii) Keep sprinkled with the Blood of the Passover Lamb of God (Ex. 12, 1 Cor. 5:7).

Obviously these principles will be a complete mystery to many people who are even now presuming on their "divine right to God's automatic protection". Such presumption is based on ignorance of God's Word and Will, with a false understanding of His love which is viewed as being unconditional. **NOWHERE in the Bible does the Lord promise unconditional, automatic protection for everyone, although it is AVAILABLE to all those who call upon the Name of Jesus** (Acts 2:21, 3:6, 4:10–12) **and trust and obey.**

SUMMARY

"**The fear of the Lord is the beginning of wisdom**" (Prov. 9:10, Psa. 111:10). That is another way of saying that anyone who does not live with the awareness that one day they will give an account of their lives to God the Judge has no wisdom, not any wisdom that matters, anyway.

> "For the Lord searches all hearts, and understands all the imaginations of the thoughts. If you seek Him, He will be found by you but if you forsake Him, He will cast you off for ever (throughout eternity)." (1 Chron. 28:9)

We need to see things from God's angle, to see the BIG picture and how we fit into it. Somehow He has to get our attention. The simple fact is that when things are going well, many feel they don't need Him. Humans are normally ungrateful for the good things they receive and we only turn to Him when things go wrong. It is not wrong to do that—to turn to Him, because that is why He allows things to go wrong—to get our attention. Then He can tell us what is going to happen in the future e.g. The Great Tribulation throughout the earth—(Rev. 7:14) so that, with His help, we can escape the worst of its consequences and the Great Judgement (Rev. 14:7,20:11–15). The fact that He perseveres with us for so long, in spite of our unbelief and wickedness just shows us how much He loves us.

There is a great GLOBAL movement on at this time in history whereby the rich and the poor nations are trying to tackle the planetary problems concerning environment, pollution and famine etc. They are moving towards a World Government to solve all the earth's problems, but of course, there is not even a hint of acknowledging Christ as World King. He is King of kings and Lord of lords but the nations do not want Him (Psalm 2). They will set up some human government with a world President and the Man of Sin will have arrived, as prophesied by the apostle Paul (2 Thess. 2:1–4). He will be charismatic[71] and popular but suffer from the great sin of UNBELIEF. He will authorise a world religion of his own, based on occult power, but he won't last long. The Anti-Christ's reign will be short-lived (read all about it in 2 Thessalonians).

But you see, if you don't pay attention to God by becoming a disciple of Jesus Christ, you would not know what the future held in store and you would drift along ignorantly and end up in Hell. The compassion of God through personal disaster is that He gives us a taste of Hell now, especially if we are unbelievers, to let us know what it is like before we get there. Of course, we can ignore the warnings and still get there (some people are rebellious to the point of utter stupidity, as King Solomon observed throughout the Book of Proverbs).

Christians cannot afford to presume on the Lord's grace either, as Paul warns us:

> "See therefore the kindness and the severity of God. On the one hand severity to those who have fallen, but on the other hand the kindness of God to you, **provided you continue in His kindness,** or you also will be cut off." (Rom. 11:22)

Many people may have a problem at first, when hearing that contracting A.I.D.S. has a very positive side to it, but people who criticise the view that this epidemic is a warning, rebuke or partial judgement of God upon a sinful and rebellious nation are no help when it comes to finding answers. Every Christian should know there is a Great Judgement to come and the trials and tribulations and judgements of this life serve to remind us of this and keep us close to God and obedient to His laws. When we are disobedient we open the door of our lives to satanic attack, which, if we have any sense at all, should bring us to the point of self-examination, followed by a renunciation of our sins, and repentance and reconciliation with the God who loves us and made us, through His Son Jesus Christ.

Little or big judgements along life's way help to straighten us out and bring us to the point of repentance so that we may escape the Great Judgement of sinners, when all of God's enemies shall be disposed of in Hell forever, as a farmer gathers and disposes of useless weeds in the furnace (Matt.13:30). But, you say, I am already contaminated

---

71 In the worldly, hypnotic sense, not by the Holy Spirit.

and diseased. Will God take away this plague? Venereal Disease (or sexually transmitted disease) is similar to the disease of the Leprosy of the Old Testament. It is a judgement upon sin in the world and even in Old Testament times there were ways of obtaining healing (Levit. 13–14, Numbers 12) even though the disease often gave the appearance of utter hopelessness, having eaten away the flesh.

If the Lord was prepared to cleanse and heal leprosy in Old Testament days, how much more is He prepared to cleanse and heal us from similar contagious, disfiguring and terminal plagues today, now, in the New Testament dispensation? (Mark 1:40–45). In all nations we now have more freely available the message of Salvation through the Blood of Jesus Christ, the Lamb of God, to overcome ALL forms of evil. If we have sinned, there is a way back for us, through Jesus (James 5:14–16). Love, pardon, peace and health CAN be our experience. If we have never been caught up in sexual rebellion then the Word of God should speak to us afresh, reminding us that God is not mocked and we indeed reap what we sow. How much better it is for you and me to trust His Word and use it to negotiate the dangers of this short pilgrimage we call "life" in safety.

We close this chapter with two (2) statements from the Christian Church in Australia about A.I.D.S. which, by and large, seem to me to contain much merit. Where I differ I have so commented at the end of each official statement, as is anyone's right. Nevertheless I believe them to be far superior to the usual public denominational statements which are sometimes prone to be public relations exercises rather than God's truth for a destructing world.

The annual National Anglican Bishops' Conference, held at Menangle from 3rd-5th April, 1987 released the following statement on AIDS.

> "As Bishops of the Anglican Church we share the concern of the whole community about the spread of AIDS.
>
> "We recognize the potential dangers which the disease poses for Australia and the world. We grieve with all those who are suffering.
>
> "We support the Australian and State governments in their determination to prevent the spread of AIDS.
>
> "There is no doubt that the spread of AIDS is directly related to casual

sex and to some extent intravenous drug use. The AIDS virus has also been transmitted by blood transfusion and in other ways can threaten the innocent. However, the principal cause is promiscuity. Promiscuity is not in itself a new thing. Yet in recent years community attitudes have tended to regard it as acceptable and without social cost.

"The spread of AIDS is not merely a medical or social problem, but also an important moral and ethical issue. Central to it is the matter of community attitudes and values. Any campaign based solely or even primarily on 'safe sex' or 'prevention' fails to address the fundamental moral issue. Indeed it may compound the problem by unwittingly fostering promiscuity.

"Casual sexual relationships have consequences that are destructive, not only to health through sexually transmitted diseases, but also to stable and fulfilling human relationships and social life.

"Some people have claimed that AIDS is a sign of the judgement of God on individual sufferers or particular groups. **We cannot accept that God wills the suffering of the innocent; but where the community has abandoned God's standards suffering is one potential result.**

"We call on all Australians to reaffirm the Christian moral value of a life-long permanent marriage relationship as the proper context for sexual expression; and to reject the assumption that temporary relationships can be accepted as a social norm.

"We call on the Governments of Australia to build into their present campaigns against AIDS a positive promotion of the moral value of permanent sexual relationships; and to strengthen their efforts to overcome the causes of all forms of intravenous and other drug addiction.

"We call on the clergy and people of the Church to care pastorally for all who have contracted AIDS regardless of their background or sexual orientation, as a true response to the example of Christ.

"As Anglican Bishops we reaffirm the teaching of Jesus Christ: **that human wholeness comes from remaining in touch with God's intention and design**, and through being filled with God's Spirit; that God has given us our sexual natures both for the expression of love between wives and husbands and for the nurture of children within faithful marriage relationships."

I would like to make two constructive criticisms on the statements (above) in bold print.

(i) It seems to me to be an exercise in mixing truth with subtlety to say that God does not will the suffering of the innocent but that suffering may result when God's standards have been abandoned. No one is innocent (perfect). All have sinned and come short of the glory of God (Rom 3:23), and many are accursed through their unbelief etc., as we have seen. We are all born with original sin (Rom. 5:12, Eph. 2:1–3) and are consigned under sin (Rom. 11:32) deserving judgement. That is the real truth.

(ii) The comment about human wholeness coming from remaining in touch with God's intention and design is altogether too wimpy and weak. It sounds like a distant relationship where God is used as an insurance policy (if the need arises).

Also there is no mention of Christ Jesus as Saviour and Deliverer, although His Lordship is implicit in the statement.

Now let us look at the statement issued by the Roman Catholic Bishops of Australia. Recognizing A.I.D.S. as having the potential to become the greatest scourge experienced by humanity in this century, the Bishops said:

"AIDS could not have spread through Australia without homosexual practices, sexual promiscuity and drug abuse.

"AIDS is a sexually transmitted disease that can also be transmitted through intravenous drug abuse and blood transfusion. Therefore, the continuation of this epidemic is neither inevitable nor unavoidable.

"In Australia, homosexual practices have been the principal cause of the transmission of this disease. Even heterosexual spread of the contagion can often be traced to earlier infection of the transmitting partner through homosexual practices. Transmission through medical accidents is now likely to be extremely rare, although a significant number of people previously infected in this way may still transmit and develop this disease.

"**We must not** make our present national situation more serious by presenting a moral teaching that is false or ambiguous; **we must not** yield to the pressures for silence. Christian moral teaching must make it clear that irrespective of their role in the transmission of AIDS, **homosexual acts are intrinsically wrong. These acts are immoral and cannot be condoned or approved.**

"**It is also wrong** to act in any way that is likely to pass on the disease to others; **it is wrong** to risk contracting the infection."

The Catholic Bishops acknowledge the Government's commitment to fighting AIDS, while at the same time it continues to tolerate the multi-million dollar pornography industry which adds to depravity and promotes promiscuity. The only effective means to combat AIDS is faithful sexual love within marriage.

The Bishops do not see AIDS as the Wrath of God, a divine judgement on a sexually permissive society. It is wrong, say the Bishops, to stand in judgement of individuals who have contracted the disease.

"Christians always have to distinguish persons from actions, and our merciful God will judge us all. To those who are ill with AIDS and to their families, the Church wishes to reveal the faith of Christ, the Good Samaritan, and extend his Helping hand.

"We must do everything in our power to prevent others falling sick with this disease, and this means that all education programmes must tell the truth. The truth is that certain types of behaviour must be avoided if the disease is to be avoided. The truth is that simply reducing the risk is not good enough; it is an inadequate strategy, which sells people short. The truth is that there are sound scientific reasons for believing that vaccination against AIDS may not become a successful procedure. Treatment is available, but cure is unlikely in the near future."

What the Bishops want in the media and in our schools are truthful and thorough programmes presenting human sexuality and family life in positive ways. Love and life-long marriage must be exercised. Casual sex with a variety of partners and marital infidelity are avenues to spreading this lethal disease and infecting innocent partners and unborn children.

Condoms for safer sex are not the answer. They provide a false security. This type of promotion, according to the Bishops, brings respectability to promiscuity.

> "If sexual responsibility before marriage and within marriage is truthfully taught and effectively practised, AIDS will ultimately cease to be a danger to anyone.

> "AIDS victims will not be abandoned by the Church, and those working with AIDS sufferers are encouraged to be compassionate.

> "The suffering must always retain their dignity and their rights and we pledge the support of the Church to them and to those helping to meet their physical, personal and spiritual needs. We condemn any move to discourage AIDS sufferers from continuing to maintain hope in life."[72]

This Roman Catholic statement has a stronger emphasis on right and wrong, and truth, and takes a very strong, Christian moral stance. However my main difference with it is its playing down of the Wrath of God. We have already seen that the Wrath of God rests on those who:

(i) do not believe (put their trust in) the Son of God

(ii) do not obey the Son of God (John 3:36)

(iii) trust in themselves (Jer. 17:5–8)

(iv) rely on (good) works of the law (Gal. 3:10)

(v) do not love the Lord Jesus Christ (1 Cor. 16:22).

These are not malicious judgements that one person makes on other persons. These are judgements made by the Word of God on the spiritual condition of other persons, and it is our Christian prophetic duty to declare the Word of God, that those who are under judgement (wrath) may repent, turn and be forgiven and restored.

---

72 As presented by Father Denis Madigan in the Sunday Telegraph, 13th Jan 1989.

The alternative is to say nothing and withhold the hope of restoration through our Lord Jesus Christ. Christians should not stand in judgement of others, of course, or in any way be judgemental, but neither should they deny the truth or neglect their prophetic and pastoral duty.

Facing up to the real problem is the only way to get the right solution.

My second point may be related to the first in that the reason many people do not like using the term "Wrath of God" is because it may seem hurtful, crushing and demeaning to a person's sense of self-worth, their sense of dignity. Hence the Bishops use the phrase, "*The suffering must always retain their dignity...*"

If by dignity we mean pride, I disagree, because it is important that any sinner comes to God with humility and a broken spirit (Ps. 51:10,17). God rejects the proud. However if the Bishops mean the sufferer should be treated with respect then we will all agree, I think, because we humans are worth more than many sparrows (Matt. 10:29–31), being made in the image of God Himself (Gen. 1:26).

Finally, if we Christians are to be really helpful, both to God and to suffering mankind, then **we must speak the truth in love** (Eph. 4:15).

I believe that the introduction to the Commination Service contained in the Anglican Book of Common Prayer (1662 A.D.) does just that — speak the truth in love:

"Brethren, in the primitive Church there was a godly discipline, that at the beginning of Lent, such persons as stood convicted of notorious sin were put to open penance, and punished in this world, that their souls might be saved in the Day of the Lord: and that others, admonished by their example, might be the more afraid to offend. Instead whereof, until the said discipline may be restored again, (which is much to be wished,) it is thought good, that at this time (in the presence of you all) should be read the general sentences of God's cursing against impenitent sinners, gathered out of the seventh and twentieth chapter of Deuteronomy, and other places of Scripture; and that ye should answer to every sentence, Amen. To the intent that, being admonished of the great indignation of God against sinners, ye may the rather be moved to earnest and true repentance: and may walk more warily in these dangerous days; fleeing from such vices, for which ye affirm with your own mouths the curse of God to be due."

Perhaps you have heard the song "Gimme That Ol' Time Religion"? Perhaps that is what we need today to save the suffering from themselves.

The bottom line is that Christians of ALL denominations are required by the Lord to HATE sin but LOVE the sinner, and He will judge us all in due course.

I do hope that any person who has read this chapter and who feels they have been, and still are, under the wrath of God, will take heart and hope and begin to reach out to "Him who … is able to do far more abundantly than all that we ask or think … in Christ Jesus to all generations for ever and ever. Amen." (Eph. 3:20–21)

I recently saw a message displayed outside our local Baptist Church at Crows Nest which, I think, makes a fitting conclusion to this chapter:

JESUS DIED FOR THE WHOLE DAMNED WORLD!!!

How true—

And that includes YOU!

5

YOUR WAY OF ESCAPE—WHAT YOU DO NEXT

5.1 IS THIS YOUR PROBLEM?

This book has been written for a very broad range of Christian people—for Pastors, Deliverance Ministers and Christians of every type. Nevertheless we realise that many people who read it may do so out of pressing personal need, not because they are seeking God or a "religious" faith.

I suppose by now you would be aware of the savage consequences of a life of sin. Not only does sin lead to eternal death, but it also pays disastrous dividends in THIS life—disease, mental sickness, hatred and heartbreak, when what you are truly seeking—and have always sought—is peace, true love, self-esteem, security and the happiness that flows from these blessings. Take, for example, the woman caught in the act of adultery (John 8:3–11). In this beautiful account of the forgiving grace of Christ to a sinner caught in the act of mortal (deadly) sin, we also learn that no one could throw the first stone of execution because every member of the mob, from High Churchman to village lackey, were brought to the realisation of their own sinful condition.

What of YOUR situation? You may be riddled with a sexually transmitted disease, or an unknown carrier, or just sick of the cheapness, tawdriness and self-degradation of your existence. Perhaps you have lived your life in the fast lane and, inevitably, became a loser.

The problem is that, although you desire dignity (worth) and self-esteem and the esteem of others, you have also sought freedom in the ways of the world and have now discovered that such "freedom" is really slavery and leads into a dead-end of uncleanness and worthlessness (2 Peter 2:18–19). At times spirits of hopelessness, despair and filth attack you. Destruction whispers to you to "end it all" and you feel very tempted to take your life. Satan would love you to do that because instead of the eternal peace you **think** you'll get (because of his lies) he knows that, without Christ, you will suffer eternal condemnation (damnation) and you will not simply have lost a battle, but you will have lost the war for your soul forever.

Suicide is NOT the way out! That would be to jump from the frying pan into the fire—literally!

All your uncleanness can be exchanged for the worth and peace you really want, for the Son of God made the exchange for you with His blood sacrifice.

Satan has deceived you into thinking that because of the environment, famine, sickness, tension in the Middle East etc., there is no hope for this world and there is no hope for YOU. But the REAL threat to you and your very existence is NOT what MIGHT HAPPEN but WHAT WILL DEFINITELY happen **if you REJECT God's offer of mercy and love through His Son, the Lord Jesus.** The order of events is:

1. You will die (**the first death**) sooner or later (Heb. 9:27).

2. You (your spirit) will immediately be taken to the torment of Hades (Luke 16:19–31) to await the Great Judgement. Your body will return to dust in the ground and your soul will disgorge all its unclean spirits which will then seek reincarnation in the living, but your SPIRIT, the REAL you, will be deposited in the place of torment.

3. When the Lord has finally overthrown all His enemies, spiritual and physical, you will appear at the Great Judgment (Rev. 20:11–15).

4. Your rejection of Christ's suffering, sacrificial death and love for you means you will be considered a rebel against God, and because your name will not be found in the Book of Life you will be disposed of in the Lake of Fire (the second death) (Rev. 21:8).

5.2 YOUR WAY OF ESCAPE

However the good news is that uncleanness, that sin of yours, whatever its form, and its awful penalty can be exchanged for the worth, dignity and future you really want. For the Son of God (who is known to Christians as the Lord Jesus Christ) made an exchange FOR YOU, that is ON YOUR BEHALF, on the Cross of Calvary. He died for your sins so as to give you the opportunity to claim Him (Jesus) as your stand in, that is, as the one who paid the price of sin for YOU. Not only did He bear YOUR burden of sin but **as you respond** to His act of self-sacrifice and love He gives YOU His robe of perfection. What an exchange!

Before the Throne of God He accepts upon Himself every sin laid to your charge, with its penalty, in exchange for His perfection or clean sheet! The Word of God describes it in these ways:

> "God commends His love towards us in that while we were still sinners, Christ died for us" (Rom. 5:8).

> "We beseech you on behalf of Christ, be reconciled to God. For our sake He made Him **to be sin** so that we might become the righteousness of God" (2 Cor. 5:20–21).

> "Christ also died for sins, **the righteous for the unrighteous**, that He might bring us to God" (1 Peter 3:18).

> "The Son of man came to give His life (soul) a ransom for many" (Mark 10:45).

> "**He himself carried up our sins** in His body onto the tree, that we might die to sin and live to righteousness" (1 Peter 2:24).

> "Certainly He has borne our sickness and carried our pains ... But **He was wounded for OUR transgressions**, He was bruised for OUR iniquities. Upon Him was the chastisement that made us whole, and with His bruise (singular) we are healed" (Isaiah 53:4–5).

So then, by the blood sacrifice of Himself for sin, yours and mine, He paid the price for all your rebellion towards God, for ALL your uncleanness; because God made Him *to be sin* and when He was nailed to that Cross, OUR sin was paid for and Christ Himself bore the curse and condemnation of the Law of God in OUR place, yours and mine.

In doing this *He defeated all the unclean spiritual rulers and authorities of this world. Every foul demonic spirit was defeated*, even the spirit of death itself. Indeed by means of His victory on the Cross, He made a public spectacle of these unclean powers and put them to shame (Col. 2:15).

This means that all your worthlessness, despair and hopelessness, all your uncleanness, can be exchanged for the inestimable worth of being a son or daughter of God. The offer is extended to EVERYONE; indeed the Word of God tells us that God COMMANDS all men (and women) everywhere to repent—that is, to drastically change the direction of their lives from their sinful ways towards God's ways (Acts 17:30).

The worth, dignity and fulfilment you seek for yourself is available—and it is ONLY available—by exchanging your present position as a crushed and hopeless possession of satan for the position of a son or daughter of God. This is where REAL worth, REAL dignity begin—when we are BORN AGAIN as children of the King and can call Almighty God our heavenly "Father!"

But you say: "Hey, now wait a minute, Peter. That sounds fine but I don't think I'm that bad a sinner" OR "My sins are too bad—God wouldn't forgive ME." Whatever your response you need to know the answer to the question: WHAT IS SIN?

5.3 WHAT IS SIN?

A breaking of God's standards is called SIN, iniquity, transgression and trespass, but mostly sin, which is defined in the Bible as "lawlessness against God" (1 John 3:4). It is also defined as being **demonic** (Gen. 4:7).[73]

Many people who follow their own standard of morality often deny that there is any such thing as sin, and this is particularly true of those folk whose lives are patterned

---

73 You will need a good translation to clarify this-say, the N.I.V. Study Bible or the NAB. (R.C. edition).

on sinful conduct. I well remember discussing this subject with a university student in Canberra whose defence regarding her many love affairs was that there was no such thing as sin. This was her way of justifying her conduct and "removing" (hopefully but unsuccessfully) her accountability to God and theinescapable consequences.

The Christian view of sin, as given by the scriptures is:

    (a) Man is born in sin (Psalm 51 5, 58:3, Romans 5:12)

    (b) Man is a slave to sin (John 8:34, 2 Peter 2:19)

    (c) Sin is hated by God (Jeremiah 44:4)

    (d) Sin is lawlessness against God (1 John 3:4)

    (e) Sin goes back to Adam and from him spread to ALL men (Romans 5:12)

    (f) This means that ALL have sinned and come short of the Glory of God (Romans 3:23, 1 John 1:10, James 2:10).

    (g) Sin springs from a man's heart (Genesis 6:5, Mark 7:21, John 2:25) i.e. he doesn't have to be taught. It comes naturally.

    (h) Sin is demonic i.e. sin is inspired by demons or unclean spirits (Gen. 4:7, Matt. 12:38–45, Eph. 2:2, 6:12, 2 Cor. 7:1, James 3:15; refer Appendix B)

What do we mean by "accountability to God"? It simply means what we have always sensed in our hearts—that there will come a day when EVERYONE will give an account of their actions and TOTAL UNERRING justice will be handed out to everyone according to their deeds (Rev. 20:11–15).

In other words, all of us will have to face a day of reckoning as the scriptures say:

"Now we know that whatever the law says it speaks to those who are under the law, so that every mouth may be stopped, and THE WHOLE WORLD MAY BE HELD ACCOUNTABLE TO GOD ... Since through the Law (of God) COMES KNOWLEDGE OF SIN" (Romans 3: 19–20) ... "where there is no Law there is no transgression" (Romans 4:15, 5:13) and "if it has not been for the Law, I should not have known sin" (Romans 7:7).

Part of the purpose of the Law of God then, is to make the whole world accountable to God and to bring knowledge of sin; the law of God thus reveals to us God's standard of morality. It can be seen then, that people wishing to set up their own moral standards are forced into the position of having to refute God's laws and in the final analysis their author-God Himself; so that the current rebellion against Christian morality is in fact a thinly veiled movement of anti-Christ aimed at God Himself, by strengthening unbelievers in their Godlessness, and destroying those of immature faith.

> *John Stott* writes—"I remember a young man coming to see me when he had just left school and begun work in London. He had stopped coming to church, he said, because he could not say the Creed without being a hypocrite. He no longer believed it. When he had finished his explanation, I said to him, "If I were to answer your problems to your complete intellectual satisfaction, would you be willing to alter your manner of life?" He smiled slightly and blushed. He had been throwing off many restraints and was having a fling. His real problem was not intellectual but moral." (Basic Christianity, pg. 17)

"But," you say, "I don't think I can keep the faith. It is too hard! I couldn't handle it!"

"Oh yes, you can" because the Lord will help you. Dr. John Stott also wrote:

> "Archbishop William Temple used to illustrate this lesson in this way: 'It is no good giving me a play like Hamlet or King Lear, and telling me to write a play like that. Shakespeare could do it; I can't. And it is no good showing me a life like the life of Jesus and telling me to live a life like that. Jesus could do it; I can't. But if the genius of Shakespeare could come and live in me, then I could write plays like that. And if the Spirit of Jesus could come and live in me, then I could live a life like that.' This is the secret of Christian sanctity. It is not just that we should strive to live like Jesus, but that Jesus by His Spirit should come and live in us. To have Him as our example is not enough; we need Him as our Saviour. It is thus through His atoning death that the penalty of our sins may be forgiven; whereas *it is through His indwelling Spirit that the power of our sins may be*

broken."[74]

Thus the Lord Jesus Christ has provided two enormous but basic victories for those who seek God's forgiveness. He has:

(i) Defeated the powers of darkness on the Cross by paying the price for sin (the disease) and sins Himself and thus making it possible for us to receive God's pardon (Col. 2:13–15).

and

(ii) He supplies the Holy Spirit (Acts 2:33) to live within our hearts, by which we can overcome every unclean spirit (already defeated, remember) within and outside us. Thus we have a potential for TOTAL victory. **Every unclean spirit can be cast out, every vile habit and every curse broken**.[75] It won't always be easy but, with the Spirit of Christ IN YOU and the power of Christ enabling you, you will begin to know in ever increasing measure, the worth of being a son or daughter of the Most High God!

Let us take a closer look at (i) above. Is it really true that on the Cross the Son of God defeated ALL your enemies? Certainly the apostle John writes **"The reason the Son of God was manifested was to loose (destroy) the works of the devil"** (1 John 3:8b).

But what does that mean? The apostle Paul's letter to the Colossians tells us that through the Cross of Christ, God has:

(a) made us (Christians) alive together with Christ

(b) forgiven us all our trespasses

(c) cancelled the written laws (of God) against us

(d) dropped His charges against us,

74 Basic Christianity pp. 104 – 105.

75 See Appendix A for a curse-breaking prayer

(e) nailed them to the Cross

(f) thereby stripped the powers of darkness of their weapons against us

(g) therefore shamefully exposed our enemies

(h) triumphed over them by the Cross of Christ (Col. 2:13–15).

What a victory! **It is a legal, spiritual victory that can be ours IF**:

(i) we are or become true disciples (John 8:31–32)

(ii) understand this legal victory (above)

(iii) know or learn how to appropriate this victory into our lives

(iv) live in the light of it

It's time for you to move into it.

5.4 WHAT YOU DO NEXT

You can begin RIGHT NOW. If the Holy Spirit has spoken to you through this book DON'T PUT HIM OFF! Read carefully the following sample prayer of REPENTANCE and RENUNCIATION:

"Dear Lord Jesus,

I am a sinner and I know that I have done things which you consider abominable. I am truly sorry, Lord, for all my sins.

Please forgive me for ALL my sins and wash me clean in your precious Blood.

I renounce the devil, the powers of darkness and all their works and I acknowledge you, Lord Jesus Christ, to be Lord of my life. I ask you, Lord Jesus, to break every foul curse upon my life, snap every unclean chain that binds me.

Please FILL ME with your HOLY SPIRIT of power and set me free to worship you and serve you as I should.

Thank you, Lord Jesus, for making it all possible by dying for me on Calvary's Cross, My Lord and my God.

Hallelujah and Amen!"

You don't have to READ this prayer out to the Lord but examine it and pray its PRINCIPLES out loud, from your HEART, using your own words if you wish. Don't say it if you don't mean it.

READY?—THEN DO IT NOW!
FINISHED?—GOOD! [76]

Now that you have made a wonderful fresh start by making a decision of the will to renounce the kingdom of satan and become a member in the Kingdom of God, and have made official application for membership by asking the Lord Jesus, and have received the seal of His Holy Spirit in your heart by faith, you may be wondering what comes next.

Firstly, I want to say that Christianity is really NOT just keeping a set of rules phrased

76 If you remain uncommitted, I suggest you copy the above prayer and keep it handy for future use.

in terms of "Thou shalt NOT do this or that." It is all about discovering how to live under the leadership of the Holy Spirit who now dwells within you, that is, in your soul, and has linked up with your human spirit in an unbeatable partnership.

Now that you are "Born Again" you are in spiritual terms a spiritual baby who has been given all the resources of the Kingdom of God (through Christ Jesus' Spirit within you) to get your life together for Jesus—to "clean up your act" and gladly obey the leading of the Holy Spirit (John 8:1–12). An expanded curse-breaking prayer for daily use is presented in Appendix A.

5.5 THE NEW TESTAMENT

You can find out a lot about what the Holy Spirit wants you to move into by reading the New Testament, which the Holy Spirit wrote by means of the Apostles etc. Begin with one of the Gospels and get into fellowship with other Christians your own age who know more about the Bible than you do. If you have questions or any other problem in understanding the Word of God check with them or your Pastor, or if you have no one to turn to right now contact me (see next pages for details).

It is obvious that now you have moved into the Kingdom of God you will want to meet and mix with and share time with other members of the Kingdom who will be able to help you grow up from being a spiritual baby into a mature man or woman in Christ, who is able to help other "babies". How quickly this happens is up to you. If you fool around and play games with the new Lord in your life you will probably end up a statistic in the (spiritual) infant mortality lists, but if you get into a Church where Christ is preached and the Holy Spirit is moving, if you get into the New Testament and begin to learn to pray simple, direct prayers in the Name of Jesus you will be surprised how quickly you will grow.

5.6 CHALLENGES

There will be plenty of challenges along the way and you need to know that being converted or Born Again is not the end of the solution to your problems but the beginning. It means the end of your old lifestyle and the beginning of the discovery of your new life in Jesus, the beginning of your discovery of the unsearchable riches of Christ. It is an exciting time. However, there is no point in kidding you. The powers of darkness will be most upset at losing their sovereign control over your life, and also panic stricken at the arrival of the Holy Spirit within you in order to (i) save your soul and (ii) begin evicting the department of sin to which they belong. They will have already lost many friends when the Holy Spirit first came into you and now those spirits that remain will gather themselves together and seek to counter attack before you can become any stronger in the faith. You may experience fear, doubt, unbelief or confusion, etc., as these spirits seek to control your soul, but do not be afraid.

Here is where you must win by continuing to make decisions of the will (i.e., choices) that are in obedience to the leading of the Holy Spirit, rather than submit to the unclean desires (feelings) and lusts of the flesh which are inspired by unclean spirits.

Thus you can understand **Christianity is NOT obedience to a set of rules but obedience to the leading of the Holy Spirit**, based upon His guidance in the New Testament. The "Thou shalt nots" are there, not to restrict your freedom to enjoy life but to spare you from being a slave to the powers of darkness, whose only interest is to draw you down the road to emotional, physical, and eternal destruction.

5.7 DELIVERANCE

There are many ministries of the Spirit of God now available to you in the Church, all of which flow from the teaching and the preaching of the Word of God. You may be conscious of the need of physical healing or deliverance, especially if you find it difficult to break with your old lifestyle. You may be handicapped by being locked up into intellectualism, unable to show warmth or love to any great degree, though hungry for it yourself. In the next chapter we seek to present the philosophical side of Christianity and compare it briefly with the more common non-Christian philosophies, bearing in mind that the Kingdom of God of which you are now a member certainly does have its code of conduct or morality. However as we have said, what we call the Law of Christ (Rom. 8:2, 1 Cor. 9:21) exists not to bind you or restrict you but to protect you, that you may steer your course through this life-time in safety, with God's Hand of blessing upon you. If you swim in shark-infested waters it comes as no surprise if you get eaten. Christians who venture into sharks' territory get eaten and taste just the same as non-Christians. Likewise when we venture into demonic circles e.g. drugs, illicit sex, etc. we must expect to be attacked. God's prohibitions then, are for OUR GOOD (Deut. 10:13) and we ignore them at our peril.

You would be wise to get into a ***Deliverance and Restoration program*** for regular deliverance ministry, even if you have to travel far afield for it. We ALL need cleansing from some form of pollution. If you cannot find a local program, let us know. If you have a problem in understanding any of this book or genuinely need help and guidance in renouncing and forsaking the past, please do not hesitate to contact the ministers of the Fellowship. We love you with the love of Jesus who died a brutal death on a Cross for you that you might be forgiven and set free from EVERY EVIL BLIGHT and CURSE upon your life (Deut. 28), and may the LORD RICHLY BLESS YOU.

Peter Hobson
Full Salvation Fellowship Ltd
P. O. Box 1020
CROWS NEST 2065 Australia

Tel. (02) 9436 3657   Fax. (02) 9437 6700

6

THE WAY AHEAD—
GOD'S MORALITY

"… keep the Commandments of the Lord, and His Statutes which I am commanding you today FOR YOUR GOOD!" (Deut. 10:13)

6.1 PHILOSOPHY

I was tempted to launch into a wider review of the more popular philosophies and their weaknesses but that would have reduced this book to the level of an intellectual exercise, which is NOT the idea. I think it was Karl Barth, the famous German Theologian and Philosopher who, when asked for the most profound thought he had ever had, quoted a famous old hymn and said:

"Jesus loves me, this I know
For the Bible tells me so!"

Many philosophers sound clever, sometimes brilliant, and others utterly ridiculous. Even those who are sometimes inspiring and are labelled Christian philosophers fall short of the standard of the fullness of truth that the Christian finds in the person of Jesus Christ, or even His apostles.

Let us consider **Karl Marx**, possibly the most revered philosopher in the world until the recent democratic revolution in eastern Europe, apart from Jesus Christ. His work "Das Kapital", though difficult to read, is considered a classic and his philosophy of the sharing of wealth, summed up in his famous motto—

**"From each according to his ability,
To each according to his needs"**

has inspired the world-wide socialist or modern labour movement. It sounds so wise, generous, compassionate, fair, just and equitable etc. etc. but Marx was an atheist who did not recognise that EVERYTHING GOOD comes from Almighty God. Those who practice his fatal philosophy quickly discover (if they can think for themselves) that what they have to share amongst each other is not WEALTH but POVERTY, and the noble slogan becomes in practice—

**"From each whether you can afford it or not
To each according to what little is available".**

Hence the old "powerful" USSR could only share amongst its citizens a standard of material living LESS THAN HALF that of the citizens of the USA. Why? She had the technology, the population, the mineral resources and the brains, but because of her idolatry of Marx, Lenin, Engels and Stalin etc., she did not have the blessing of Almighty God but rather His curse. Ethiopia followed the gods of Marx and Lenin for 14 years and experienced drought and wholesale starvation for 12 of them. China exchanged her many gods for Marx and Lenin and after more than 30 years was still way, way behind—only fractionally better off than desperate India with her millions of gods.

Mother Russia had two-thirds of a century—a man's life time—to fulfil the glorious promises made to the workers, and no one can say she didn't try very hard to make her philosophical system work, but it is just like satan to promise everything, demand your soul and give almost nothing in return. The promised Utopia is never realised because Godless philosophies are under the curse of God, (Deut. 8:19–20). What good is a "clever" philosophy of life if the heavens do not bring forth their life-giving rains or the sun its creative warmth to the creation? The only philosophies or moralities that are any good are those which recognise that Almighty God (El Shaddai) holds us all in the palm of His Hand, and He has revealed His truth, His ways, to us through Jesus Christ His Son. All else is a waste of time and emptiness (Eccl. 1:2, 14). We now move from political philosophy to moral philosophy.

6.2 MORALITY

Most philosophies or religions lay down a code of moral conduct for people to live by.

What is Morality? The dictionary gives us the following helpful definitions:

MORALITY: A system of morals, moral conduct (especially good)

MORAL SENSE: A distinguishing between right and wrong, dealing with the regulation of conduct.

IMMORAL: Morally evil.

From these definitions I think it is fair to conclude that for the vast majority of people something moral means something right and good, and immoral means something wrong or bad.

6.3 ARE THERE ANY GUIDELINES?

Every day we have to make moral decisions about what is right and what is wrong, and we use different approaches in making our decisions. People use the following as key words to determine their behaviour:

1. **Freedom**. (The Existential or Humanistic approach)

   If you live in the West you have probably seen some people wearing tee shirts with the slogan "If you feel like it—do it!" This was reportedly the philosophy of Charles Manson and his "Family" of seven killers sentenced to death in 1972, later commuted, for the motiveless murders of nine people in 1969.

   This philosophy is often mistakenly thought of as democracy but it is really classical Anarchy. Democracy has rules and makes us accountable to the majority. Anarchy acknowledges no rules (laws) and therefore no responsibility or accountability.

   The philosophy behind anarchy is that man is completely alone in the universe and is free to act in any way he chooses. He can do one thing or he can do the very opposite. Both are equal for there is no right or wrong. Actions are only free or not free, not right or wrong. If we say, "I just do what I feel is right" we are expressing this type of philosophy (cf. Judges 17:6, 21:25).

The Bible exposes the irresponsible "freedom" that we know as anarchy as in fact being enslaved by sin and corruption (John 8:31–34, 1 Peter 2:16, 2 Peter 2:19).

2. **Pleasure.** (The Hedonistic approach)

This view states that what gives pleasure is right, therefore we must live for pleasure and self-satisfaction. However it is an irresponsible and destructive philosophy of life which ruins all that is worthy. Our flesh becomes a god to be satisfied and makes us totally selfish.

3. **Niceness and Good Taste.** (The Aesthetic approach)

As long as something is nice and doesn't offend society unduly it is, according to this theory of morality, quite all right. On the other hand, ugly and distasteful things are wrong. Such a system of morality is very subjective because everyone has different ideas about what is nice and good in taste, depending on our ruling unclean spirits.

4. **Law.** (The legalistic approach)

This considers that all human behaviour is to be determined by a fixed set of principles or laws, such as the Ten Commandments. The value of this approach is that a person has a definite code of conduct. However there can be problems because there are no God-given sets of laws or set down courses of behaviour for every single situation of life. Many Christians fall into the trap of making extra lists of "dos" and "don'ts" and then claim that these rules are the law of Christ. Jesus called this "the leaven of the Pharisees" (Matt.16:6–12)

5. **Love, Situation Ethics or the New Morality.**

For the New Morality or Situation Ethics, "love" is the key-word when we make moral decisions. The questions asked are "What would love do here? Is it a loving action or not?" No line of action can be prescribed beforehand, because every situation is different and what may be right in case A may be wrong in case B. Hence the name "Situation Ethics".

The chief errors with the New Morality are that it assumes all people have a high idea of what true love is, it presumes a person's ability to always make the correct decision for himself, and it detracts from the glory and authority of God by making man the decider of his own behaviour.

Several of these philosophies obviously contribute greatly to the religion of Humanism, which we should now contrast with the mind of Christ.

6. **GOD'S WORD** (The New Testament of the Bible)

The New Testament speaks of the glorious freedom experienced by those who are children of God. It reaffirms and upholds the MORAL Law of Moses (as distinct from the RELIGIOUS LAW). It also contains powerful teaching about the essence and expression of love. Biblical morality is unique because it achieves a right balance between these positive elements of Freedom, Law and True Love. Love is the guiding principle for a Christian's conduct and *a Christian will express his love towards God and his fellow man by obeying God's moral Laws*. Moral Law and love complement each other. Moreover the Christian, freed by Christ from the penalty and power of sin will experience freedom in its richest sense in loving and serving both God and neighbour.

6.4 PROBLEMS

Distinguishing a right course of action from a wrong one is a problem none of us can escape. It is a common fact of experience that issues are not always clearly labelled black and white. Often a grey region makes the right decision difficult to discern.

We have already seen that in our Western society there are several approaches to moral decisions, and that each approach, except the Biblical one, emphasises a single basis for moral decisions; for one it is **freedom**, for another **pleasure**, for another **niceness** and **good taste**, for another **law**, and for yet another **love** is the keyword. But each of these bases is either wrong by Biblical standards or incomplete in itself. Various people differ in their views as to what is moral and what is immoral. Dr. Germaine Greer (of Women's Liberation fame) has been quoted as saying that "marriage is immoral" and that marriage weakens society because the sum of two people joined together (making one unit) is less than two distinct individuals. One might label that as mathematical philosophy. On the other hand Christian and Biblical morality which successfully integrates the principles of freedom, law and love, is the only valid one for the Christian and is expressed in the view of Dr. Bonhoeffer who wrote:

> "Marriage is more than your love for each other. It has a higher dignity and power, for it is God's holy ordinance, through which He wills to perpetuate the human race till the end of time. In your love you see only your two selves in the world, but **in marriage you are a link in the chain of the generations**, which God causes to come and to pass away to His glory..." (The Christian Family—Christenson, Pages 9–10).

The Rev. Larry Christenson adds:

> "The Christian family, therefore, does not exist for its own benefit. It is created to bring glory and honour to God. The blessing of man is a derivative, a by-product. **Those who stubbornly hold that their own happiness and convenience are the highest goals of family life will never understand God's plan for marriage and the family**, for they do not grasp the underlying structure, the basic starting point."

One doesn't need a string of statistics to know that the divorce rate in our western ("democratic", "Christian"?) societies is extremely high, and this is happening even though marriage statistics are being affected by "de facto" relationships. Over the last few years even Christians have found it more difficult to persevere with a troubled marriage and have joined the queues for obtaining divorce.

The pressures of this world through its immorality, promiscuity and so-called sexual "freedom", its selfishness, "independence" and ambition have achieved an erosion of Christian principles, so that people do not even get married but live in sin because of the alleged hassles of marriage generally and its high failure rate.

But wait a minute! Is it MARRIAGE that has failed? If you like driving cars and bought the car of your dreams at great expense surely the commonsense thing to do would be to read the instructions as to how to drive it, care for it and otherwise use your precious possession. If the manufacturer says NOT to drive at over 60 Kms an hour for the first 1000 Kms or over 90 Kms an hour for the next 5000 Kms you would follow those instructions and all the other instructions because you want your new car to go well, to last and to enjoy for a long time to come.

But if you thought you knew better than the manufacturer, or didn't care about it or its future so long as you got plenty of "fun" out of it NOW, in the short term, and you began to race the engine continuously, ignore regular servicing by writing your own set of rules to suit yourself and generally abused your new car in your quest for immediate pleasure, then when it began to fall apart at the "seams" and finally blew up, would you blame the car? Or would you be honest enough to blame yourself?

You see, it is not MARRIAGE that is the problem, it is the way men and women USE it. We do not read the Manufacturer's instruction manual (the Bible) and even when we do, so often we ignore the Maker's advice and do it OUR way, chasing instant pleasures of the flesh, without truly caring and loving. If we want to get good mileage out of our marriage, we need to rediscover GOD'S morality, for therein lies, with God's help, the path of true love, peace, joy, security and fulfilment. To sum up the Christian viewpoint the Bible says ***"Let marriage be held in honour amongst all***..." (Hebrews 13:4). It is immediately plain that there is a clash of moralities and therefore at least one must be false. Therefore our next problem is by what authority do we declare the morality of God?

6.5 AUTHORITY

We need to examine the grounds for our morality, our authority for our moral standards. Who is the judge of what is moral or immoral? What absolute standard can be applied? Many men would say "conscience" but one man's conscience may give a different answer to a moral question than another man's. For example, conscientious objection to taking up arms would not be a course of action for many men whose country was under attack by a tyrannical aggressor, yet both opposing opinions would be respected today as the exercise of conscience. Can both be right (moral) or is one (at least) necessarily immoral? And if one is immoral, by what standard or authority is this ascertained?

For the Christian, Jesus' standards present true morality or true good and anything less is less than good. Jesus Himself said *"Why do you call me good? Only God is good"* (Mark 10:18) and this means to us that only God is moral and therefore only God's standards as revealed by Him through His Word, the Bible, reveal TRUE MORALITY. Man has no authority to set moral standards and his conscience is inadequate, by itself, as we shall now see.

6.6 CONSCIENCE

Doesn't conscience help non-Christians to know God's morality? In a sense, yes, as Paul explains:

> "All who have sinned without the law will also perish without the law, and all who sinned under the law will be judged by the law. For it is not the hearers of the law who are righteous before God, but the doers of the law who will be justified (reckoned righteous). When Gentiles who have not the law do by nature what the law requires, they are a law to themselves, even though they do not have the law. They show that **what the law requires is written on their hearts, while their conscience also bears witness and their conflicting thoughts accuse or perhaps excuse them** on that day when, according to my gospel, God judges the secrets of men by Christ Jesus (Rom. 2:12–16).

There is a sense in which the moral Law of God is written on the hearts of all men but because of the demonic nature of our hearts, this is in a covered or veiled way which is not clear enough to be an authoritative guide against temptations. We know it as a general feeling about what is right and what is wrong, but when we are pressured there is not usually sufficient authority or strength in our feelings to enable us to stand firm. In fact Paul says that some "Christians" can make shipwrecks of their faith by REJECTING conscience (1 Tim. 1:19). Many libertines do this today.

They have a conscience but they can refuse to obey it. To be free from the demands of conscience is to be "liberated" (they think) not realising their so-called liberation is in fact slavery to sin (1 Peter 2:16, 2 Peter 2:18–19). Other consciences have been so completely corrupted that they are no longer able to exercise moral choice "... to the corrupt and unbelieving nothing is pure, *their very minds and consciences are corrupted*. They profess to know God, but deny Him by their deeds, they are detestable ... " (Titus 1:15–16) and again Paul speaks of the pretensions of liars whose consciences are SEARED." (1 Timothy 4:2)

But as we have seen in the previous chapter *there is hope for people with corrupted consciences*—thanks be to God. We are invited to *"purify your conscience* from dead works to serve the living God" through the blood of Christ (Hebrews 9:14) and to have "our hearts sprinkled clean (by the blood of Jesus) *from an evil conscience*" (Heb. 10:20). All this brings us back to "love that issues from a pure heart and good conscience and sincere faith" (1 Tim. 1:5) and where the EYES OF OUR HEARTS ARE ENLIGHTENED. (Eph. 1:18)

All these good things BEGIN to happen when we are surrendered to Christ. In short, our consciences are not always a safe guide. They can, and will let us down as far as true morality is concerned unless they are ENLIGHTENED BY God's Word which reveals to us God's standard. An interesting point is made by Paul regarding practical morality. The Apostle says we ought to obey the governing authorities, pay taxes etc, *not only to avoid God's wrath but for conscience' sake also.* (Rom. 13:1-7) Perhaps they had "Conscience money" in those days too? Therefore paying taxes is NOT immoral, as some people think today, although we may smile and sympathise with that point of view.

6.7 WARNINGS FROM GOD

We have already seen that to attempt to destroy God's true morality and replace it with our own inevitably involves attempting to remove God from the picture altogether, for to recognise that God exists is to imply we are **accountable** to God. And should our accountability reveal a deficiency in our obedience, it follows logically, and is stated explicitly in God's Word, that we can expect a reaction from God, as under:

> "He who conquers shall have this heritage, and I will be his God and he will be my son. But as for the cowardly, the faithless, the polluted, as for the murderers, fornicators, sorcerers, idolaters, and all liars, their lot shall be in the lake that burns with fire and brimstone, which is the second death." (Rev. 21:7–8)

> "Do you not know that the unrighteous will not inherit the kingdom of God? Do not be deceived; neither the immoral, nor idolaters, nor adulterers nor homosexuals, nor thieves, nor the greedy, nor drunkards, nor revilers, nor robbers will inherit the kingdom of God. *And such were some of you*. But you were washed, you were sanctified, you were justified in the name of the Lord Jesus Christ and in the Spirit of our God. (1 Cor. 6:9–11).

The warnings clearly underlined by both these passages (stating the eternal consequences that will follow the habitual breaking of God's Morality) are also added to in similar passages in Romans 1:26f and Colossians 3:5,8. Such warnings are severe and to the point and many of the sins listed are easily recognisable as being on the increase today. ALL are demonically inspired.

The important thing for Christians to keep uppermost in their minds and spirits is that the worse things get with the rule of antichrist in the world the closer we are to the fulfilment of the promises of God. We can deplore the wickedness of the world and at the same time rejoice in the soon coming King and His Kingdom and therefore our total deliverance and victory. The World may be losers, and it is sad there have to be losers, but we who are in the Kingdom of God and acknowledge Jesus as Lord are winners, and try as they may, no one and no thing can take that from us (Rom. 8:31–39), so let us do as the New Testament bids us:

> "God commands *all men everywhere* to repent ... " (Acts 17:30)

> " ... you have come to Mount Zion and to a city of the living God, to a

heavenly Jerusalem and to innumerable angels, to an assembly and a church of the first-born who have been enrolled in (the) heavens and to God the judge of all men, and to the spirits of the just who have been perfected and to the mediator of a New Covenant, Jesus, and to the sprinkling of blood which speaks of better things than (the blood of) Abel.

See that you ***do not refuse Him who is speaking***. For if they did not escape when they refused him who warned on earth, much less shall we escape if we reject Him who warns from heaven. His voice shook the earth then, but now He has promised saying 'Yet once (more) I will shake not only the earth but also the heaven'.

Now the (phrase) 'Yet once (more)' declares the removal of the things being shaken, the things that were made, in order that the things not being shaken may remain."

Therefore **let us have grace in receiving an Unshakable Kingdom through which we may serve and be well-pleasing to God, with devoutness and awe,** for indeed our God is a consuming fire." (Heb. 12:22–28)

" ... speaking loud boasts of vanity (emptiness) they entice with excessive lusts of the flesh, those who are nearly escaping from **those living in error, promising them freedom—but they themselves are slaves of corruption**, for whatever overcomes anyone, to that they are enslaved. (2 Peter 2:18–19)

6.8 PURIFY YOURSELVES

I'll just let the Word of God speak to you on this:

"***Blessed are those who wash their robes*** in order that they may have the right to the tree of life and they may enter by the gates into the city. Outside are the dogs and the sorcerers and the fornicators and the murderers and the idolaters and everyone who loves and practices a lie. I Jesus have sent my messenger to witness these things to you ... " (Rev. 22:14–16)

"Do not become unequally yoked with unbelievers, for what do right-eousness and lawlessness share? Or what fellowship has light with darkness? What agreement has Christ with Belial, or what part has a believer with an unbeliever? And what union has a temple of God with idols?

"For we are a temple of the living God, as God said 'I will dwell in them and will walk among them, and I will be their God and they shall be my people. Therefore *come out from the midst of them and be separated,' says the Lord, 'and touch no unclean thing*. And I will welcome you, and I will be a Father to you, and you shall be sons and daughters to me,' says the Lord Almighty.

"Therefore having these promises, beloved LET US CLEANSE OURSELVES FROM ALL POLLUTION of flesh and of spirit perfecting holiness (separation for God's purposes) in the fear of God." (2 Cor. 6:14–7:1)

"God resists the arrogant but gives grace (favour) to the humble. Submit yourselves therefore to God but resist the devil and he will flee from you. Draw near to God and He will draw near to you. You sinners cleanse your hands, and *purify your hearts you (that are) two-souled*." (James 4:6–8)

"... straighten the weary hands and the paralysed knees and make *straight paths for your feet,* lest the lame be turned aside rather than be healed." (Heb. 12:12–13)

"Flee youthful lusts and pursue righteousness faith, love, peace with those who call on the Lord out of a CLEAN heart" (2 Tim. 2:22)

"Blessed are the *clean in heart*, for they shall see God" (Matt. 5:8)

"Beloved, now we are children of God and it has not yet been shown what we shall be. We know that when He (Jesus) is manifested WE SHALL BE LIKE HIM, because we shall see Him as He is. And everyone having this hope concerning Him PURIFIES HIMSELF as He is pure." (1 John 3:2–3)

From these scriptures you can understand how important the deliverance ministry of Christ is today for our personal cleansing.

6.9 SOME PRACTICAL GUIDANCE

No one can keep God's moral laws without the help and the power of the Holy Spirit. Pray EVERY DAY to be filled with the Spirit, for He does indeed supply the power from within us to be faithful disciples. If we try in our own strength we will surely fail and perhaps become discouraged and fall away from the Faith.

However the Word of God explicitly tells us that we "can do all things (that we are supposed to do) through Christ who strengthens us" (Phil. 4:13, 2 Cor. 12:9, Eph. 3:16,20, Col. 1:11).

International evangelist Dr. Billy Graham wrote some wise words for young people (and new Christians) way back in 1968.[77] They are even more relevant today than they were then:

TEN SUGGESTIONS FOR YOUNG PEOPLE

"One mark of a Christian is self-control and self-discipline. I don't know how a modern young person can keep pure outside of Jesus Christ. Some may do it by sheer will power—they are very few. But with Christ we have supernatural forces at our disposal to help us to overcome the temptation.

On sexual matters I have ten suggestions for young people today:

1. Avoid wrong company. If you run with a rough crowd, some of it will rub off on you. The Bible says, "Come out from among them, and be ye separate ... and touch not the unclean thing."

2. Avoid the second look. You can't help the first look, but you can avoid the second look that becomes lust.

3. Discipline the conversation. Avoid the dirty joke, the off-color story.

---

77 Decision Magazine, June 1968

"Evil communications corrupt good manners." (And today, blasphemy and profanity!)

4. Be careful about dress. It is up to you, before God, as to how you attire yourself. A young lady who was converted in one of our Crusades wrote us a note, "From now on I am going to dress as though Jesus were my escort."

5. Choose carefully what shows you see and what television programs you watch. (*And today, switch off all blasphemy!*)

6. Be careful what you read. Much contemporary reading material appeals to the sex instinct. Dr. O. Hobart Mowrer of the University of Illinois, in his book The New Group Therapy, writes, "It is interesting to wonder just how much responsibility those who slyly or blatantly advocate the new freedom for young women feel they ought to take when this freedom boomerangs. Perhaps I'm ill-informed, but to the best of my knowledge movie producers, lewd novelists, artists, and perfume and liquor manufacturers do not commonly found or support lying-in homes for unwed mothers, protective services for illegitimate children, clinics for the treatment of venereal disease or psychiatric services for those lives they have helped to disorganize."

7. Be on guard concerning your leisure time. David had time on his hands and it was then he saw Bathsheba and fell into trouble.

8. Make it a rule never to engage in heavy petting. Christian young people ought to have prayer before every date. I believe that a girl who has Jesus Christ in her heart has a supernatural power to enable her to say "No" to the advances of any fellow, no matter how smooth a line he has. And I believe a boy who knows Christ is able to discipline his life.

9. Spend much time in the Scriptures. The Psalmist said, "Thy word have I hid in my heart, that I might not sin against thee." Memorize the Scriptures, and when temptation comes, quote them. The Word of God is the one thing the devil cannot stand up against.

10. Have Jesus Christ in your heart and life. Do you know him as your Saviour? I want to tell you that God loves you, and that a strong faith in God has kept many a man and woman from committing immorality. Joseph had such a faith, and he refused the advances of Potiphar's wife even though he knew it probably meant prison (Gen. 39:7–20).

WE DON'T HAVE THE STRENGTH BY OURSELVES

You might say to me, "I'm afraid I am guilty. I have broken this commandment against immorality," but every one of us is guilty. We don't have the strength by ourselves to keep this commandment or any of the other nine. But at the Cross of Christ we find forgiveness of all the past and a new dynamic to live purely.

Do you remember the sinful woman who washed Jesus' feet with her tears? She received Jesus as her Lord, and He said, "Your sins are forgiven." He will say that to you tonight. Christ died on the cross for you. He shed his blood for you. ***But you have to receive Christ for yourself.***"[78]

(Decision, June 1968)

SUMMARY

Please remember that ALL wrongdoing is sin and REQUIRES THE CONTINUING FORGIVING GRACE OF GOD THROUGH JESUS CHRIST OUR LORD.

We have already made it plain that "all have sinned and fall short of the glory of God (Romans 3:23), and that the whole world is accountable to God" (Romans 3:19).

The morality of the world reflects the sad fact that "the whole world lies in the power of the evil one" (1 John 5:19). Jesus said,

> "And this is the judgement, that the light has come into the world, and men loved darkness rather than light, because their deeds were evil. For

---

78 Remember the Sinner's Prayer in section 5.4?

everyone who does evil hates the light, and does not come to the light, lest his deeds should be exposed. But he who does what is true, comes to the light, that it may be clearly seen that his deeds have been wrought in God." (John 3:19–21)

The solution for the men and women of the world then is to come daily to Him who is the Light of the World, and have their sins forgiven, for *"the blood of Jesus the son cleanses us from ALL sin"* (1 John 1:7), and be FILLED with the Spirit of God, and learn to walk in the Spirit daily.

For the NON-Christian there may appear to be other forms of morality to follow but the bottom line is that he or she will still be held accountable before God and judged according to GOD'S standards, (i.e., the God of the Bible), NOT their own. Thus for the Christian, the one who belongs to Jesus and follows Him, there can be no morality other than CHRISTIAN MORALITY. To follow Jesus and to be like Him who loved us and gave His life for us on that stark wooden cross more than 19 centuries ago is the highest calling of God for you, for the Bible says "He who BELIEVES in the Son has eternal life; he who does not OBEY THE SON shall not see life, but the wrath of God rests upon him" (John 3:36).

JESUS' WAY IS THE ONLY TRUE MORALITY

for He is the Way, the Truth and the Life.

APPENDIX "A"

CURSE-BREAKING PRAYER

GREETING AND IDENTIFICATION

Dear Lord Jesus ...

CHOOSING YOUR KING/KINGDOM

[a] 2 Cor. 4:2
Eph. 6:12
[b] Rom. 1 21
John 20:28

[a]I renounce the devil and all his works. I renounce the powers of darkness and all their works, and [b]I acknowledge You, Lord Jesus Christ, to be my Lord and my God.

BREAKING THE CHAINS

[c] Job 36:5-11
Acts 12:7
Heb. 13:3
1 John 3:8
[d] Ex. 20:5
[e] Luke 10: 19
[f] Gal. 3: 13
[g] Luke 24:49
Acts 1:1

I ask You to [c]break every chain which binds me; remove from me every foul curse that has been laid upon my life, even [d]to the third and fourth generation, and before that if necessary. I now [e]take my authority and break every curse upon me, in the name of Jesus of Nazareth, because [f]Jesus became accursed for me. I thank You dear Lord for this [g]power and this authority to break every curse.

INNER CLEANSING

[h]Heb. 12:15
[i] Matt. 6:12–15
[j] Heb. 3:12
[k] 2 Cor. 7:1

I ask You to take out of my heart every [h]root of bitterness, [i]unforgiveness and [j]unbelief, indeed [k]every unclean thing that hinders me from leading a godly life.

I FORGIVE-PLEASE FORGIVE

[l]Matt. 6:12–15
Matt. 18:21-35
[m] Heb. 2:3

[l]I forgive those who have hurt me and grieved me in the past, and I ask You to forgive them also, even as You have forgiven me, and bring us all into [m]Your Full Salvation.

n Luke 9:23–26
  John 3: 16
  1 Cor. 6: 19–20
o Jer. 17: 14
  Ps. 107:19–20
p Ps. 51: 1 0
  1 John 1:7–9
q Ps. 41: 1–3
r Acts 3:21
s Rom. 8:29
  2 Cor. 3:18
  1 Cor. 11:11
  1 John 3:2–3
t Eph. 5:4
  Col. 2:7

COMMITMENT AND DIRECTION

And now gracious Lord [n]I yield my life into Your hands: [o]heal me and [p]cleanse me: [q]deliver me and [r]restore me; and make me [s]like the Son of God.

THANKSGIVING

[t]Thank You Lord Jesus.

Amen.

SEVEN COMMON CURSES TO BE BROKEN
See 4.5 (b) and (c)

THE CURSE OF-

1. UNBELIEF

Spouse of Disobedience — Adam and Eve's disastrous role model.

He who BELIEVES in the Son has eternal life; but he who DISOBEYS the Son will not see life but the wrath of God remains upon Him. (See also Lev. 26:14–39; Deut. 28:15–68, 29: 19–28)

GEN. 3:17-19
ROM. 5:12
JOHN 3:36

...Without faith it is impossible to please Him   (Heb. 11:6)

...For whatever is not of faith is sin (Rom. 14:23)

Why is faith (and obedience) so important to God?

... He who does not believe God's testimony to His son has made Him a liar (1 John 5:10)

2. HATING ISRAEL

> The Lord had said to Abram, "I will make you a great nation ... I will bless those who bless you, and I will curse him who curses you . . . (Gen. 12:1–3,27:27–29; Num. 24:5,9; Isa. 41:8–16)

3. THE OCCULT

> ... For all who practice these (occult) things are an abomination to the Lord. (Deut. 18:12, Isa. 41:21–24)

4. HUMANISM-SOCIALLSM-IDOLATRY

> Cursed is the man who trusts in mankind, and makes flesh his strength ... (Jer. 17:5; Deut. 8:19)

5. FAILING TO RETURN THANKS IN TITHES AND OFFERINGS

> ... You are under a curse, the whole nation of you, because you are robbing Me. Bring the whole tithe ... (Mal.3:8–18)

> Famine is a disgrace to a nation (Ezek. 36:28–30)

6. "GOOD" WORKS WITHOUT CHRIST

> All who rely on works of the law are under a curse (Gal. 3:10)

7. NOT LOVING THE SON OF GOD

> If anyone does not love the Lord Jesus Christ, let him be accursed (1 Cor. 16:22)

> Compare the first and great commandment. "Thou shalt love the Lord your God..."

ALL CURSES ARE BROKEN THROUGH THE BLOOD OF JESUS (GAL. 3:10–13)

APPENDIX "B"

THE STOICHEIA-
THE CAUSE OF UNCLEAN SEX

Let me begin by expressing the belief that the Revised Standard Version of the Bible is correct in translating the New Testament word **stoicheia** as *elemental spirits* (Gal. 4:3,9; Col. 2:8,20). This is also the conclusion of the International Critical Commentary on Paul's letter to the Galatians.

In everyday terms this means that the word **stoicheia** covers a range of unclean spirits which seek to control and dominate the tribes of the earth and their social structures. In my opinion they include **ancestral**, **familiar**, **control**, and **territorial** spirits, and therefore make up a considerable part of the unclean baggage each of us brings into this world from earlier generations (Rom. 5:12), as well as being the inspiration for animism and all pagan religions.

Please forgive me if I do not spend much time in establishing the sinful and/or demonic nature of the human heart. This has been covered before in several other publications[79] and I would ask you to accept the truth of that statement as it stands, i.e. that the human heart is, by nature, sinful and that its spiritual disease of sin is caused by a ruling unclean spirit presiding over an empire of various kingdoms of unclean spirits, revealed in the Bible under the blanket names of Sin and Death. If you do not accept or like this initial premise and you do not have a copy of one of our other books to refer to, perhaps you could quickly look at Romans 5:12,17,21 and 7:13–25 and tie in these references to the REIGN (as kings and princes) of Sin and Death with other verses which clearly teach the inescapable warfare of life is SPIRITUAL. The apostle Paul tells us that—

> "We are not contending against blood and flesh but against the Rulers, against the Authorities, against the world rulers of this darkness, against the SPIRITUAL (HOSTS) of evil in the heavenlies."   (Ephesians 6:12)

---

79 "The Re-incarnation Deception" "End-Time Deliverance "Your Full Salvation"

"For though we walk in the flesh we do not wage war in the flesh (realm or world), for the weapons of our warfare are not fleshly but powerful in God (spiritual) to overthrow strongholds ... "   (2 Corinthians 10:3–4)

When we stop to think about this and begin to take Paul's words seriously, we find they strongly infer that the whole struggle of life is a struggle against unclean, invisible, spiritual enemies, i.e. unclean spirits or demons.[80] It is obvious that every day carries its own challenges—indeed Jesus taught us that every day presents us *"with more than enough evil"* (Matthew 6:34), we begin to realise that we are literally surrounded by the hosts of darkness seeking to trap us wherever possible. Is this being negative? No, we are only saying what the Bible says and the Bible is not a negative book—it is the revelation of God's victory over the rulers and authorities through Jesus Christ. Thus Christians who are "in Christ" have nothing to fear—there is no need to hide one's head in the sand rather than look the enemy in the eye. The enormity and complexity of satan's hosts (armies) are being revealed by the Holy Spirit today in a way that no generation before us has ever experienced. We have never understood or even scratched the surface of another well known Bible phrase **"the whole world lies in (the power of) the evil one."** Would you please read that phrase — slowly — three times — and really let it sink in? If you have done that you will more readily and easily understand something of the variety of unclean spirits or demons encountered during deliverance ministry, and how a very large proportion of their attacks against humans are aimed at our vulnerable sexual natures.

Let us now look at the army of satan as revealed to us in Paul's letter to the Colossians. Perhaps the best way to do this is for me to translate the passage as literally as I can from the Greek New Testament and insert my own comments along the way, because it is very hard to improve on Paul's insights as he links the spiritual powers of darkness with the human fleshly behaviour of our "normal" lives. So, please bear in mind as you read the following scripture passage from Colossians, chapter two, that:

---

80 The terms "unclean spirits", "demons" and "the powers of darkness" are considered interchangeable for the purposes of this book, throughout.

1. It is a literal translation,

2. Alternative choices of words are in brackets,

3. My personal comments are in brackets,

4. Words inserted to make sense of the English are in italics.

I think it will be clear as to what are "words inserted" for grammar, what are alternate choices and what are my comments as we read through the passage. One other thing. For the sake of brevity and clarity, I have only included sections of verses which are relevant to our study—sufficient to give us the context and meaning of the apostle's letter, viz.:

v.8 "See that no one robs you through philosophy and empty deceit according to the tradition of men (which has woven such an enormous deceptive web of falsehood and has enmeshed the minds of mankind with the snobbish pursuit of intellectualism for pride's sake) according to the ***elemental spirits of the world*** (which inspire so much of the creation's sickness, death and various evils), and not according to 'Christ ...

v.10 "... who is the Head of all rule and authority (clean and unclean, with special reference to the evil spiritual rulers and authorities against which we ALL wage war, although much of mankind is unaware—Ephesians 6:12)

v.12 "... and you (Christians) were buried with Him (Jesus) in baptism, by which you were also raised with Him (Jesus) through the (your) faith of (in) the working of God who raised Him from the dead.

v.13 "And ***you*** being dead in trespasses and in the uncircumcision of your flesh He (God the Father) made alive together with Him (Jesus), forgiving you all the (*your*) trespasses

v.14 "wiping (cancelling) out the handwriting (of Moses' Law and all its pharisaic additions) which was (stood) against us with its ordinances (legal dogma and bondage) and has taken it (Moses' Law etc.) out of the midst (way), (by) nailing it to the Cross.

v.15 "(God the Father) put off (disarmed) the **rulers and authorities** (especially those in the ***spiritual*** realm—Eph. 6:12—because they inspire those rulers and authorities in the physical world, such as Caiaphas, Annas and Pilate to do the evil they do). **He exposed them openly, triumphing (over) them by Him** (Christ Jesus and His Cross).

v.16 "Therefore, let no one judge you about eating and drinking or in respect of a feast or new moon or Sabbaths.

v.17 "These things are (*only*) a shadow of things to come, but the body (reality) is of the Christ.

v.18 "Therefore ... let no one judge against you with (*false*) humility, requiring (*the*) worship of the angels and intruding with visions, being puffed up by the **mind of his flesh**

v.19 "and not holding (*fast to*) the Head (Christ) from whom the whole body will grow with the growth of God by means of being supplied and joined together with its joints and bands (ligaments etc.)

v.20 "If you died with Christ from the **elemental spirits of the world** (carnal, physical creation) why do you live (*as if you still belonged*) in the world (*controlled by the elemental spirits*) as if subject to its legal dogmas and bondages (which are, after all, **inspired by the same unclean spirits, whether rulers, authorities or elemental, to which Christ died and YOU with Him, and which spirits He totally defeated**)? ...

v.23 "These (precepts and **teachings of men** under the control of the spirits) are of no honour (value) (except) for satisfying **the flesh** (and all the unclean spirits which control mind and flesh)."

I do hope you have read this scripture passage carefully because it has so much to tell us. May I suggest that you read it again, or even more than twice, until you feel that you have grasped what the apostle is saying to us. I think you will agree that Paul draws some surprising parallels. He warns us against the deceit of the **stoicheia** (elemental spirits) of the world (2:8) who use philosophy and human tradition and the things that they inspire such as the bondage of legalism to festivals and Sabbaths and (monastic?) self-abasement (2:16-19). Christ, he says, has made a public spectacle of and triumped over the rulers and authorities, **putting them off (disarming or unclothing them) by His Cross** (2:15).

From the context of this passage there would appear to be *a clear link between the elemental spirits and the rulers and authorities*. It is interesting to note that Paul disparagingly uses stoicheia which is translated "elemental spirits," and then "rulers and authorities" which seem more respectful terms for the powers of darkness. A possible alternative to seeing these terms as interchangeable or synonymous is to understand that "rulers and authorities" are higher-ranking leadership spirits (kings and princes) and the elemental spirits as the workers under their command, for clearly both sets of terms apply to the powers of darkness. Or, if you don't like the allusion to rulers and workers, perhaps it would be more accurate to refer to them in military terms such as "Princes", Officers, NCOs and Privates. My own view is simply to see elemental spirits and rulers and authorities as *mutually inclusive*.

Because of Christ's finished work on the Cross, we Christians (those belonging to Christ—Rom. 8:9) are also supposed to have *put off* the old man with his practices (Col. 3:9) because *we died with Christ from the elemental spirits of the world* and all their miserable traditional "religious" bondages (Col. 2:20). *These religious regulations* have "an appearance of wisdom in promoting rigour of devotion ... but are of no value, serving only to *indulge or satisfy the flesh*" (Col. 2:23 RSV Footnote). What a stunning indictment of Christ-less religiosity!!!

There can be no doubt that religious, homosexual and even pedophile spirits have invaded major denominations, especially those which emphasise a showy, outward, formal style of religion (cf. 2, Tim. 3:1–6) instead of requiring an INWARD change of the heart.

What you see is NOT always what you get. Please note carefully the apostle's arguments:

1. IF the "stoicheia" are related to or interchangeable with "rulers and authorities", and

    IF Christ put them off (rulers and authorities) by His death on the Cross, and

    IF WE positionally, legally died (were crucified) with Christ (at our conversion)

THEN THIS MEANS that WE ALSO have put off the Old Man (the satanic or satanized man — Matt. 16:22–23?) with all his practices. Hallelujah!

2. The apostle also presents to us a very important spiritual equation. The powers of darkness = The stoicheia and/or rulers and authorities.

3. These powers of darkness inspire false religion and false belief within mankind, using

   (i) philosophy (intellectualism)

   (ii) human tradition (bondages of habit and history)

   (iii) legalism

   and these "weapons" produce, for example, the following religious observances or conduct:

   (i) festivals

   (ii) sabbaths

   (iii) self-abasement

   (iv) legalistic religion

   —which only indulge or satisfy the FLESH! — the polluted part of us.

   Let me put all that another way:

   Now, since (a) Christ put off (disarmed) and triumphed over the rulers and authorities and the *stoicheia*, i.e., ALL the powers of darkness by His Cross (2:15)

   and since (b) we Christians who have been crucified with Christ have also put off the Old Man with his practices (3:9; cf. Eph. 4:23–24, Rom. 6:6)

   so also: (c) we died with Christ from the stoicheia (2:20) (cf. Rom. 6:2,11, Gal. 2:20).

RESULT! So then, *the superstitious religiosity of the human heart serves only to indulge the flesh* (typical witchcraft syndrome with all its lusts and passions) and this worldly religiosity is inspired by the *stoicheia* (2:20).

I suggest that the links between the rulers and authorities, the flesh, the stoicheia and the old (satanized) man are clearly drawn for us. Likewise, we should take into account the scripture:

> "For you have died, and your life is hid with Christ in God ... Put to death therefore what is earthly in you: fornication, uncleanness, passion, evil desire (lust) and covetousness, which is idolatry. On account of these the wrath of God is coming upon the sons of disobedience." (Col. 3:3,5,6 RSV)

This is followed by a further short list of works of the flesh (Col. 3:8,9) which very often accompany unclean sexual demons.

Confused? Well, it appears that while (in Christians) our old (satanized) man is supposed to be dead, crucified with Christ, we still have to keep putting him to death every time he raises his ugly head—dying daily to sin (Rom. 6:2,11; Luke 9:23). This "members and/or flesh" problem we call sin and/or rebellion and I am saying that ***it is all inspired by the spiritual rulers and authorities*** (which we are supposed to have put off when we became Christians), and the ***stoicheia*** (elemental spirits) to which we are supposed to have died.

One thing more needs to be said before we leave "the Old Man". Jesus made a very interesting remark to the Pharisees in the context of successful deliverance when He said "Or how can anyone enter into the house of the ***strong man*** and seize his goods (lit. *vessels*) unless he first ***binds the strong man?***" (Matthew 12:29). This teaching draws attention to the importance of binding and loosing (Luke 13:16) and perhaps the reference to the strong man and his house is more than just an illustration but ***a direct allusion to the old man or ruling spirit which controls an empire of vessels (lesser spirits).***

APPENDIX "C"

HOMOSEXUALITY AND
THE NEW SOUTH WALES PARLIAMENT

The N.S.W. State Government has been forced to pour in millions of dollars for research and related measures to combat AIDS in recent years, yet the N.S.W. Parliament passed the Premier Mr. Wran's Private Member's Bill to legalise sodomy and male soliciting in a record nine days. This was "achieved" in May 1984, nearly a year AFTER an outbreak of AIDS had been reported by Sydney Hospitals.

The Rev. Fred Nile, M.L.C. spoke in Parliament strongly opposing the Bill as follows:

> "We should not ignore the teachings of the Bible. We would do so at our peril and at the peril of our society. God could not have given a more dramatic warning than He did with Sodom and Gomorrah. In spite of overwhelming opposition from all sections of the community, religious and non-religious, representing millions of New South Wales electors, the Government allowed this Bill to be brought before the House, even though it is introduced as a Private Member's Bill. The contents of the Bill are essentially the same as those of earlier Bills that have been fully and well debated in this House, and particularly in the other place, over the past three years. As some honourable members have said, one cannot avoid the observation that the Government has placed such a high, perhaps strange, priority on this Bill. I feel sure future historians will comment on that fact. Why has the Government allowed this state of affairs? Why has it allowed a Bill presented in the name of Mr. Wran to take precedence over government business?"

What is the Purpose of Laws?

> "What is the purpose of our making laws in the Parliament? Do we do it in our own interests? The Parliament makes laws for the peace, welfare and good government of this State. We emphasize that role by beginning each

day with a solemn prayer seeking the blessing and guidance of Almighty God for the advancement of His glory and for the true welfare of the people of this State. That practice simply follows the biblical teaching in Roman 13. It teaches us:

"All who govern or rule do so as God's ministers or delegates, to punish evildoers and promote good actions."

In the First Book of Timothy, chapter 2, the desire is that society may lead a quiet and peaceable life, Godly and respectful in every way. Honourable members can see the importance of a moral foundation in what they do. I believe that foundation is a biblical one—which has been taken up by the church and its teachings down through the centuries.

The question has to be asked: Who will benefit from this bill? How will this bill advance God's glory in society? The answer is that it will not advance God's glory or the true welfare of the people at all. The only possible advance by this private member's bill will be the granting of freedom to consenting males eighteen years and over to engage in acts of sodomy or, as it is described in the Act that this bill seeks to amend, buggery. How can that be for the advancement of the true welfare of society?

A great deal could be said on the question of health and disease. That matter has already been referred to by some honourable members. In Australia at present is Dr. Dowdle, an expert on these matters from the Atlanta Disease Centre, the most highly regarded disease centre in the world, specializing in compiling records on acquired immune deficiency syndrome and so on. A report that appeared in the Sydney Morning Herald on Wednesday, 16 May, 1984 reads:

"There are now more than 4,000 cases of A.I.D.S. in the United States. There are people with severe signs of the disease, but Dr. Dowdle says now that a laboratory test is going to be available to detect people carrying the virus, the number will increase. He is then reported to have said: 'We are probably working at the tip of the iceberg.'"

Perhaps it is the tip of a volcano because of the disease factor involved in homosexual practices such as sodomy.

It is wrong for anyone to equate homosexuality with heterosexuality. To do that is a moral perversion, and it must be rejected. What does this bill seek to do? The Premier simply described it as a bill to decriminalize homosexual acts between consenting adults in private. That is a soft way of putting it. I believe it has misled the community, even though there has been a backlash by the majority of people. Many people still do not understand fully what the bill seeks to do.

"AUSTRALIAN CHRISTIAN SOLIDARITY"

24th March, 1985.

APPENDIX "D"
MORAL SINS IN THE NEW TESTAMENT

MORAL SINS	Romans 1:26, 13:13 Rev. 21:7–8	Gal. 5:19–21 Col. 3:5,8	Mark 7:21–22 Eph. 5:3–5	2 Tim. 3:2–5 1 Tim. 1:9–10	1 Cor. 6:9–10 2 Cor. 12:20–21
unrighteousness	*		*		
wickedness	*				
covetousness	*	*	greediness		
evil (malice)	*				
envy	*	*		*	
murder	**		*		
strife	*	*		*	
guile	*				
malignity	*	*			
whisperers	*				
railers	*				
God-haters	*			haters of good	
insolent	*				
arrogant	*		*		
boasters	*				
inventers of evil things	*	passion, evil desire, evil thoughts			
disobedient to parents	*				
undiscerning (foolish)	*		foolish talk, foolishness,		
faithless	**		levity		
without natural affection (heartless)	*			*	
ruthless	*				
fornication	debauchery	**	**	*	**
uncleanness	polluted	**	*	*	
lewdness (lasciviousness AV) (licentiousness RSV)		*	*		*
idolatry	*	*			*
sorcery (witchcraft)	*	*			
enmities		*			
jealousy (see envy)					
anger		**			*

MORAL SINS

	Romans 1:26, 13:13 / Rev. 21:7–8	Gal. 5:19–21 / Col. 3:5,8	Mark 7:21–22 / Eph. 5:3–5	2 Tim. 3:2–5 / 1 Tim. 1:9–10	1 Cor. 6:9–10 / 2 Cor. 12:20–21
dissension		*			
party spirit		*			
drunkenness	*	*			*
carousing	*	*			
thefts			*		*
adulteries			*		*
an evil eye (envy)			*		
blasphemy		*	*	*	
lawless				*	
disobedient				*	
ungodly				*	
sinners				*	
unholy				**	
profane				*	
parricides				*	
matricides				*	
sodomites–perverts	homosexuals			*	effeminates
kidnappers				*	
liars	*	*		*	
perjurers				*	back-biting
slander		filthy abuse		*	
revilers			*		*
gossip				*	*
conceit					*
disturbances					*
self-lovers				*	
money lovers				*	
boasters				*	
ungrateful				*	
implacable				*	
profligates				*	
fierce				*	
treacherous				*	
reckless				*	
pleasure-lovers				*	
cowardly	*			*	

PETER HOBSON BOOKS

ISBN 0947252150

MENTAL ILLNESS - WHAT CAN CHRISTIANS DO?

IF WE ARE NOT WITH HIM WE ARE AGAINST HIM! — Said Jesus after healing the blind and dumb demoniac. Christian ministers are facing ever increasing challenges today as they seek to help the damaged and afflicted, and never has the saving and healing grace of our Lord Jesus Christ been more widely and obviously needed. We need to learn how to restore the human mind, soul and the body from all the damage of the enemy. This book plots the path to Victory and, as always, desperate and hungry seekers get the best results.

ISBN 0947252010

MAKE YOURSELVES READY, VOL. 1

Deliverance is a genuine ministry provided by Jesus Christ on the cross for the day in which we live. It is too late in God's timetable to hold back this truth any longer. God's revelation and solution to our addictions, our fears and our torments must be made known as a matter of urgency. The time is short. The world is in big trouble and Jesus is coming soon for a beautiful bride – the Universal Church. Unfortunately, if He came today, He would be marrying a very troubled, divided, unclean lady. The Bride must make herself ready.

ISBN 0947252029

ENGAGING THE ENEMY, VOL. 2

This second book in Peter's Deliverance series deals with such topics as: Instructions to Demons (Binding, Commanding Spirits, Names & Discernment of Spirits, Talking With Demons, etc), Opening Prayers, Where to Send Demons, The Transference of Spirits (Beware During Ministry, Beware at Death, Beware When Counseling, Beware of Occult Demonstrations), About The Drama & Manifestation and the Lord's Answer, Self-Deliverance (Beware Lack of Discipline, Lack of Honesty, Lack of Support), & more!

ISBN 0947252037

WALKING IN VICTORY, VOL. 3

This third book in Peter's Deliverance series deals with such topics as: the Battle Tactics of the Enemy & The Deliverance Cycle, Teaching on Maintaining Deliverance (Relapses, Human Will, Attitude, etc) Teaching on Prayer Weapons (Forgiveness, Continuous Deliverance, Protection of the Blood, the Fullness of The Holy Spirit, Prosperity), Teaching on Fellowship (Worship & Praise, Sharing, Conduct, Discretion), and more!

ISBN 0947252142

WE ALL HAVE OUR DEMONS!, VOL. 4

This fourth book in Peter's Deliverance series deals with such topics as: Mind Control, Multiple Personality Disorder (MPD), Hearing Voices, Dissociate Identity Disorder, False Memory Syndrome, and Icons and Images. Includes examples of various spirits including; Spirit of fear, Spirit of stupidity, Spirit of rebellion, Spirit of Epilepsy, Spirit of superstition, Spirit of blasphemy, Spirit of bitterness, Spirit of murder, Spirit of anger, Spirit of lust, Spirit of pride, Spirit of gluttony, the Spirit of death and deliverance from cancer.

ISBN 0947252061

END-TIME DELIVERANCE & THE HOLY SPIRIT REVIVAL

A Vision for End-Time Deliverance, including Pursuing Christlikeness, Victory Over Sin, and The Real Renewal. The book ties Jesus' ministry of deliverance with the need for cleaning house in the Church to prepare for the End-Times. Topics include: A Vision for the End Time, the Magnitude of Human Demonization, God's Unfolding Plan of Continual Deliverance, Spiritual Gifts of Healing & Discernment Along With End-Time Deliverance Ministry, and more!

YOUR FULL SALVATION

Are you ready for the coming of the Son of God? Whoever you are - wherever you are - this book will give you the direction you need in your life to be ready for Him! Through his studies in the Bible, Peter Hobson has discovered that evangelism, healing and deliverance were part of the Saviourhood of our Lord Jesus. And they are all an effective part of God's end-time plan!

ISBN 0947252045

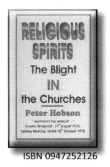

ISBN 0947252126

RELIGIOUS SPIRITS: THE BLIGHT IN THE CHURCHES

Find the harm that religious spirits can do - and are doing - in our churches today. Topics include: Religion & Christianity, Religious Spirits in the Churches, Personal Religiosity, Pharisaism, Dangers in Renewal, Outside the Churches, Counterfeits of the Name Above Every Name, and more!

PETER HOBSON BOOKS (CONT)

ISBN 0947252096

GUIDANCE FOR THOSE RECEIVING DELIVERANCE

This book meets the needs and questions of someone seeking deliverance. It discusses: Interpreting symptoms, Prayer and Restoration, the Christian armor, Discretion, and Opposition from the Church and the World to Deliverance.

ISBN 094725210X

SURVIVING THE DISTRESS OF NATIONS

A Peter Hobson Booklet on End Time events and signs. He explains what a person can do to be prepared for the soon coming of Jesus Christ. Includes a salvation message and a call to seek deliverance. Specific Topics include: The End of This Age (Israel, Weather Changes, Pole Shifts, Earthquakes, etc), Details of the End of the World, More Warning Signs (Pestilences & Plagues, Stockmarket, Ozone Levels, Identity Cards, Crime, Famine, Pollution, etc), and God's Solution.

ISBN 094725207X

HEADCOVERING AND LADY PASTORS & TEACHER

A sensitive treatment of this delicate subject. Peter Hobson discusses the for and against of head covering in the Church today. Hobson includes topics on: Relationships Between Men and Women, the Relevance of Paul's Teaching Today, Reasonings for Head Covering, Opposing Views to Head Covering, and the Appointment of Women and Lady Pastors/Teachers. A must for anyone with questions on this topic!

ISBN 0947252118

TORONTO

"Probably the most vigorous and definitive defense - and criticism - of the Toronto Blessing yet published." This book explains WHY the Toronto experience began and WHERE it will inevitably lead for those who have been praying and expecting the Lord to move powerfully through the Church. If you have questions about this experience, or are wondering its significance, this book is for you!

ISBN 0947252169

BEWARE HYPOCRISY!
THE CASE FOR TRUE RENEWAL...

The purpose of this book is to turn Bible-loving Christian from being unintended Hypocrites into True Disciples of Jesus Christ - for the challenging days ahead!

What do you think is a good description of a Christian who (rightly) opposes homosexual practice because it is against the Word of God, but then explains away as out of date the two full chapters on the right use of tongues and prophecy (1 Cor. 12 & 14)? Hypocrite?

How would you describe a "Bible-believing Christian" leader who opposes Christ's command to heal the sick and cast out demons, essential ministries of the Great Commission with which the Lord has charged His Church? Pharisee? False teacher? Rebel? Scatterer (wolf) - Matt. 12:30? If we are not with Him we are against Him - said Jesus after healing the blind and dumb demoniac.

ISBN 0947252053

CHRISTIAN AUTHORITY, POWER,
AND THE STIGMATA

Ever read a study so power-packed with revelations of God that it kept you in an attitude of near-continual repentance all the way through? This is such a study.

Peter Hobson opens up key Christian truths in a way that reveals breathtaking new heights and dimensions of God's provision, especially in relation to our equipping against problems, those not caused by remnant fleshly bad habits or lack of positive confession, but rather through Satanic inroads.

DISTRIBUTOR

MR. STEPHEN BANKS, President
Impact Christian Books, Inc.
332 Leffingwell Ave., Suite 101
Kirkwood MO 63122
USA

PHONE: (314) 822 3309   FAX: (314) 822 3325
EMAIL: Stephen@impactchristianbooks.com
WEBSITE: www.IMPACTCHRISTIANBOOKS.com

INTERNATIONAL CONTACTS

REV. ABRAHAM VICTOR BABU
Abundant Grace Ministries
Viravada, Pithapuram
E. G. Dt 533450
Andhrapradesh
SOUTH INDIA

EMAIL:
victorbabuad@rediffmail.com

EVANG. FRANK WILLIAMS ABOAGYE
P. O. Box Se 2254
Kumasi - Suame
Ghana
W. AFRICA

EMAIL:
frankwilliamsaboagye@yahoo.com

SUPT. P. YESHAIAH
Full Salvation Fellowship Of India
#5-25-27B, J. P. Nagar
Ithanagar
Tenali 522 201
A.P.
SOUTH INDIA

PASTOR BENWEL ASIAGO
Full Salvation Ministry
P. O. Box 3438, Kisii 40200
Kenya,
EAST AFRICA

FAX TO BOX: (254) 381 31194
PHONE: (254) 735 071 824
EMAIL:
Fsm_kenya2005@yahoo.com

PASTOR EMMANS WANG
The Prophetic Hill
P. O. Box 4 Vom
Jos
Plateau State
Nigeria
W. AFRICA

EMAIL:
Emmanswang@yahoo.com

PASTOR GRACE OKURUT
Full Missions Ministry
P. O. Box 584
Soroti
Uganda
E. AFRICA

EMAIL:
Okurutg@yahoo.com

PASTOR EMMANUEL SARFRAZ
AFM Church
Hali Public School
Haji Pura
Jamilabad Ad Road
Chungi No. 1
Multan

PAKISTAN

EMAIL:
Sadiqhali@Hotmail.Com

BISHOP ERNESTO BALILI
265 Vamenta Blvd.
Carmen
Cagayan de Oro City
PHILIPPINES

EMAIL:
bishopbalili@yahoo.com

Made in the USA
Lexington, KY
16 April 2015